Yuck!

Life and Mind: Philosophical Issues in Biology and Psychology
Kim Sterelny and Robert A. Wilson, editors

Cycles of Contingency: Developmental Systems and Evolution, Susan Oyama, Paul E. Griffiths, and Russell D. Gray, editors, 2000

Coherence in Thought and Action, Paul Thagard, 2000

The New Phrenology: The Limits of Localizing Cognitive Processes in the Brain, William R. Uttal, 2001

Evolution and Learning: The Baldwin Effect Reconsidered, Bruce H. Weber and David J. Depew, editors, 2003

Seeing and Visualizing: It's Not What You Think, Zenon W. Pylyshyn, 2003

Organisms and Artifacts: Design in Nature and Elsewhere, Tim Lewens, 2004

The Mind Incarnate, Lawrence A. Shapiro, 2004

Molecular Models of Life: Philosophical Papers on Molecular Biology, Sahotra Sarkar, 2004

Evolution in Four Dimensions: Genetic, Epigenetic, Behavioral, and Symbolic Variation in the History of Life, Eva Jablonka and Marion J. Lamb, 2005

The Evolution of Morality, Richard Joyce, 2006

Evolutionary Psychology as Maladapted Psychology, Robert C. Richardson, 2007

Describing Inner Experience? Proponent Meets Skeptic, Russell T. Hurlburt and Eric Schwitzgebel, 2007

The Native Mind and the Cultural Construction of Nature, Scott Atran and Douglas Medin, 2008

Color Ontology and Color Science, Jonathan Cohen and Mohan Matthen, editors, 2010

The Extended Mind, Richard Menary, editor, 2010

Yuck! The Nature and Moral Significance of Disgust, Daniel Kelly, 2011

Yuck!

The Nature and Moral Significance of Disgust

Daniel Kelly

A Bradford Book
The MIT Press
Cambridge, Massachusetts
London, England

For information about special quantity discounts, please email special_sales@mit-press.mit.edu

This book was set in Stone Sans and Stone Serif by the MIT Press. Printed and bound in the United States of America.

Library of Congress Cataloging-in-Publication Data

Kelly, Daniel R. (Daniel Ryan)
Yuck! : the nature and moral significance of disgust / Daniel Kelly.
    p.   cm.—(Life and mind: philosophical issues in biology and psychology)
"A Bradford Book."
Includes bibliographical references and index.
ISBN 978-0-262-01558-5 (hbk. : alk. paper)
1. Aversion. 2. Emotions. I. Title.
BF575.A886K45   2011
152.4—dc22
                                                                            2010053625

10 9 8 7 6 5 4 3 2 1

To Mike, Lynn, and Erin

Contents

Acknowledgments   ix

Introduction   1

1   Toward a Functional Theory of Disgust   11

2   Poisons and Parasites: The Entanglement Thesis and the Evolution of Disgust   43

3   Disgust's Sentimental Signaling System: Expression, Recognition, and the Transmission of Cultural Information   61

4   Disgust and Moral Psychology: Tribal Instincts and the Co-opt Thesis   101

5   Disgust and Normative Ethics: The Irrelevance of Repugnance and Dangers of Moralization   137

Notes   153
References   165
Index   189

Acknowledgments

If memory serves, this book, and the dissertation that it grew out of, was sparked by an eye-opening seminar on biological and cultural explanations of human behavior I attended while in graduate school, a great conference on moral psychology in the summer of 2004 at Dartmouth College, and a number of conversations with my advisor, Steve Stich, at least one of which occurred at a Chinatown restaurant over a meal made up of dishes like blood tofu and duck tongue soup, which he was clearly enjoying, and which I was unsuccessfully trying to not be disgusted by. From there, the project unfolded slowly and in stages, and I have benefited along the way from the help and encouragement of many people.

My biggest debt is to Steve, whose professional guidance and support have been invaluable in navigating the early stages of a career in academia, whose vision of what philosophy is and can be has helped shape my own, and who, by virtue of this, has perhaps unknowingly provided reassurance that a life in academic philosophy can be both invigorating and worthwhile. Many thanks also to the members of the Moral Psychology Research Group; the exposure to so many perspectives, the stream of opportunities, and the intellectual companionship and camaraderie have been, and I am sure will continue to be, fantastic. I am also thankful to everyone who has given me many useful sorts of feedback on this project, either in conversation or by commenting on earlier written drafts. Those whom I can remember include Anne Barnhill, Damon Centola, Christine Clavien, John Doris, Luc Faucher, Geoff Georgi, Alvin Goldman, Matt Guschwan, Colin Jager, Edouard Machery, Ron Mallon, Brian McLaughlin, Shaun Nichols, Jenefer Robinson, Ted Sider, and Eric Wesselman, as well as Tom Stone, Philip Laughlin, and two anonymous reviewers at the MIT Press. Suggestions and criticisms on talks based on this material have also been extremely helpful, and my gratitude goes out to the members of the philosophy departments at Illinois Wesleyan University, Rice University, the University of Houston, and the University of Utah, as well as the participants at the 2006 Conference for the International Society for Research on Emotions in Atlanta; the 2007 Cognitio Conference on Connected Minds and the 2008 Summer Institute on Societies and Minds, both at the University of Quebec at Montreal; the Purdue Social Psychology Brownbag Speaker Series; the 2008 workshops on the evolution of signaling and emotion and commitment at Australian National University; and the 2009 Rocky Mountain Ethics Conferences at the University of Colorado at Boulder. Finally, I am indebted to Purdue University, especially to my colleagues in the philosophy department, for providing a diverse and hospitable intellectual environment.

Finally, I need to thank Melissa Will. It occurs to me that I have not always been my usual sunny and pleasant self when I was really immersed in this project, and so, over the years, she has probably suffered more for my art than I have myself.

Introduction

Pick a random person off the street and ask him to name five disgusting things off the top of his head, and you are likely to get an earful about filth, disease, death, bugs, and perhaps the mention of some sort of exotic food he finds particularly unpleasant, like pickled snake or boiled sea cucumber. These are the types of things mention of disgust most immediately brings to mind, and they are concrete and manifestly physical. The experience of the emotion, as opposed to the things that commonly induce it, is fairly primal itself: the visceral sense of revulsion, the slight feeling of nausea that unsettles the stomach, the worries about physical contact and contamination, the gaping facial expression that could so easily tip into actual retching. The response and the sort of things that typically trigger it appear to be matched in their involvement with the body, the organic and physical.

On the other hand, consider Henry Higgins's reaction to Eliza Doolittle's diction when they first meet in the play *Pygmalion*:

A woman who utters such depressing and disgusting sounds has no right to be anywhere—no right to live. Remember that you are a human being with a soul and the divine gift of articulate speech: that your native language is the language of Shakespear and Milton and The Bible; and don't sit there crooning like a bilious pigeon.

Professor Higgins appears to have been fully disgusted by nothing more than what he takes to be an improper accent. Most of us, I am guessing, do not have such refined sensibilities that we are often revolted by mere pronunciation, but the fact that something as intangible as idiolect could induce disgust is probably not completely unfamiliar, either. Think of the most egregious rhetoric of your least favorite public figure or political commentator, and you can probably induce a quick flash of revulsion in yourself without much effort. George Orwell infamously claimed that the bourgeois think that "the lower classes smell"; he was implying that for all the highfalutin debate and reasoning about political theory, one of the most difficult hurdles to achieving real social equality is that the middle and upper classes are slightly disgusted by the working classes. The upshot is that in addition to its focus on the slime and filth of the physical world, disgust involves itself in more abstract matters as well. When it comes to rival groups or political opponents, actual odor is usually not the source of the offense, however. Rather, it is the very ideology and value system of those whom one is set against that can come to be deeply disgusting. In these cases, it is not unusual for disgust to take on a moral valence.

The arena of disgusting things ranges from the concrete and physical to the abstract and social, but it exhibits variation in other ways as well. Everyone is disgusted by something or other, but common sense and casual observation suggest that different things will disgust people with different sensibilities and different cultural backgrounds. One group's delicacy is another group's object of revulsion. Each of us has his or her own personalized and idiosyncratic objects of disgust as well.

Even were he to admit that the emotion is somewhat puzzling, the man on the street could be forgiven for being surprised or even skeptical that disgust is of much academic interest or the object of serious scholarship. Such an opinion would be understandable, perhaps, but at this point it is simply wrong. A swell of recent work has raised disgust from relative obscurity to new levels of visibility, and novelty alone does not account for the attention. Instead, disgust has become relevant to discussions across the humanities, especially those engaging the cognitive sciences and those in the midst of the "affective turn." It is very much a subject of interest in cognitive science, and is already prominent in debates that take place where psychology intersects with philosophy and moral theory. This newly elevated profile increases the potential for a book on disgust to reach a wide and interdisciplinary audience. This, in turn, raises its own difficulties for the author of such a book, concerning tone of voice, ideal terminology, and how much, and what, can be presupposed in the course of any particular line of thought. With this in mind, I have tried to presuppose as little as I thought I could get away with, without becoming overly tedious or pedantic. How well this tack ultimately succeeds will inevitably be left up to its readers, but I hope to have made the book at least accessible to as many different types of audience as possible.

As just alluded to, disgust has become prominent in three distinct projects, based in cognitive science and moral psychology, normative and applied ethics, and metaphysics and metaethics, respectively. All three projects examine disgust in one way or another, but each differs with respect to why the emotion is relevant to its aims. The first project is the primary concern of much of this book. It is firmly rooted in the cognitive sciences, it is empirical and integrative in spirit, its methods are descriptive and explanatory, and its aim is to understand the nature and evolution of the emotion itself. The project is integrative because understanding disgust requires the use of different tools drawn from disciplines that make up the cognitive sciences, including the philosophy of mind, the philosophy of psychology, a variety of different subdisciplines in psychology, and work on culture and gene-culture coevolutionary theory. The project is also empirical in that it draws on information and evidence gathered from a variety of approaches, including various branches of experimental psychology (social, developmental, etc.), behavioral economics, cognitive neuropsychology, cultural anthropology, and comparative evolutionary biology.

One goal of this project is to develop a proximate explanation that characterizes the psychological mechanisms underlying the main features of the emotion, including the mechanisms that produce the different components of the response, as well as those responsible for the ability to acquire new elicitors of disgust. Another goal is to produce an ultimate explanation of the evolutionary pressures that molded the emotion into its current form. Ideally, this latter type of explanation will help illuminate the primary and auxiliary roles that disgust in fact plays in the cognitive economy of modern humans, including those roles related to morality.

The book is largely organized around these goals. Chapter 1 is, in effect, a review of the empirical literature germane to disgust. While there is no single overarching debate or research program to canvass, an enormous amount of work touches on the emotion. Data and insight have been gathered from so many different directions that a compilation of results, presented in an unadulterated fashion, would risk appearing completely piecemeal and disjointed, the conceptual equivalent of a bad cubist painting that tries to represent its object from every angle at once. The burden of the first chapter, then, is not only to gather and review the relevant research, but also to impose some structure on it. To this end, I first create what I call the disgust *behavioral profile*. The first half of the behavioral profile clarifies the core disgust response and its characteristic features, and points out some of the most prominent downstream effects of that response on other behaviors. The second half attempts to specify the different kinds of elicitors of disgust in as plain a manner as possible, so as not to presuppose anything of theoretical interest. From the behavioral profile, I also derive three constraints that a complete theory of disgust should satisfy; each of the second, third, and fourth chapters ends by showing how it has met one of these desiderata.

Chapter 1 ends with the presentation of a functional model of the human disgust system. It depicts a cognitive architecture comprised of the different mechanisms that make up the human disgust system and which can account for the features of disgust cataloged in the behavioral profile. It charts the flow of information between those mechanisms and associates aspects of disgust behavior with components of that cognitive architecture. Its three main divisions are between an execution system, which maintains a database of disgust elicitors and produces the central aspects of the emotion itself; an acquisition system, which is responsible for the acquisition of those disgust elicitors that are not innately specified; and the variety of common downstream effects that disgust often has on other psychological and behavioral activities.

While the model posited at the end of chapter 1 represents a proximate psychological explanation, chapter 2 is devoted to the evolution of disgust, and so begins to sketch an ultimate explanation of the types of evolutionary forces that assembled this emotion. Here I am concerned with the question "How did disgust evolve, and what is its primary function?" My answer to the second part of this question, which is encapsulated in what I call the Entanglement thesis, is that it does not have a single primary function, but a pair of them. According to the Entanglement thesis, different components of the disgust execution subsystem themselves have fundamentally different evolutionary etiologies. At the heart of the human disgust system, I claim, are two distinguishable mechanisms, each with its own distinct origin and function: one that has to do with diet and the avoidance of toxic foods, and another that has to do with avoiding pathogens, parasites, and the reliable indicators of their presence. Mechanisms that evolved to handle each of these problems are present in other animals (the corresponding adaptive problems are not unique to humans), but for a variety of reasons that I draw out in the course of the argument, those mechanisms have merged into a single system only in humans.

Adopting this view suggests answers to many puzzling issues surrounding disgust, most obviously why it has been thought by some researchers to be uniquely human, while others see clear homologies in other primates and animals. Moreover, it offers a plausible account of other much-discussed but hitherto-unexplained aspects of disgust, including, but not limited to: the types of false positives that typically trigger disgust; why conspecifics are so salient to this emotion and why it plays so prominent a role in regulating social interactions; why the defining characteristics of the response form a nomological cluster; why such a diverse set of entities and objects all trigger this single response; and why certain of those elicitors are universally disgusting. I discuss each of these aspects in turn, and show why competing accounts of disgust—namely, the Simple Continuity view and Terror Management theory—are unable to account for them.

Finally, chapter 2 ends by offering a preliminary list of the factors that might have driven these two mechanisms, with their distinct functional and evolutionary trajectories, together into the single integrated emotion we now recognize as disgust. This argument is extended to suggest why a similar instance of descent with modification did not take place in the cognitive architecture of other animals, even our closest primate cousins.

Chapter 3 focuses on what I call disgust's sentimental signaling system. I begin by considering a range of intriguing facts about the typical ways in which people express their disgust, and how we are able to recognize that others are disgusted by something. Expressions of disgust, in body language and most clearly in its characteristic facial expression of the gape, are largely automatic and potentially unconscious. They are also difficult to completely suppress; if I see something that disgusts me, an understated gape will often leak out onto my face even if I am consciously trying to hide how I really feel. Recognizing disgust in others can likewise be both automatic and potentially unconscious. This is particularly striking in light of the fact that recognition of disgust in others is also often empathic: recognizing someone else's gape face as an expression of disgust often involves the activation of one's own disgust system, and thus a mild episode of the emotion in the recognizer.

After describing the research that has been done on these features of disgust's sentimental signaling system, I consider two different models that might explain those features, and thus give an account of what the signaling system evolved to do. The first of these, which I call the Classic Commitment model, takes its cues from Robert Frank's seminal work on social emotions and commitment devices. This model understands emotional expression in terms of commitment problems. It would explain the expression and recognition facts about disgust in terms of the dynamics of cooperation and deception, and the types of signals needed to make commitments like threats and promises credible. The second model, which I call the Cultural Transmission model, is taken from the literature on the psychology of cultural transmission. This model would construe facts about expression and recognition in terms of natural pedagogy and social learning, and would thus cast disgust's sentimental signaling system as a complex mechanism that underpins the easy acquisition and transmission of important cultural information.

After motivating and spelling out the core ideas behind each of these models, I argue that the Cultural Transmission model is a much better fit for disgust, on both theoretical and empirical grounds. Building on the Entanglement thesis, I show that disgust's sentimental signaling system allows individuals to learn about crucial, but often parochial, information about what is edible or poisonous and what is potentially contaminating, in the local environment. I go on to show how this model is also consistent with preliminary evidence showing how disgust can influence cultural evolution. Finally, I conclude by arguing that this sentimental signaling system is a key component of disgust's multifaceted *acquisition* system, and how, together with some of the other forms of acquisition, it can help account for the patterns of cultural variation associated with disgust elicitors.

Chapter 4 attempts to shed light on the further roles disgust has come to play in modern human moral psychology. The discussion here presupposes the Entanglement thesis, which linked disgust to poisons and parasites, and builds on it. Disgust is involved in more than food and disease, and to clarify the roles that outstrip food and disease, particularly those that are associated with morality, I place disgust in the context of work on gene culture coevolution. This theory sees humans as being distinctive in the extremely different types of environment they can successfully inhabit, their forms of sociality, and their reliance on culture. In navigating this large literature, I focus on the tribal instincts hypothesis, which holds that gene cultural coevolution has resulted in modern humans having a unique set of tribal social instincts. In unpacking this idea, I elaborate on two of the main components of this package of psychological capacities. The first is a capacity for social norms, which allows individuals to acquire social norms from others, and produces motivations both to comply with the acquired norms and to punish others who violate them. The second component is a sensitization to boundaries between different tribes, and the types of symbols and cues that are likely to mark in-group from out-group members.

Having articulated this theoretical context, I return to disgust and argue for what I call the Co-opt thesis. This thesis holds that disgust has been recruited to perform novel functions associated with both of the previously mentioned components of human tribal instincts, but despite being co-opted, it has also retained most of its core structural features. The features of disgust, especially the rigidity of the behavioral response and the open-ended flexibility of the acquisition system, made it an apt candidate to be co-opted when early humans faced the novel conditions produced by their increasingly complicated reliance on culture. The role of disgust in many moral judgments can be explained by the disgust system working in conjunction with a norm psychology that evolved to help coordinate social interactions and produce behaviors that are locally adaptive, given the specific demands of different niches and circumstances. Ethnic boundary markers are often highly emotionally charged, and attitudes and behaviors associated with ethnocentrism, xenophobia, and prejudice often follow the logic of disgust, depicting out-group members not just as wrong or different, but as tainted, contaminating, even subhuman. This is explained by appeal to an ethnic psychology that evolved to maximize interactions between in-group members, but in some cases draws on the disgust system to provide the motivation to avoid members of other tribes.

After first highlighting some of the difficulties that are faced by attempts to demarcate the domain of morality and addressing a skeptical view that talk about moral disgust is merely metaphorical, I show how my account of so-called moral disgust suggests a by-product hypothesis that can explain some of the more puzzling effects that recent research on disgust and moral judgment has been discovering. The picture that emerges is of a universal, multifunctional cognitive system that is uniquely human in a number of ways.

Though the fifth and final chapter of the book follows naturally from the first four, it shifts gears from the first project relevant to disgust to the second. As the focus moves from empirical moral psychology to normative and applied ethics, it crosses the traditional boundary between the descriptive and the prescriptive as well. Rather than defend this move in the abstract, I am content in allowing the proof to remain in the pudding; no individual step in the argument I make in this chapter strikes me as methodologically illegitimate. If the sort of reasoning I employ there is spoiled by a failure to keep its *is*'s completely separate from its *ought*'s, I doubt I am the only offender. As I show, several philosophers who take part in the debate I focus on have one foot on each side of the alleged empirical–normative divide themselves.

These ethicists are addressing a cluster of normative issues that surround what has come to be known as "the yuck factor." In its starkest form, the core question is whether or not being disgusted by something provides good reason to think it is immoral or morally problematic. This can sharpened up in a number of ways. What justificatory role should disgust be given in considered moral judgment? How should feelings of disgust be weighted in moral deliberation? If someone is attempting to achieve a state of ideal reflective equilibrium, for instance, what should she do with the fact that some relevant activity, particular social practice, or type of lifestyle disgusts her? How should our legal system and other institutions handle feelings of disgust? If a majority of the population is disgusted by a social practice, should this fact influence or be reflected in the policies that guide our social institutions? How? Distinct but related issues about the ideal role of disgust in morality are raised by questions with a slightly different focus: Is disgust ever the morally ideal response to certain attitudes or practices? Is it morally permissible or problematic to intentionally invoke disgust in the service of altering behaviors or changing minds? For instance, would there be anything wrong with a campaign aimed at lessening racism that used the latest advertising and marketing techniques to depict racism and racists as not just wrong, but disgusting?

I argue that the recent debates about the role disgust deserves in ethical thought have been impoverished by an inadequate understanding of the emotion itself. I first describe the respective positions of what I call *advocates*, who hold that disgust alerts us to the morally important boundary between the natural and the unnatural, and should thus be considered a trusted source of moral guidance, and *skeptics*, who hold that at best disgust should be discounted in reflection and moral deliberation, and at worst is a powerful instrument of oppression that should be regarded with outright suspicion. Next I show how the arguments given in favor of each position thus far rely on extremely different but equally implausible views of the nature of disgust. I briefly recount the most important aspects of my own view, developed in the first four chapters, then go on to argue that my view provides new and more plausible foundations for skepticism about the idea that disgust deserves some kind of special epistemic credit or moral authority, that the emotion is a trustworthy guide to justifiable moral judgments, or that there is any deep wisdom in repugnance. I also make a case that in addition to the emotion's disreputable historical track record in the service of oppression and discrimination, appreciating the character of disgust should make us extremely wary of invoking it, even in the service of uncontroversial and morally admirable ends.

Finally, the third project to which disgust is relevant centers primarily on metaphysics and metaethics. Those engaged in this project are often interested in disgust, and the corresponding property of disgustingness, in the hopes that it can serve as a model, helping to shed light on core questions about ontology and how various properties might be located in nature. Understanding the relationship between disgust and disgustingness, the line of thought goes, might help clarify a variety of issues, including what it might mean to say that a property is response dependent, dispositional, or projected, as well as related issues about the character of judgments and claims about response-dependent, dispositional, and projected properties.

For example, disgust has attracted the attention of those seeking to update and extend the Humean sentimentalist tradition, whose basic idea is that evaluative concepts and properties, including moral ones, crucially depend (somehow) on the human sentiments. This reflects a commonly held view that disgustingness is a paradigmatic example of something projected onto the world by the mind, a property that can easily seem to be an independent feature of external reality, but which is in fact produced by our minds and projected outward, like the colored images that a film projector adds to an otherwise blankly white screen. Sentimentalists—and metaethicists of many persuasions, actually—have recently turned to disgust and disgustingness, using it to illuminate the structure and semantics of evaluative discourse (or content of evaluative experience) more generally. In what ways are judgments about disgustingness analogous to judgments about, for instance, rightness and wrongness? Are judgments of disgustingness intrinsically motivating in the same way moral judgments are often claimed to be? When two parties argue about whether Whoppers are disgusting or not, what are they disagreeing about? Are they talking past each other? If not, what determines which person, if either, is right? Are there truth conditions for ascriptions of disgustingness? If so, what are they?

I have little to say directly about this cluster of issues. Explicitly tackling the questions central to this third project is no small undertaking, and doing so would have produced a very different book. While writing this one, however, it did not escape me that developing a systematic analogy between disgust and morality has the potential to prove quite edifying. Others have looked to gain insight into morality via the *linguistic analogy*; an alternative *disgust analogy* could prove equally fruitful, and perhaps more apt. An obvious difference between the two approaches, however, is that in the case of linguistics, there is already a large body of well-developed, sophisticated theory for those interested in the nature of morality to draw on. In the case of disgust, no corresponding systematic theory has been available from which to build the analogy. This book should begin to remedy that situation. As a result, I also hope that much of what I have to say will be of interest, and of use, to those who wish to explore the disgust analogy further, so that this book can ultimately help in the larger project of understanding the nature of morality in general, from its evolution, psychology, and cultural transmission, to its justification and ontology.

1 Toward a Functional Theory of Disgust

1.1 Introduction

One interesting fact about disgust is that it is a piece of human psychology that does not sit easily on either side of the traditional nature–nurture divide. On the one hand, the capacity to be disgusted, together with a small set of things that appear to be universally and innately disgusting, is a part of the species' typical psychological endowment. These are a part of human nature; one does not have to learn *how* to be disgusted, and one does not have to be taught to be disgusted *by* certain things, either—like the pungent smell of rotting garbage on a hot summer day, for instance. On the other hand, the variation evident in what different people find disgusting reveals a considerable role for nurture as well. In other cases, people do learn what to be disgusted by through individual experience, through social interactions with others, and through the type of education that constitutes the refinement of their moral and aesthetic sensibilities.

This fact about disgust is just one reason that the emotion has attracted the attention of a wide range of researchers, so that it is now relevant to a number of discussions taking place in different parts of academia. These include philosophic debates about metaethics, sentimentalism, and response dependence (McDowell 1985, 1987; D'Arms and Jacobson 2000, 2005; Knapp 2003; Nichols 2004; Gert 2005), the empirical investigation of morality (Haidt et al. 1993; Haidt et al. 1997; Rozin et al. 1999; Moll et al. 2005; Schnall et al. 2008), examinations of social history (W. Miller 1997), normative and applied ethics (Kass 1997, 2002; Nussbaum 2004a,b; Hauskeller 2006; Douard 2007), and a variety of research projects across the spectrum of psychology. Most of these will come under consideration in the course of this book. In this first chapter, though, the psychological research will serve as the point of departure.

The recent surge of interest and empirical work on the psychology of disgust has been accompanied by only the mildest convergence in theoretical views. Beyond agreement that disgust is a specific type of aversion, the proverbial "dizzying array" of conjectures have been made about its fundamental nature: disgust is a reaction formation, a defense against or rejection of emotional intimacy (S. Miller 1986, 1993); it is a socially constructed moral emotion of exclusion most closely linked to touch and smell (W. Miller 1997); it is a food-based emotion most closely linked to the mouth (Rozin et al. 2008); it is an innate system evolved to protect us from parasites, germs, and disease (Curtis and Biran 2001; Curtis 2007); it is, at least in part, a pan-mammalian adaptation that regulates sexual conditioning (Fessler and Navarrete 2003a, 2004); it underlies a particular kind of social stigmatization (Kurzban and Leary 2001); it helps in demarcating ethnic boundaries (Boyd and Richerson 2005a); it is governed by the laws of sympathetic magic (Nemeroff and Rozin 2000). After only a cursory glance, one might be tempted to wonder whether everyone is talking about the same thing. Closer inspection shows, I believe, that many of these fragments of theory are compatible with each other in interesting ways, but the fact remains that at present there is no single received view, accepted by all interested parties. The closest thing to orthodoxy was Paul Rozin's view (Rozin et al. 2008). Even that has come under direct attack from various quarters, however; see W. Miller 1997; Charash and McKay 2002; Curtis et al. 2004; Fessler and Navarrete 2005; and chapter 2 of this book.

A number of factors have led to the current situation in cognitive scientific work on disgust. One is the seemingly contradictory nature of disgust itself. Another is that the present state of research is marked by a trend familiar from other areas of science and periods of development—the data have recently been accumulating faster than theory has been able to keep up. A final factor responsible for this proliferation of different views is that, like most emotions, disgust is "level ubiquitous" (De Sousa 1987). Roughly speaking, something interesting can be said about its character from nearly every level of analysis, from its associated patterns of neural activation to its role in large-scale cultural dynamics and most points between.[1] From the perspective of a theoretician, this is a particularly exasperating source of confusion, since appreciation of level ubiquity can make it unclear where to even begin in thinking about the emotions. Moreover, disgust appears to present an especially acute case of this difficulty. As reflected by the views cited earlier, analyses offered about disgust from different levels of inquiry often seem to have little to do with each other.

In light of this, a primary goal of this book is to consolidate and organize the research on disgust. Disgust is puzzling and intriguing in a variety of ways, but despite this—or more likely, *because* of it—no coherent account has yet emerged to resolve the puzzles or systematically accommodate the data. One of my central aims is to construct a theory that can bring order to the chaos. As will become apparent, doing so will require use of ideas drawn from a number of different research programs. If this strategy is successful, one of the corollary benefits will be that the resulting theory of disgust can also serve as a model, showing how diverse conceptual tools can be integrated and put to use to construct theories in other areas of cognitive science.

The journey of ten thousand miles, we are told, begins with a single step. But what is the correct first step toward these no doubt ambitious goals? The standard place to begin such an endeavor would probably be to survey all currently available accounts of disgust in turn. After subjecting each to criticism and evaluation, one might then decide on the most plausible or promising view, and proceed to defend, supplement, or develop it in new directions.

I will not be proceeding in this manner, though. As hinted at earlier, the fragments of theory that have been put forward so far are tantalizing and frustrating in about equal measure. Their sheer number would make weighing them all against each other burdensome at best, futile at worst. In light of this, the most promising approach is to avoid becoming entangled in the vagaries of those speculations and begin by returning to the ground floor of what is known, to the facts. Therefore I will set aside all theoretical proposals, at least to begin with, and instead focus on the large body of data that has been gathered about disgust. The first step will be to gather those facts together in one place and construct what I call the behavioral profile of the emotion of disgust. The second will be to sketch out a model of the cognitive architecture that can help explain the data gathered in the behavioral profile.

1.2   The Behavioral Profile of Disgust

Since it is a compilation of the known facts, the behavioral profile will proceed, in essence, like a review of the empirical literature germane to disgust. Speaking of "the" literature on disgust is a bit misleading, however. Just as there is no single theory, there is also no single overarching debate, experimental paradigm, or research program specifically devoted to the emotion. The amount of empirical work that *touches* on disgust, however, can seem overwhelming, and data are being gathered and reported by researchers from numerous disciplines, with little overlap by way of shared background assumptions or methodological protocol. As a result, the scope of what follows is not just far ranging but unabashedly interdisciplinary. Moreover, beyond an allegedly shared subject matter, this body of research is marked by a striking lack of conceptual unity.

I have three main aims in compiling this behavioral profile. First and foremost, I will gather together and review all the relevant research of which I am aware. Second, my discussion will focus mainly on the data that have been gathered, and to a lesser extent on the experimental setups used to gather those data. Nor will I, in this chapter at least, devote much attention to whatever theoretical frameworks (Piagettian, Freudian, evolutionary psychological, social constructivist, etc.) were originally used to interpret the results. In doing this, I will try to characterize disgust in straightforwardly behavioral terms, so as not to beg any questions about theory or the psychological mechanisms underlying the emotion. I cannot remain completely agnostic, however, since the discussion needs to be organized in some way. The third task, then, is to impose some degree of structure on this otherwise sprawling body of data. In choosing how best to systematize and present the empirical research, I have been guided by the structure of the emotion itself. The central division in what follows is between the data about the disgust *response*, on the one hand, and data about the *elicitors*, the types of things that induce the response, on the other.

The first half of the behavioral profile clarifies the basic disgust response and its characteristic components and points out some of the most prominent downstream effects of that response on other behaviors and judgments. This section includes some neurological data as well; in calling it the behavioral profile, I use "behavior" in a loose sense, and so include data about the way a person's brain "behaves" when she is disgusted. The second half attempts to specify the different types of elicitors of disgust in as plain a manner as possible, so as to not presuppose anything important.

Two last caveats: first, I am sketching the capacity as it typically manifests in normal, fully formed, adult human beings. I will address issues of development and varieties of malfunction only when relevant, which sometimes involves deferring discussion until in later chapters. Second, the behavioral profile contains only data explicitly about disgust. I save other, relevant subject matter—comparative research on other species or conceptual tools borrowed from work on cultural evolution, for instance—for later chapters, as well.

1.2.1 The Response

Roughly speaking, the response is the way people react once they have detected something that they find disgusting. It is the pattern of behavior they exhibit when they are disgusted by something. The core response has long been thought to be universal, found in all cultures and normally functioning adult humans. Darwin initially provided evidence that all normal, mature humans have the capacity to be disgusted, and that facial expressions of disgust are recognizably the same across cultures (Darwin 1872). Evidence supporting these claims to universality has continued to accumulate ever since, and few have found grounds to disagree (see Ekman 1992; Rozin et al. 2008). The exact parameters of "normal" remain unclear, however. Among the many deficiencies alleged to be found in humans raised in extreme isolation is the lack of a fully developed disgust response and elicitor set (Malson 1972).

Researchers have dedicated considerable effort to mapping out the different affective, cognitive, and behavioral facets of the disgust response. It has become evident that the pattern of behavior making up the response is idiosyncratic, in that the components of that pattern do not always share any clear thematic unity. In what follows, I break down the properties of the response into three parts, what I call the affect program, core disgust, and downstream effects. These parts, and the order of their presentation, roughly correspond to their relative distance downstream from the initial detection of an elicitor.

1.2.1.1 The Affect Program

The term "affect program" is a conspicuously theoretical notion that wears its commitment to the computational theory of mind on its sleeve. The term is used in psychological research to characterize a family of the most basic emotions. In general, affect programs are emotional responses that are complex and highly coordinated. The responses are reflexlike in that they are often triggered automatically and have a quick onset and brief duration. Moreover, individual affect programs are triggered by entities and events that have recurring adaptive significance, and to which each particular response is well suited. The historical roots of the conception lie in Darwin and can be traced through the notion of innate, fixed action patterns used by classical ethologists such as Konrad Lorenz and Nikolaas Tinbergen, into its current form in the more contemporary work on emotions done by Paul Ekman and other prominent psychologists (see Griffiths 2001 for references and discussion). Most of these researchers agree that affect programs are likely to be related to homologous response patterns found in other primates, and are likely to be pan-cultural among humans.

Structurally, an affect program comprises a number of parts: (a) a trigger or stimulus, which elicits (b) a signature behavioral and (c) signature physiological response, each of which has its own components, including, most prominently, a characteristic facial expression, and finally (d) an attendant qualitative feeling. The response itself is (usually) automatically elicited, and the different elements of that response cluster together. That is, once an affect program is set off, it automatically triggers not just one or a few of the distinguishable elements of response but all of them.[2]

The relation of affect programs to emotions in general, especially to more complicated or cognitive emotions, is a tricky one that has been treated at length elsewhere (Griffiths 1997, esp. chaps. 4 and 9). Paradigm examples of affect programs, however, include anger, fear, joy, sadness, surprise, and disgust. For the most part, the components of the disgust affect program are easy to identify and separate out. Behaviorally, disgust produces an immediate aversive or withdrawal response, wherein the disgusted person attempts to distance herself from the offending entity. This rejection need not always manifest as moving away, however, but can often result in motivation to get rid of the offending entity in some other way. The associated facial expression of disgust is known as the "gape face." It is characterized by a nose wrinkle, extrusion of the tongue and expelling motion of the mouth, and wrinkled upper brow. The gape face mimics the facial movements that precede or accompany actual retching, the behavior from which the expression is thought to derive. Like other affect program facial expressions, it is thought to be universal and universally recognizable as such (Ekman 2003).

In terms of its physiological component, triggering disgust causes a slight drop in temperature, and it is the only affect program marked by a drop in heart rate (albeit a minor one), rather than a rise (Ekman and Davidson 1993). In addition, disgust increases salivation and gastrointestinal activity. Together with heart rate deceleration, these components have been taken to indicate activation of the parasympathetic nervous system, which plays a broadly inhibitory role in the functioning of an organism (Levenson 1992).

Finally, the qualitative component of the disgust affect program is a particular feeling of aversion, the all-too-familiar experience of revulsion and repulsion. From a subjective point of view, feelings of disgust can vary in intensity and texture from instance to instance, and more intense episodes are phenomenologically similar to nausea.[3] In fact, this is no accident, as the disgust response includes many *physiological* concomitants of nausea (Ekman 1992). The connection between the digestive system and the affect program of disgust suggested by the previously mentioned increase in salivation that accompanies disgust, together with these similarities with nausea, has been further elucidated with brain imaging techniques. Evidence gathered using fMRI technology links disgust to the anterior insular cortex, which is thought to be involved in gustatory responses on independent grounds (Phillips et al. 1997). Indeed, the anterior insula is often called the "gustatory cortex" and is active in processing offensive tastes in both humans and other primates (Kinomura et al. 1994; Rolls and Baylis1994). This connection to the gustatory cortex also marks disgust as having a neural substrate distinct from other affect programs like fear and anger, which are more closely associated with amygdala.

1.2.1.2 Core Disgust

The emotion of disgust outstrips the affect program, however. While disgust appears to bear all the distinguishing characteristics of affect programs in general, there is more to it; the cluster of elements that make up the entire disgust response cannot be captured using only the resources of the affect program template. Another set of features that are slightly less reflexive and more cognitive in character is also produced. Following Rozin's terminology (Rozin et al. 2008), I call this set of elements of the response *core disgust*. The three central features of core disgust are a sense of oral incorporation, a sense of offensiveness, and contamination sensitivity.

The sense of *oral incorporation*—this terminology is also borrowed from Rozin and his colleagues—is perhaps most closely related to the affect program. Aversion can take several forms, but the disgust response generates aversion with a pronounced oral feel. As previously noted, disgust employs many of the same bodily systems employed in digestion and food consumption; nausea, increased salivation, and the activation of the gustatory cortex and gastrointestinal system are centered on the mouth and digestive system. Strikingly, these components accompany all disgust reactions, even those induced by entities that are not potential food or have little to do with eating or the mouth. This fact, in turn, can create a strong cognitive association between the mouth and oral functioning, on the one hand, and an elicitor of disgust, on the other—whether or not the elicitor has anything to do with the mouth or food in the first place. Indeed, research has found the aversion produced by disgusting entities can be made more intense by considering those entities as food, or as present in the mouth (Rozin et al. 1995). Feces are disgusting enough; imagining eating them is downright vile. Thus, though perhaps the terminology itself is less than ideal, nebulous associations between disgust and the mouth may very well present, at a phenomenological level, as something like a visceral "sense of oral incorporation."

Studies that do not specifically focus on this feature of disgust can nevertheless shed light on the types of mechanisms that produce a sense of oral incorporation. For instance, when the anterior sector of a subject's insula, the brain area associated with disgust, was electrically stimulated during neurosurgery, it evoked nausea and the feeling of being sick, as well as the sensation of the stomach moving up and down—in other words, the kind of feelings that often immediately precedes vomiting (Penfield and Faulk 1955). More recently, researchers implanted depth electrodes to electronically stimulate the anterior insula, producing sensations in the throat and mouth that participants described as difficult to stand (Krolak-Salmon et al. 2003; see also Wicker et al. 2003).

Moving on, a more cognitive, sustained sense of *offensiveness* is also evoked by entities that induce disgust; those entities are thereafter treated and thought about in a certain characteristic way. The term "offensiveness" is here used to capture a specific element of the aversion associated with disgust, but it goes beyond merely pulling away or expelling an item from the mouth. The very presence and proximity of disgusting entities are upsetting; they tend to capture attention, and are both memorable and difficult to ignore; they are perceived as unclean, somehow dirty, tainted, or impure; and disgusted people often seek to distance themselves from those entities, either by fleeing or by removing the entities from their immediate vicinity. In addition, such behavior is often accompanied by a motivation to cleanse or purify oneself. When the elicitor is more symbolic than concrete, people will often try to distance themselves symbolically from the disgusting ideas or perpetrators, or will attempt to expel what is offensive by whatever symbolic means seem appropriate (see Rozin et al. 2008).

This feature of core disgust more clearly outstrips the affect program template. Where the affect programs are reflexlike, marked not only by their quick onset but by brief duration, the sense of offensiveness is more enduring. Once a particular entity has triggered a person's disgust system and has thus been marked or encoded as disgusting, that person tends to treat the entity as offensive not for just a brief period of time, but indefinitely, all other things being equal. For instance, she continues to be offended by the item well after the reflexlike withdrawal is complete or she stops gaping at it.

Finally, the third component of core disgust is what I call *contamination sensitivity*. This term captures the fact that once an item is marked as disgusting and offensive, it is cognized as having the ability to infect other items with its offensiveness; it can pass on its disgustingness and contaminate otherwise pure and undisgusting entities. The means of contamination can vary, but the most common routes are via physical contact, both real and merely perceived, or via a known history of physical contact or close physical proximity (see Nemeroff and Rozin 2000; Siegal 1988; Siegal and Share 1990). Contamination sensitivity has a few strikingly idiosyncratic properties. First, contamination is a means by which disgustingness can be *transmitted* from one entity to another. Contaminated entities are thereby disgusting, and so induce disgust and are treated in the same way as other disgusting entities. Contamination sensitivity, in this sense, is fairly robust. There need not be any perceivable physical residue left by the source entity on the contaminated, receiving entity in order for an agent to find, and continue to consider, the receiving entity disgusting. Once considered contaminated, an entity is then treated as disgusting, and thus elicits all the features of the disgust response, including contamination sensitivity—they are treated as being able to transmit their own disgustingness to still other entities.

Second, contamination sensitivity is *elicitor neutral*. Any elicitor of disgust, regardless of the actual nature of the elicitor or which "domain" of disgust it falls in (physical, social, moral, or otherwise), has contamination potency of the same basic sort. If any item is disgusting, it is thereby considered contaminating and can transmit its disgustingness to other entities in the same way.[4]

Much of the experimental work of Paul Rozin and his colleagues investigates these properties, while also documenting the surprising strength of contamination sensitivity. Some experiments demonstrate participants' refusal to drink juice that has come into contact with disgusting items, such as a cockroach or human hair. Others use the same format to show that there need be no actual physical contamination to trigger the contamination sensitivity of the disgust response. For instance, some participants refused to drink juice that had come in contact with demonstrably clean, *uncontaminated* entities, such as a cockroach that had been chemically sterilized, a brand-new comb or a brand-new flyswatter, removed from the hermetically sealed plastic right in front of the experimental participants (see Rozin et al. 1985; Rozin, Hammer et al. 1986; Rozin et al. 1989). Still other experiments demonstrated how participants treated different sweaters, all of which had been thoroughly cleaned but had different histories.

For instance, one sweater was brand-new, whereas another was laundered after it had been worn only once by a perfectly healthy stranger. Unsurprisingly perhaps, participants showed greater reluctance to put on the used sweater, which they treated as if somehow contaminated, although it had been laundered. Even more interesting was that participants' reluctance to put on a sweater increased substantially when they were told that the previous owner had experienced a misfortune such as a leg amputation or had a disease such as tuberculosis. Contamination sensitivity appears responsive to moral taint as well: participants also became increasingly reluctant to put on a sweater when told that the previous owner was a convicted murderer. Indeed, most aversive of all items in their considerable repertoire, claim Rozin and his colleagues, is a sweater that once belonged to the twentieth century's ultimate moral monster, Adolf Hitler (Rozin et al. 1994). Not only is this striking on its own terms, but it is also a vivid demonstration of elicitor neutrality, the fact that disgusting entities are all contaminating, regardless of the character of whatever elicited the particular episode of disgust. In other words, Hitler's moral disgustingness appears to be at least as contaminating as the more concrete disgustingness of a cockroach or a human hair.

Third, there is an important *asymmetry* between disgustingness and non-disgustingness when it comes to contamination potency. This asymmetry is often talked about in terms of purity. Consider that it is far easier for something pure to become contaminated than it is to purify something that is already contaminated. This is illustrated in a telling observation made by several researchers: a single drop of sewage can spoil an entire jug of wine, but a single drop of wine doesn't much help in purifying a jug of sewage (Rozin and Fallon 1987; W. Miller 1997). Evidence suggests that the common sense expressed by this quip is on the right track and that this asymmetry is indeed a cross-cultural feature of the disgust response. For instance, when given a range of potential purifiers for a contaminated glass of juice (adding color to the juice, boiling it, having mother take a sip and indicate it to be okay, etc.), neither American nor Hindu Indian children (4–8 years old) treated any as effectively rendering the contaminated juice "clean" or pure again (Hejmadi et al. 2004; see also Nemeroff and Rozin 2000 on the cross-cultural ubiquity of the "laws of sympathetic magic").

In sum, contamination sensitivity, even more obviously than the sense of oral incorporation and offensiveness, does not comfortably fit anywhere in the affect program template. It is more cognitive than the brute physiological or reflexive components of the response. The sensitivity to a disgusting entity's contamination potency endures long beyond the immediate reaction it produces, but production of that longer-term sensitivity is nevertheless a component of the disgust response. Thus, in addition to the reflexlike features grouped together in the affect program, the three properties of core disgust identified by Rozin and his colleagues are also part of the cluster of elements that make up the disgust response.

Together with the lingering sense of offensiveness and, to a lesser extent, the nebulous sense of oral incorporation, contamination sensitivity makes up what can be thought of as the *inferential signature* of the disgust response. In addition to its typical patterns of overt behavior and typical patterns of physiological reaction, the disgust response also includes these typical patterns of thought or inference; people tend to think about things that disgust them in this characteristic way. Keeping this in mind, an important distinction can be made explicit. It is worth emphasizing that though "offensive" and "contaminating" are properties often ascribed to *items* that trigger disgust, a sense of offensiveness and contamination sensitivity and the patterns of inference and behavior associated with them, in the sense discussed here, are parts of the *response* to such items. Indeed, one of the most insidious aspects of disgust is that once an item triggers it, that item is thereby thought about and treated as if it were offensive and contaminating—whether or not it is genuinely or "really" offensive (if there is such a thing) and whether or not it is objectively contaminating (which there certainly is). Put another way, part of the disgust response is that the properties of offensiveness and contamination potency are *projected onto* whatever elicits it.

1.2.1.3 Downstream Effects
It might help to first explain what "downstream effects" is meant to capture. To do this, I need to step back and reflect on the project from a distance. In compiling this behavioral profile, I am using experimental data to sketch the contours of a capacity, namely, the capacity to be disgusted. Schematically speaking, the behavioral profile provides an explanandum, the set of data that a theory of disgust will explain. The resultant theory will, roughly, amount to a psychological explanation. As such, it will appeal to the structure and functioning of psychological entities, namely, a set of underlying cognitive mechanisms, to explain the capacity and the typical patterns of behavior and inference in question.

The first step in giving a psychological explanation, then, is to clearly characterize the capacity being explained. However, as many commentators on psychological methodology have pointed out, individuating a capacity, discovering the boundaries between one capacity and another, is far from trivial (see, e.g., Cummins 2000; Prinz 2004, chap. 1). The immediately relevant upshot of this difficulty is that we do not always have a straightforward way to distinguish between one capacity and another, between the essential features of a capacity and its downstream effects, understood as the ways that a capacity's operation typically affects other, distinct activities and capacities—cognitive, behavioral, or otherwise. Carving the human mind at its joints is no easy task.

This general worry about individuating a capacity and isolating the primary target of explanation can be raised for the emotions, including the particular case of disgust. To deal with this worry, I proceed on the assumption that the features of the affect program and core disgust can be treated as the features that make up the capacity to be disgusted. The behavioral data to be described in this section, on the other hand, can be separated and relegated to the status of common downstream effects, often caused by, but distinct from, the disgust response proper. This means that rather than components of the capacity to be disgusted, these data reveal the systematic effects of disgust on other, distinct cognitive and behavioral capacities.

Several considerations justify the assumption that it is exclusively the elements of the affect program and core disgust that make up the capacity to be disgusted. First, this portion of the response exhibits consistency; whenever disgust is induced, whatever the nature of the elicitor and the context, the coordinated response that is produced reliably includes the elements of the affect program and core disgust.[5] The straightforward fact that these elements all regularly covary with each other, forming what philosophers of science sometimes call a nomological cluster (Boyd 1991), indicates the presence of a psychological natural kind. Second, while researchers are unable to agree on much of theoretical substance about disgust, all seem to *identify* the emotion they are interested in by reference to the features I have gathered under the headings of the affect program and core disgust. Third, many of the remaining behavioral features that I classify as downstream effects clearly involve the operation of other capacities. Indeed, most of the data presently considered are drawn from experiments explicitly designed to test how inducing disgust influences the operation of other, distinct capacities and psychological systems. Even if these considerations do not, by themselves, definitively establish the division drawn here, I will adopt it as a working hypothesis. The theory developed later, if on the right track, will help to vindicate the assumption on which it is predicated.

Interpreted in light of this working hypothesis, the data on downstream effects give clues to the structure and functioning of the capacity itself.

For instance, part of the offensiveness of disgusting entities is that once detected, they tend to capture attention, stick in the memory, and increase sensitivity to other potentially disgusting entities. A series of correlational studies found attention and memory biases for disgust elicitors; all else being equal, people pay more attention to, and are better at remembering, disgusting things than neutral ones (Charash and McKay 2002). Those studies also found evidence of a more general phenomenon called *mood congruency*: being in a particular mood or emotional state makes one more sensitive to elicitors of that emotion. In this case, participants primed with disgusting stories were better at recalling, and paid significantly more attention to, disgusting things than nondisgusting things.

Memory and attention biases are probably related to the fact that disgust also tends to induce a bias toward information sharing, making people more likely to tell others about things that disgust them. Once again, experiment has supported casual observation on this score. One study (Heath et al. 2001) focused on urban legends: embellished stories about recent, often lurid events, which sometimes contain a grain of truth (but often do not), are popularly believed to be true, and spread quickly through a population either way. The study found that participants were more likely to pass along an urban legend that was disgusting than one that was not, and were more likely to pass along particular urban legends the more disgusting they were. In addition, the more disgusting a story was—the more disgusting motifs it contained—the more likely it was to show up on a set of urban legend Web sites.[6] Another study that indirectly supports the existence of this sort of information-sharing bias looks at those etiquette manuals that have been most prominent over the course of the last few centuries (Nichols 2002b). Nichols found that etiquette norms prohibiting behaviors that are likely to trigger disgust (spitting while at the dinner table) were more likely to survive and be passed down through generations than those that are not (using the wrong fork to eat a salad).

The emotion, of course, has a powerful phenomenological component, and this gives rise to a proprietary, florid, and perhaps all-too-familiar vocabulary. Examples of this type of colorful vocabulary inevitably appear scattered throughout this book. For a more sustained look at some of the most historically famous and extreme instances, see William Miller's social history *The Anatomy of Disgust* (1997); see also Vasquez et al. 2001 for a discussion of the role of this type of vocabulary in different "moral rhetorics," and Smith 2007 for a discussion of the language of stigma.

Some of the most notorious downstream effects of disgust involve the influence it can exert on evaluative judgment about a variety of subjects.

For example, merely having high disgust sensitivity has been found to coincide with a general aversion to people who violate norms, a phenomenon dubbed "moral hypervigilance" by Jones and Fitness (2008). Another study, which used a number of clever indirect measures to gauge "intuitive disapproval," found disgust sensitivity to correlate with intuitive disapproval of homosexuality (Inbar et al. 2009). Occurrent disgust, as opposed to the mere disposition to be disgusted easily, can negatively influence a person's assessment of many things, making those evaluations harsher and more severe. What is particularly striking about this downstream effect is that it is extremely *persistent*, in that it survives through a number of conditions. In the simplest case, the object that triggers disgust and the object being evaluated (be it an entity, action, practice, etc.) are one and the same, and the person making the evaluation possesses a justification for her judgment. In such cases, people make more negative evaluations and are able to articulate good reasons that support their assessments.

More eyebrow raising are cases where the disgust elicitor and object of evaluation are the same, but the reasons the person offers in support of her negative judgment can be defeated. In such cases, disgust again produces, or at least militates in favor of, a negative evaluation. Moreover, the bald disgust response has a powerful enough effect on judgment that people often continue to endorse their initial negative evaluation even upon reflection. That is, people will maintain their negative judgment of the object of evaluation even when they admit that, by their own lights, they are unable to articulate any good reasons supporting that negative evaluation. Jonathan Haidt and others who continue to explore the influence of disgust (and other emotions) on moral judgment (Haidt et al. 1993; Murphy et al. 2000; see also Haidt 2001) have dubbed this phenomenon *moral dumbfounding*: people persist in endorsing certain moral judgments even when they are dumbfounded as to what might justify them. For instance, many participants held fast in their condemnation of disgust-inducing activities such as consensual sibling incest or masturbating with a dead chicken, even when they had been convinced that none of the reasons they initially gave in support of their judgments were credible (Murphy et al. 2000).

Also unsettling is the fact that disgust, once induced, can negatively affect judgments even when the object of evaluation is *distinct* from whatever object or objects triggered the disgust response. One rather devious setup used hypnotism and disgust to produce negative and relatively more severe judgments of blameless, innocuously described vignette characters. Those who experienced hypnotically induced disgust (triggered by otherwise neutral words in the vignettes) were unable to articulate or pinpoint why they disliked the characters in question, but judged them to be suspicious and untrustworthy nonetheless (Wheatley and Haidt 2005). Participants were hypnotized to feel a flash of disgust at arbitrarily chosen words such as "often" or "take." They were then given a series of vignettes describing scenarios, some involving paradigmatic moral transgressions, each of which they were to rate for moral wrongness and disgustingness. Across the board, ratings were more severe when disgust was induced. Participants in whom disgust had been hypnotically triggered gave more severe ratings, for both moral wrongness and disgustingness, and for both moral transgressions that involved viscerally disgusting actions (cousin incest and eating one's dog) and those that did not (a politician who takes bribes, an ambulance-chasing lawyer). Most interesting were the participants' reactions to the following neutral vignette, which describes no moral transgression nor hints at anything wrong or disgusting: "Dan is a student council representative at his school. This semester he is in charge of scheduling discussions about academic issues. He [tries to take/often picks] topics that appeal to both professors and students in order to stimulate discussion." Use of the disgust-inducing word in the vignette, however, increased judgments of disgustingness and moral wrongness by factors of roughly 10 and 6, respectively. Participants maintained their unfavorable judgment of Dan despite their complete lack of justification for it, dubbing him a "popularity-seeking snob" who "just seems like he's up to something"; one participant even wrote simply, "I don't know [why it's wrong], it just is" (ibid., 783).

Moreover, this type of persistent downstream effect on evaluative judgment appears to be produced even in less devious experimental setups, where it is—or should be—*obvious* that the source of disgust and object of judgment are distinct, and when it is clear that the two have little or nothing to do with each other. The carryover effects of this so-called "extraneous disgust" have been found to affect judgments and decisions on a wide variety of subject matters, including moral judgments. In one particularly vivid example, participants were first given a survey to determine how sensitive they are to bodily signals when deliberating, and how much affect influences their decision-making process. Those who scored high on this survey again made more severe moral judgments when they had been subjected to an extraneous disgust prime that putatively had nothing to do with the vignettes they were asked to rate (Schnall et al. 2008). For instance, in one study, disgust was primed by having the participants rate the vignettes at a desk that was intentionally made filthy:

An old chair with a torn and dirty cushion was placed in front of a desk that had various stains, and was sticky. On the desk there was a transparent plastic cup with the dried up contents of a smoothie, and a pen that was chewed up. Next to the desk was a trash can overflowing with garbage such as greasy pizza boxes and dirty-looking tissues.

Again, for the participants sensitive to their own body signals, even judgments about morality were more severe in this disgust-inducing condition. This held true for vignettes that described disgusting moral violations, and more surprisingly, it was also true for judgments of the moral violations that had nothing to do with disgust. Schnall and her colleagues found similar results when extraneous disgust was induced using other creative means, including having participants recall a physically disgusting experience of their own, or subjecting them to fart spray.

Disgust has been shown to affect other sorts of cognition in similar ways. One study found that disgust has an impact on risk aversion, at least in women (Fessler et al. 2004). This experiment was inspired by evolutionary considerations, and rather than focus on disgust, it looked at the downstream effects of multiple emotions on various types of reasoning. The experimenters found that extraneously induced disgust reduced risk-taking behavior in women participants. In another, participants who were primed with disgust in a "normatively unrelated" setting (by watching the four-minute scene involving an absolutely nasty toilet from the film *Trainspotting*) failed to exhibit what behavioral economists know as the endowment effect (Lerner et al. 2004). The endowment effect is the much-studied phenomenon wherein the minimum price at which participants are willing to sell an object after it has been given to them (the object is "endowed" to them) is significantly greater than the maximum price they would be willing to buy it for in the first place. Lerner et al. showed that when disgust had been induced in participants beforehand, the typical asymmetry was eliminated; the prices that participants consented to in the selling and buying conditions were roughly identical. Moreover, both prices were lower than either the buying or selling conditions in the neutral condition, when no emotion was primed, or in the condition that involved the emotion of sadness (in which the endowment effect was not eliminated but *reversed*).

Note that in all these cases—the example involving the dirty desk, the example involving risk aversion, and the example involving the endowment effect—participants can be fully aware that the object of their evaluation and the elicitor of their disgust are distinct. Nevertheless the emotion demonstrably and systematically altered their reasoning in all three cases, exemplifying the persistent influence disgust can exert on evaluative judgments.[7]

1.2.2 The Elicitors

The other half of the disgust behavioral profile is the set of things upstream from disgust responses, namely, the elicitors, or the cues that trigger the emotion. While the makeup of the disgust response exhibits a firm consistency across the types of things that induce it, the pool of elicitors is remarkably diverse. Many have speculated about the nature of disgustingness and the thread that all disgusting things have in common. For instance, theorists have hypothesized that triggers of disgust are pollutants, or matter out of place (Douglas 1966), or they are reminders of death and our animal nature (Rozin et al. 2008). For now, I will not adjudicate between these attempts to capture what all disgust elicitors have in common. I avoid this for methodological purposes, but also because they all rely on what I take to be a highly implausible assumption, namely, that disgust elicitors all share some property above and beyond triggering disgust. Rather than argue against that assumption here, however, I will continue in the spirit of Joe Friday, again staying as close as possible to (just) the facts, and simply reporting the known elicitors as specifically and concretely as I can.

Going forward, it will be useful to keep in mind how easy it is to confuse the projective character of the disgust response with the actual properties of its elicitors. However natural or correct it sounds, saying something like "disgusting things induce disgust" is not much help in characterizing the set of elicitors, since it begs the question on the face of it, and is as informative as being told that opium puts people to sleep because of its dormitive virtue. Given that the response includes elements like contamination sensitivity, a sense of offensiveness, slight feelings of revulsion, and so on, it is no more help to merely say that contaminating things, offensive things, or revolting things induce disgust. Rather, these better describe the effects that elicitors have on people who are disgusted by them (though, for instance, some things that are *treated* as contaminating are *actually* contaminating as well). Part of the disgust response is that one experiences revulsion, and that contamination potency and offensiveness are projected onto the elicitors via disgust's inferential signature and the patterns of behavior to which it typically leads.

Finally, it should be mentioned that the gape face is an elicitor, but one of a slightly different sort than those discussed hereafter. Recognition of the gape face (and other aspects of disgust expression) can be said to elicit disgust because recognition is often *empathic*: it involves the recognizer actually producing the emotion she recognizes as being expressed by another. Moreover, voluntarily making a gape face often triggers the entire cluster of elements and produces a mild episode of the emotion in the person making the gape. The significance of these aspects of disgust will be discussed in more detail in chapter 3.

1.2.2.1 Some Candidate Universals

An undeniable affinity holds between disgust and various sorts of organic materials. Hence at the most concrete end of the spectrum of elicitors are what Rozin and others have suggested as the best candidates to be universals: feces, vomit, blood, urine, and sexual fluids (Rozin et al. 2008; see also Angyal 1941). Equally plausible as universals are corpses and signs of organic decay, which are also some of the most potent elicitors of disgust (Haidt et al. 1994). Bodily orifices—and via contamination, things that come in contact with bodily orifices—are likewise powerful and potentially universal elicitors (Rozin et al. 1995). More generally, artificial orifices or breaches of physical bodies such as cuts, gashes, lesions, or open sores (in Rozin's terms, violations of the "ideal body envelope") are also good candidates for disgust universals. These can trigger disgust if they occur to one's own body—in which case they probably also cause pain—or in someone else's. In this sense, disgust appears universally sensitive to the boundaries of organic bodies and in many cases is activated when those boundaries have been, or are in danger of being, breached.

Bodily boundaries are operative in triggering disgust not only when they are in danger of being violated, however. Items and substances once within those boundaries, which were once inside or part of the body, but then exit or are detached from the body, constitute a related class of potentially universal elicitors of disgust. Severed limbs and externalized innards, either your own or those once belonging to others, fit this description; so too do the waste products mentioned earlier. Other classic examples of this type of elicitor are blood and saliva. Swallowing the saliva that is currently in your mouth is innocuous; even imagining drinking a glass of spit, even if it is (was?) your own, is usually revolting. The blood in your or anyone else's veins is fine; an unchecked nosebleed or spurting artery is disgusting. Fingernails and hair are other good examples of body parts that are innocent enough when still attached, but become aversive once separated from a body—especially when they are in danger of reentering via the mouth (W. Miller 1997).

In this sense, disgust not only polices the boundaries of the body but also enforces a "no reentry" policy; anything that exits or becomes detached triggers it.[8] These elicitors involve bodies, their structure, composition, and the ways they can break down; as such, they also look to be plausible candidates for universals. In addition to intuitive plausibility and persuasive preliminary evidence, these also all involve organic features of bodies that are themselves human universals, and by and large do not vary with age, physical environment, culture, or ethnicity.

Finally, marks of disease and parasitic infection provide another plausible set of disgust universals. Signs of disease include those exhibited by other humans who are infected, as well as environmental cues that reliably indicate the presence of infectious agents. Indeed, knowledge that a person is infected with disease can make that person disgusting to others, even others who are fully aware that the disease in question is not contagious (Rozin et al. 1992). While many have previously pointed out the associations between disgust and infection, recent experimental work has marshaled overwhelming evidence supporting the connection between the two, gathering input from over forty thousand participants from 165 countries. In one study that used Web-based techniques, participants rated a range of photographic stimuli on how disgusting they were. The study found a similar pattern from participants the world over: photos of objects indicating potential disease were judged more disgusting than similar images that lacked disease-typical signs (Curtis et al. 2004). In another study, people from a variety of cultures were asked what disgusts them, and researchers then ran a statistical comparison between the reported elicitors and a list of infectious diseases. They found that "for every disease, one or more elicitors of disgust was mentioned as playing an important role" (Curtis and Biran 2001).

1.2.2.2 Some Common Themes

One of the better-known features of disgust is that it exhibits substantial individual and cross-cultural variability. Thus the remaining types of elicitors involve more variation than those listed earlier, and so make less-plausible candidates for universals. Within the evident variability, however, some common themes stand out. For instance, disgust is often induced not just by people who exhibit reliable indicators of disease but by a more general set of morphological irregularities and phenotypic abnormalities. "Phenotypic abnormality" appears to be a theme with considerable room for variation, however, and has been hypothesized to include, in some cases, people who are disfigured, handicapped, obese, elderly, and even members of an out-group who are unfamiliar or foreign looking.

One group of researchers performed a meta-analysis looking at data from a variety of previous studies and argued that activation of the disgust system underlies the aversion some feel toward the disfigured and handicapped. They further speculated that the same holds true of aversion to the elderly, obese, and perhaps any persons whose appearance deviates too far from the morphological ideal of the local culture (Park et al. 2003). A study by the same group suggests that heightened disgust sensitivity correlates with xenophobia; unfamiliar or foreign-looking people can be disgust elicitors as well (Faulkner et al. 2004). It is not clear what this amounts to, or what "unfamiliar" or "foreign looking" denote, but plausible candidates include whatever characteristics—morphological, physiognomic, or otherwise—might mark people as members of an out-group or different ethnicity (see also Navarrete and Fessler 2006).

Brain-imaging techniques have shed further light on this link between disgust, ethnocentrism, and prejudice toward out-group members. While filling in important neurological details, they have also revealed a particularly troubling aspect of the phenomenon: a correlation between disgust and dehumanization. In an experiment run by Harris and Fiske, participants were shown pictures of members of a variety of social groups. In the cases of prejudice where disgust was the accompanying emotion, and only in the cases involving disgust, the medial prefrontal cortex (mPFC) failed to activate (Harris and Fiske 2006, 2007).[9] The mPFC is the brain area associated, on independent grounds, with higher-level social interactions with other *people*, and is thought to underlie the capacities for mind reading and attribution of agency. Harris and Fiske's finding suggests not only that disgust is elicited by members of certain low-status out-groups, but that it is elicited particularly by those out-group members who are dehumanized, not even thought of as people or agents.

Another common theme in disgust elicitors, one that Paul Rozin has emphasized for many years, is food. Though all cultures deem some foods disgusting (and, on the other side of the coin, embrace foods that other cultures find strange or disgusting), the particular foods falling into these categories vary from location to location and from culture to culture. Moreover, these foods are often considered disgusting for conceptual or symbolic reasons. Rozin and his colleagues point out that in this context, disgust is distinct from mere inappropriateness or distastefulness (Fallon and Rozin 1983; Rozin et al. 2008). A person might refrain from eating something because it is simply inappropriate to eat, in that it is inedible, like a chair or a pebble. Most people do not eat chairs or pebbles, but it is not because they find chairs or pebbles disgusting. Likewise, disgusting foods are distinct from distasteful ones in that people refrain from eating distasteful food because they dislike the way it tastes. In contrast, a person can be disgusted by foods that she has never tried, and so does not *know* how they taste. In both cases of merely inappropriate or distasteful foods, neither is typically considered fully disgusting, and so neither is considered offensive or contaminating.[10]

Not all foods have the same potential to become objects of disgust, however. Meat, it seems, is particularly liable to elicit the emotion and is a common theme in the varieties of foods that different cultures find disgusting. In light of the salience of physical bodies to disgust, it is not altogether surprising that meat is a common elicitor. A comparison of food taboos across seventy-eight different cultures found meat consumption to be more regulated and restricted than consumption of other foods. Fessler and Navarrete (2003b) conclude that this is due in large part to the role of disgust.

Some living animals, and not just their products or corpses, are liable to elicit disgust as well. These include many "creepy-crawlies" and animals that are highly associated with disease, decay, and death, which are perhaps linked to disgust mainly by virtue of this association. Flies, maggots, worms, rats, and cockroaches are obvious examples. Others, which are in fact parasitic on humans, include lice, fleas, and ticks. In addition, Davey and colleagues have identified another group of animals that humans often find aversive, and whose aversion is driven by disgust. This group includes slugs, snails, and caterpillars, as well as animals that can be dangerous to humans but are not predators: snakes and especially spiders (see, e.g., Davey, Forster, and Mayhew 1993; Webb and Davey 1993; Ware et al. 1994).

Another common theme in disgust elicitors is sex and reproduction. For instance, menstrual blood is typically more disgusting than other types (Rozin et al. 2008). Disgust is also triggered not just by sex-associated fluids but also by many of the sexual activities that produce them. The most discussed instance of this is incest (Fessler and Navarrete 2004; Lieberman, Tooby, and Cosmides 2003; Westermarck 1891/1921), but other types of deviant sexual activities evoke disgust as well. While "deviant sex" induces disgust most everywhere, what counts as deviant is, to some extent, dictated by particular cultures and can differ from one culture to the next. For instance, homosexuality might be considered deviant and disgusting, as in many parts of the United States, or might be perfectly acceptable, as in other parts of the United States or in ancient Greece (see Haidt and Hersh 2001). As in the case of food, constraints and biases appear to influence the variation. For instance, more extreme varieties of deviance such as bestiality and necrophilia are more likely to be deemed disgusting.[11]

A final common theme in disgust elicitors includes activities, and their perpetrators, that involve breaking certain social norms. While the particular activities that fall into this category vary from culture to culture, all cultures appear to find some social transgressions disgusting. One subclass of disgust involving norms contains the social rules regulating activities that involve something that is antecedently disgusting. For example, violation of social norms governing the locally correct way to deal with corpses or dispose of fecal matter, the proper way to prepare food, or the appropriate forms of conducting oneself at the dinner table or in the bedroom are likely to induce disgust merely by virtue of the subject matter being regulated. Several studies provide more examples and details. For instance, the meat taboos mentioned earlier (Fessler and Navarrete 2003b) are social norms of this type. In addition, Shaun Nichols (2002a) found that violations of only some etiquette norms involve disgust, for instance, those against picking one's nose in public or spitting into a glass of water and then taking a sip while at a dinner party. Another study found that many different languages have words that roughly translate to "disgust," and that those words are likewise applied to social activities of this sort (Haidt et al. 1997). Many of the vignettes used to explore the effect of disgust on evaluative judgments, such as consensual brother–sister incest or masturbating with a chicken carcass, also involve violations of social norms of this kind (Haidt et al. 1993).

Again, while rules (and the behaviors that constitute their corresponding transgressions) of this very general sort make up a common theme in disgust elicitors, the details of the prescriptions and proscriptions expressed by these taboos and social norms can vary from culture to culture. The variation can be found along a number of dimensions, including their specificity—whom they apply to, when they apply, or where they apply—as well as in the importance and centrality of such norms to the local sociomoral code (see Shweder et al. 1997; Rozin et al. 1999).

However, another subclass of disgust involves norms and violations that appear to have little or nothing to do with the types of antecedently disgusting elicitors just noted. The common theme of this subclass is quite abstract but centers on group membership: violating a particularly central social norm or flouting one of the defining values of a group can induce disgust in members of that cultural in-group. For instance, the Hopi value the environment, the ancient Greeks prized self-control, the Japanese place a high value on duty and social cohesion, and Americans assign importance to egalitarianism, personal integrity, and rugged individualism. Behaviors or social activities that disrespect or run counter to those values have been found to elicit disgust in members of each culture, respectively. In the United States, Republicans and Democrats define themselves against and in opposition to each other; those in the opposite party, loudly and proudly espousing the opposing ideology, are liable to elicit disgust in their counterparts.

One particularly interesting cross-cultural study looked at, among other things, disgust and the violation of defining social norms (Haidt et al. 1997). Examples of these in the United States, listed when participants were asked the open-ended question of what they find disgusting, included acts of racism, hypocrisy, violations of important social relationships, dishonest politicians, and opposing political attitudes. In their own words, "Lawyers who chase ambulances are disgusting. People who abandon their elderly parents are disgusting. Liberals say that conservatives are disgusting. Conservatives say that welfare cheaters are disgusting" (116). Japanese participants mentioned situations where they failed to meet their own standards, when they felt shamed or abused by others, and when they felt others had failed to meet their needs or expectations. Historians tell us that ancient Greeks felt disgust toward those who flouted social norms and conventions due to lack of self-control, or those whose transgressions were unaccompanied by shame; such behaviors and their perpetrators were barbarous and inhumane (Parker 1983). Perhaps the most telling description of this subclass of disgust-inducing activity comes from the Hopi, whose specific elicitors include disregard for the environment and any form of aggression: "Anything that would be deviant to Hopi teachings and belief could be seen as disgusting to some degree" (Haidt et al. 1997, 120).

1.2.3 Shaping the Theory: Three Constraints

I began the chapter by remarking on the reasons that disgust has become a focal point of research in philosophy and psychology, and noted that for all the data that have been gathered, sophisticated theory construction has lagged behind. Rather than begin by examining the various conjectures that have been made, my strategy has been to start with the facts and construct a clean set of data that a theory of disgust needs to explain.

In addition to the facts, the character of the behavioral profile and the proliferation of competing accounts of disgust can also offer guidance about how to proceed from here. It is not unreasonable to want an adequate theory not just to explain the data, but also to provide some insight as to why so many different but plausible things can be said about this emotion. Seeing the embarrassment of riches in this way points to three key desiderata:

Unity of the response The characteristic disgust *response* comprises a number of distinct features. These features form a stable or homeostatic cluster. That is, the features occur together as a package; regardless of what triggers disgust on any particular occasion, once it is triggered, the production of one element of the cluster is regularly accompanied by the production of the others. What accounts for the clustering of this particular, idiosyncratic set of features? Why have these specific cognitive, behavioral, and physiological elements merged into a single, unified, and apparently universally human response type?

Variation of the elicitors   While the disgust response itself, along with a small set of elicitors, is a human universal, a large amount of variation exists in what is found disgusting, and so in what types of elicitors activate individual disgust systems. Indeed, disgust allows for variation at both the cultural and individual level. What accounts for this feature of the emotion?

Diversity of the elicitors   There is also a wide and surprisingly diverse range of elicitors that trigger disgust, ranging along one dimension from the concrete to the abstract, and along another from the brutely physical and inert to the highly social and interpersonal. What accounts for the pairing of such a diverse range of triggering conditions to this one specific type of response?

Each of these is a constraint that any viable theory of disgust should satisfy. I take it that the first is self-explanatory, but perhaps the second and third are less so. To see the difference between variation and diversity in elicitors, consider two people who are disgusted by exactly the same set of things, from the smell of festering dog doo to the taste and texture of fried tofu, to (what they consider to be) decadent liberal views on sexual mores, to Democratic political agendas. Despite there being no variation between the two, there is still great diversity in the things that elicit disgust in both of them. One still might wonder, about both people, why the single emotional response is elicited by such diverse types of things as organic waste, on the one hand, and, say, increased regulation of the financial system, on the other. Aside from triggering their disgust, these elicitors seem to have little else in common. Once again, though, there is no *variation* in what elicits disgust in these two people.

Now imagine a third person, who loves tofu but is disgusted by beef, (what she considers to be) barbaric and oppressive conservative views on sexual mores, and Republican political agendas. This is still an impressively *diverse* range of things to be disgusted by, but now we can also point to significant *variation* between what disgusts this third person and what disgusts the first two. An acceptable theory of disgust should be able to explain this, too, and thus meet all three of the desiderata. That said, while it is useful to distinguish between variation and diversity, it is altogether likely that many of the same cognitive mechanisms are operative in producing both.

1.3   A Psychological Model

The first step in building an account that can satisfy my three desiderata and explain the data in the behavioral profile takes the form of a psychological model of the cognitive architecture and proximate mechanisms that underlie disgust. As such some brief remarks need to be made concerning the general character of these sorts of theoretical tools and how they are understood to do their explanatory work.

1.3.1   Background Assumptions

First, the type of explanation I offer here is a proximate explanation, rather than an ultimate one. The distinction between proximate and ultimate explanations first came to prominence in the context of biology (Mayr 1961; see also Ariew 2003), but it can be brought to bear on psychological explanations, as well (Barkow et al. 1992). In the psychological case, a proximate explanation explains an organism's behavior by reference to stimuli in its immediate environment and the structure and functioning of internal, information processing psychological mechanisms whose operation eventuates in the relevant behavior. Ultimate explanations, alternatively, are evolutionary and thus historical. In the psychological case, various behaviors, behavioral tendencies, and often the character of the underlying psychological mechanisms themselves, are explained by appeal to the selective pressures that helped shape them and the adaptive problems they evolved in response to. Although it is important not to confuse one for the other, ultimate and proximate explanations can complement each other. As such, I consider an explanation of each type to be crucial to a complete theory of disgust. Accordingly, the model sketched in this chapter will provide the heart of a proximate explanation, and chapter 2 will begin developing an ultimate one.

The explanatory relations between the behavioral profile and the psychological model were briefly discussed at the beginning of section 1.2.1.3, but it will help to say a bit more here. With the behavioral profile, I have sketched the contours of a particular capacity, namely, the capacity to be disgusted. This capacity comprises a set of coordinated physiological responses, behavioral tendencies, and an inferential signature, and is thus described in behavioral terms, broadly construed. To explain that capacity, the model used in the proximate explanation of disgust will be couched in psychological terms, and the description of the model will refer to the likes of cognitive architecture and cognitive mechanisms. The operation of the psychological entities posited in the model produces the physiological responses, behavioral tendencies, and inferential signature described in the behavioral profile. Again, the capacity is the explanandum, and the psychological model the explanans (Cummins 2000).

Although the usage here will conform to the standard conventions, it is also best to be explicit about what the various elements of the model are being used to represent. The model depicts a cognitive architecture. The term "cognitive architecture" simply provides a graphic way of talking about the structure of minds. Talk about mental structure, in turn, can be understood as talk about regularities in the types of causal interactions that typically take place between different mental states. It is a functional-level model that attempts to account for the various types of data compiled in the behavioral profile with a cognitive architecture composed of different but interlocking subsystems and mechanisms. It does this by charting the flow of information and causal influence between the various subsystems and associates various aspects of disgust behavior with corresponding components of the cognitive architecture that help produce them. As such, it is depicted as what is sometimes called a boxology. Different "boxes" represent functionally distinct components of the mind, with the arrows representing causal influence between them.[12] Each box contains a propriety body of information that leads to the production of the patterns of behavior with which it is associated. Most boxologies are founded on the twin doctrines of functionalism and the computational theory of mind. Roughly speaking, functionalism is the ontological thesis that mental properties are functional properties, whose identity conditions are determined by their functional role and specified mainly in relation to other mental states, typical upstream causes, and the behaviors they cause or could cause. The computational theory of mind is based on the computer analogy, the idea that the relationship between the brain and the mind is very much like the relationship between the hardware of a computer and the programs it runs. The computational theory of mind supplements functionalism's ontological picture with the more specific claim that mental processes are computational processes performed on mental representations.[13]

1.3.2 The Disgust System

The model itself is pitched at a fairly high level of abstraction. It is in this abstraction from detail that much of the model's utility resides, as one purpose it serves is to impose a map on an otherwise sprawling body of evidence. The model divides the cognitive architecture into three main parts. The first part is an acquisition subsystem. This component is responsible for acquiring disgust elicitors that are not innately specified. The significance of the acquisition subsystem stems from the need to account for the cultural and individual variation found in disgust elicitors. That variation indicates many elicitors are acquired from the environment, either from individual experience or from social learning. Cognitive mechanisms that underlie the ability to acquire new disgust elicitors by either means are component parts of this acquisition subsystem.

The second main division in the model is dedicated to producing disgust, and is called the execution subsystem. In addition to generating the core elements of the disgust response, as mapped out in the behavioral profile, the execution subsystem also maintains a database of elicitors. That database contains representations of items, entities, or behaviors that trigger the disgust response when they are detected in the environment (or vividly described or imagined). The third part of the cognitive architecture depicted in the model does not represent a component of the disgust system proper but shows the variety of other psychological and behavioral activities on which disgust has been found to have systematic downstream effects (see fig. 1.1).

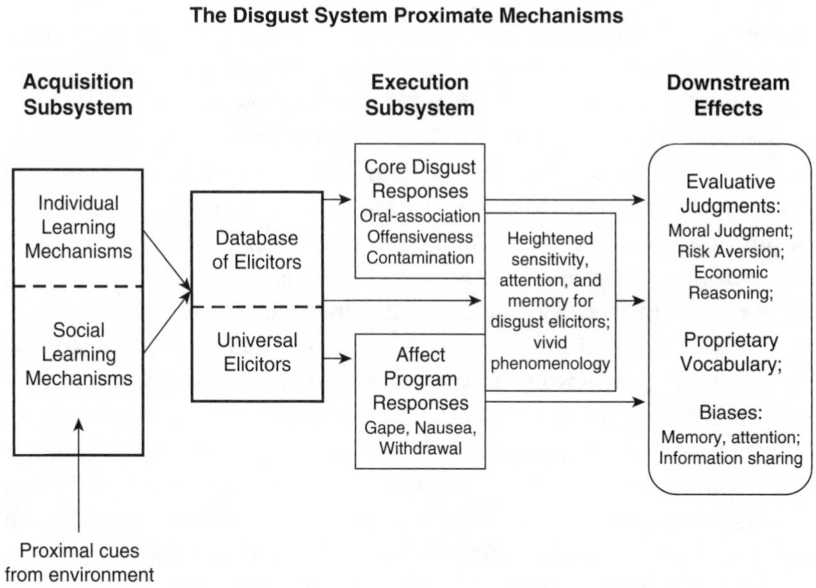

The Disgust System Proximate Mechanisms

Figure 1.1
A functional-level model of interlocking mechanisms that make up the human disgust system. The arrows represent causal links between the various mechanisms.

It will be useful to carefully walk through the model, beginning on the left with the acquisition subsystem. This is represented as containing a number of distinct, independently operating cognitive mechanisms. A division is made between mechanisms that rely on individual learning and those that rely on social learning. The broad function of mechanisms on both sides of this divide is to pick up on relevant cues and patterns from the surrounding environment, social or otherwise, and infer from them new contents for the disgust database. Mechanisms are divided by the kinds of proximal cues to which they are sensitive: the former of these involve acquisition of elicitors via direct interaction with or experience of them, unmediated by social transmission or other people. The latter involve acquisition of elicitors from other people, via imitation, explicit learning, or other forms of social transmission. Individual and social learning, in this respect, probably represent poles along a continuum rather than a sharp functional distinction. The difference is clear enough to be useful for organizational purposes, however; thus the dotted rather than solid line.

As it stands, the depiction of the acquisition subsystem allows for a plurality of acquisition routes and mechanisms but remains agnostic as to their number and individual character. It is likewise agnostic with respect to how restricted or open are the conditions under which an elicitor may be acquired via each mechanism; some mechanisms may deliver a new elicitor only under very specific circumstances, while others may be able to do so in a wider variety of conditions. This pluralism accounts for one sense in which the disgust acquisition subsystem itself is quite flexible. The model is committed, however, to the fact that at least some of the mechanisms of acquisition have some degree of innate structure and are likely to exhibit many of the characteristics associated with innate cognitive mechanisms, such as domain specificity, automaticity, and stable developmental trajectory. What unites all the diverse acquisition mechanisms is that they are all able to deliver new elicitors to the disgust execution subsystem. The execution subsystem, then, is able to receive new elicitors from a number of different acquisition mechanisms, and enter them into the "disgust box."

This brings us to the disgust execution subsystem. Moving from the left, the first component is the database of elicitors. It is depicted as a box, which "contains" a functionally distinguished set of representations of entities or activities that trigger disgust when they are detected in a person's environment or are vividly described or imagined, and so on. More specifically, when an item represented in the database is detected (described, imagined), and the execution system is activated, it leads to the production of the full suite of affective, behavioral, and cognitive components that make up the disgust response.

The database is divided into two sections by a dotted line that separates elicitors by their source, rather than their function. Again, once represented in the database, all elicitors, when detected, lead to the disgust response, regardless of how they got there, be it individual or social acquisition or innate specification. On one side are the elicitors acquired from experience. On the other are the innately specified, universal elicitors. Additionally, the latter side may contain several forms of innate information about the sorts of things that trigger disgust. More specifically, the model reserves this spot for innately specified information that might take forms *other* than representations of specific elicitors. Such information might be in the form of constraints, biases, or more general guidelines. Information represented in formats such as these may also interact with information drawn from the environment or may require information from the environment to activate, complete, shape, or edit it in some way.

Interlocking with this database are the integrated cognitive mechanisms that produce the characteristic features of the disgust response. There are two distinct mechanisms in the execution subsystem. One corresponds to the affect program and gives rise to associated elements of the response like the gape face, nausea and revulsion, and a reflexlike quick withdrawal. The other corresponds to core disgust and gives rise to the associated elements of the response, namely, the sense of oral association, offensiveness, and contamination sensitivity.

These mechanisms and the database make up the execution subsystem, whose broad function is to produce the characteristic behavioral and inferential features of the disgust response whenever one of the elicitors in the database is detected, vividly described or imagined, and so on. These architectural components of the execution subsystem are assumed to be innate and universal among normal, mature humans, and this assumption is again justified by appeal to the fact that the disgust response is found in humans of all cultures. Moreover, the operation of the execution subsystem is largely automatic and involuntary when triggered.

By producing the disgust response, the execution subsystem also leads to common downstream effects on other behavioral and psychological activities. These effects appear systematic in some cases but are less coherent and tightly integrated than the central features of the response. Thus the model simply illustrates that these appear to be causally preceded by the activation of the execution subsystem. Other than suggesting a broad pluralism, the model remains agnostic as to the types of mechanisms involved in those downstream effects or the nature of their interaction with the mechanisms of the disgust system. Some of the most striking effects from the behavioral profile are depicted in the model. Also depicted in the model is a spot for the collection of coordinated mechanisms that increase sensitivity, attention, and memory specifically to disgust elicitors, which were also mentioned in the behavioral profile. Along with a vivid phenomenology, these appear to be more immediate and consistent downstream effects than the others and are shown closer to the execution subsystem accordingly.

1.4 Conclusion

The model presented is the first major component of my theory of disgust and provides proximate explanations of many of the emotion's features. Moreover, it makes some headway in satisfying our triad of desiderata. Recall what they are:

Unity of the response The characteristic disgust *response* comprises a number of distinct features. These features form a stable or homeostatic cluster. That is, the features occur together as a package; regardless of what triggers disgust on any particular occasion, once it is triggered, the production of one element of the cluster is regularly accompanied by the production of the others. What accounts for the clustering of this particular, idiosyncratic set of features? Why have these particular cognitive, behavioral, and physiological elements merged into a single, unified, and apparently universally human response type?

Variation of the elicitors While the disgust response itself, along with a small set of elicitors, is a human universal, a large amount of variation exists in what is found disgusting, and so in what types of elicitors activate disgust systems. Indeed, disgust allows for variation at both the cultural and individual level. What accounts for this feature of the emotion?

Diversity of the elicitors There is also a wide and surprisingly diverse range of elicitors that trigger disgust, ranging along one dimension from the concrete to the abstract, and along another from the brutely physical and inert to the highly social and interpersonal. What accounts for the pairing of such a diverse range of triggering conditions to this one specific type of response?

The psychological model addresses the "unity of the response" desideratum by showing that the features of the disgust response cluster because the proximate cognitive mechanisms underlying the elements of that response are in fact interlocking and tightly integrated. It suggests a way to begin thinking about the "variation" and "diversity of the elicitors" desiderata in that it allows for a variety of acquisition mechanisms, which, despite differences in the conditions and types of proximal cues they are sensitive to, all function to deliver new elicitors to the disgust database. Thus different people, exposed to different cultural conditions and with unique individual histories, can end up being disgusted by a wide range of different entities and activities.

Of course, while this does make some progress, none of the desiderata have completely been met. Indeed, the solutions offered by the model can seem to be more restatements of the respective problems than satisfying solutions. Why are the different mechanisms thus integrated? How did the disgust system come to have several different routes of acquisition? Such questions are legitimate, but only to be expected at this stage, since the theory of disgust is not yet complete. The next step to providing a more satisfying and complete account requires supplementing this proximate explanation with an ultimate one, which looks to the evolutionary origins of the disgust system.

2 Poisons and Parasites: The Entanglement Thesis and the Evolution of Disgust

2.1 A Puzzle about Disgust

A few comparative questions will help frame the discussion in this chapter. First: is the emotion of disgust found only in human beings? This question is interesting not only for the insight an answer might shed on human nature but also because different theorists working on the emotions have given it different answers. On the one hand, a group of prominent researchers who have focused on disgust in particular answer the question in the affirmative. In the view they recommend, disgust is "a very old (though uniquely human) rejection system" (Haidt et al. 1997), which "is absent in nonhuman primates, yet extremely frequent and probably universal in contemporary humans" (Rozin et al. 2008). Proponents of this view are impressed by a number of distinctive features of disgust that they have uncovered in their work, including its decidedly cognitive, symbolic, and conceptual character; the role it plays in regulating human social interactions; its wide cultural variation; and its link to a plurality of domains, including morality. Additionally, they note that despite the confidence of some theorists, many who actually work closely with animals fail to observe anything that fits the description of disgust in those other species (Chevalier-Skolnikoff 1973; see also Morris et al. 2007).[1]

Additionally, some supporters of this view also endorse an argument that suggests *why* disgust might be unique to humans. The motivation for the argument comes from the work of the cultural anthropologist Ernest Becker (1973), author of *The Denial of Death*. Becker, like Nietzsche and Freud before him, assigned great import to the fact that humans, alone among the animals, must psychologically confront the knowledge of their own inevitable deaths. He argued that recognition of our own mortality and eventual death induces existential anxieties and even, in extreme cases, terror. Feelings and attitudes such as these constitute an adaptive threat, the line of thought goes; they can be at worst paralyzing but even in milder cases can stifle or disrupt normal, fitness-enhancing behavior. Building on this idea, Rozin and his colleagues maintain that due to cultural evolution, conceptual and symbolic disgust now mainly serves to protect against such paralyzing and fitness-reducing thoughts, repressing anything that reminds us that we are animals and are thus mortal. This, in turn, is thought to help explain why only humans have disgust: "Only human animals know they are to die, and only humans need to repress this threat" (Rozin et al. 2008). Following the literature, I call this view the *Terror Management theory*.

Another set of factors pulls in a different direction, however. Consider a second comparative question: are there homologies of disgust in primates and other animals?[2] Some researchers of the emotions have thought so, and in their view it would be quite surprising if there were not homologies of disgust in all sorts of other animals (Ekman 2003; Griffiths 1997; Darwin 1872; cf. Fessler and Navarrete 2003a). While those sympathetic to this view tend to focus on emotions in general rather than disgust in particular, their confidence in the assertion is bolstered by a number of specific considerations. These include the presence of clear homologies of other basic emotions such as anger and fear in primates and other mammals. Those holding this view also tend to see disgust as serving to monitor food intake and protect against ingested toxins. They thus point to the presence of something approximating the gape face (the characteristic facial expression associated with disgust) in primates and the existence of acquired taste aversions in many other animals. Perhaps more than anything else, though, they emphasize the broad evolutionary continuity that exists between humans and primates to support their contention. Accordingly, I call this view the *Simple Continuity view*.

At first, these two views appear to be opposed to each other. If they are indeed incompatible, it would be nice to know which one is correct. However, one may not be forced to take sides; there are other stances to take with respect to the issue. For instance, there may be an irenic conclusion that could be endorsed, holding that each view is partially correct when understood properly. On the other hand, it could also be the case that neither is correct, and both should be rejected.

In what follows, I argue for this last option. To say why, however, I must first motivate and defend the alternative view that I favor. Once that has been accomplished, I will briefly return to this puzzle posed at the chapter's outset and show why both the Simple Continuity view and Terror Management theory should be rejected as ultimate explanations, and so deserve no part in an account of the fundamental nature of disgust.

2.2 The Entanglement Thesis

Here, in short, is the hypothesis I defend and elaborate on in the remainder of this chapter: underlying disgust are two distinguishable cognitive mechanisms that were once distinct but became functionally integrated—entangled with each other—in the cognitive architecture of modern human beings. In the face of the sorts of selective pressures I describe hereafter, those two mechanisms combined to form what we now recognize as a single emotion, whose character is shaped by the adaptive problems each mechanism initially and separately was designed to solve. While homologies to each individual mechanism can be found in primates and other animals, only in humans have the two mechanisms become functionally integrated, and thus only in humans do we find this particular emotion. Since I am hypothesizing that two mechanisms became so entangled as to form a single emotion, I call this idea the *Entanglement thesis*.

To make the case for this hypothesis, I build on the work done in the last chapter. That chapter culminated with a psychological model that helps explain the facts compiled in the behavioral profile. Here I proceed on the assumption that the model is by and large correct and offer a set of ultimate explanations for some of the mechanisms posited therein. In addition to describing the adaptive problems that gave rise to the distinct mechanisms underlying our capacity for disgust, I also consider a hypothesis about the conditions and evolutionary pressures that drove those mechanisms together, reshaping and fusing them into a single, integrated emotion.

According to the proximate model, the two distinct mechanisms (aside from the database) that underlie the disgust response are associated with the affect program and core disgust, respectively. We will see that each of these mechanisms is not only behaviorally but also evolutionarily distinct, and the elements associated with each mechanism can be traced back to their distinct evolutionary pasts. That is, each is evolutionarily ancient: the mechanisms and problems they evolved to mitigate originate far back in human phylogeny, and mechanisms homologous to each can be found in other species. However, each has followed a different evolutionary trajectory: each initially arose to perform a different function. This remains the case despite the fact that they have become deeply intertwined in humans, and apparently only in humans.

One mechanism, associated with the affect program, evolved as an adaptive response to the ingestion of toxins and harmful substances. The other, associated with core disgust, evolved as an adaptive response to the presence of disease and parasites in the broader physical and social environment. I discuss each of these in turn.

2.2.1   Food Intake: The Omnivore's Dilemma, Acquired Taste Aversions, and the Garcia Effect

According to the Entanglement thesis, the mechanism underlying the affect program is closely linked to digestion and evolved specifically to regulate food intake and protect the gut against ingested substances that are poisonous, toxic, or otherwise harmful. It was designed to expel substances entering or likely to enter the gastrointestinal system via the mouth, and has been call a "food rejection system" (Darwin 1872; Rozin et al. 2008).

Rozin's work on disgust emphasizes the relevant adaptive problem, which he calls "the omnivore's dilemma." All species that are "nutrition generalists" face this dilemma, given that some potential foods are more nutritious than others, and still others are detrimental. The problem itself is quite simple: the organism must eat, but it must be selective in what it consumes, because many things that seem edible are actually harmful when ingested. Rozin distinguishes a number of ways in which this problem might be mitigated. For instance, simple distaste prevents some foods from being consumed based on their sensory properties, namely, because they taste bad, or are excessively bitter, sour, and so on. (Disgust, as pointed out in the previous chapter, differs from mere distaste in that it can prevent modern humans from ever tasting potential food in the first place.)

One common way to navigate problems raised by the omnivore's dilemma is provided by acquired taste aversions. These provide a way to narrow down culinary options by implementing a "once bitten, twice shy" rule. In humans, this variety of "shyness" manifests as an intense aversion directed toward the offending food type. Thus, a type of food that has induced sickness in the past comes to be avoided in the future. If, for instance, an individual has a meal that involves a generous slather of hollandaise sauce, and then becomes violently ill not long afterward, she is likely to find hollandaise sauce distinctly unpleasant in the future. In extreme cases, the mere smell of it may make her more than a little queasy. Her culinary options have thereby been narrowed.

Much interest in taste aversions focuses on their proprietary mechanism of acquisition. These were first systematically investigated in rats (Garcia, Hankins, and Rusiniak 1974), but similar effects have since been found in an astounding number of other animals, ranging from garden slugs through primates to humans (Bernstein 1999). While some tastes, such as extreme sourness or bitterness, are innately distasteful, full aversion in this sense must be learned through experience with the relevant type of food. However, the proprietary learning mechanism requires only a single trial to acquire an aversion to a new type of food. If consumption of a particular food is accompanied by gastrointestinal distress, even as long as twelve hours after consumption, an aversion to that food is developed.

This domain-specific acquisition mechanism for taste aversions allows for what is sometimes called "one-shot learning," and it is not uncommon for it to yield false positives. If a person experiences gastrointestinal stress in the relevant time frame after eating, she is apt to develop a strong dislike for what she ate. It does not seem to matter if the stomach unpleasantness was actually caused by the food—because it was poisonous, spoiled, contaminated, or otherwise toxic—or if the upset gut was due to something altogether unrelated; a new taste aversion toward the salient food is likely to be acquired. What food or flavor is salient may vary from case to case, but it appears that aversions are more likely to be developed toward foods with strong tastes and pungent smells. The susceptibility of the taste-aversion-learning mechanisms to false positives in this respect is often called the "Garcia effect"; the taste aversions themselves are sometimes called "Garcia aversions." Comparative evidence reveals the capacity to form Garcia aversions in a great many other animals, including those phylogenetically distant from humans, which suggests that the underlying cognitive machinery is evolutionarily quite ancient. This also stands to reason, as the ability to guard against consuming poisons and toxins would have been highly adaptive in the past, as it is now.

Perhaps most relevant to disgust and the Entanglement thesis is the means by which avoidance of a specific food is ensured once a taste aversion is acquired. When the previously offending type of food is presented to an individual, say eggs Benedict with hollandaise sauce, she responds aversively. The specific aversive response is produced by many of the same systems involved in ingestion itself, and the resulting feeling is of nausea. This, of course, serves immediately to deter an organism from consuming the substance in question, but it is in the specific character of the aversion, in the connection to nausea and ingestion, that the link between taste aversions and human disgust is most manifest.

In humans, the behavioral elements of the disgust response, specifically those associated with the affect program (as well as the sense of oral incorporation noted in core disgust), almost all involve bodily systems also associated with food and the digestive system. For instance, extreme disgust can result in outright vomiting, but even in milder cases it includes not just quick withdrawal but the physiological element of nausea. Also, the characteristic facial expression, the gape, involves movements associated with oral expulsion, as well as the constricting of the nasal passages used to smell food. This facial expression clearly mimics the patterns of muscular contraction in the mouth, nose, and face that are involved during the actual behavior of retching, which nausea so often precedes. Finally, in distancing oneself from the offending items, quick withdrawal serves to lessen the intensity of the smells that can trigger nausea.

All these elements of the disgust response, especially those associated with the affect program, bear the mark of a system designed to monitor nutrition and consumption. Facts concerning the other side of the disgust system, the types of things that commonly trigger it, help fill out the picture. That food itself is one of the common themes in the elicitor set only strengthens the conclusion that human disgust, the omnivore's dilemma, and taste aversions are all deeply linked. Thus the ultimate explanation of the properties of the affect program will be found in the evolutionary logic of monitoring food consumption and preventing ingestion of poisons and toxin. As such, the first component of the Entanglement thesis is now in place: one of the two main mechanisms composing the execution side of the human disgust system is what I will henceforth call, in shorthand, the *poison mechanism*.

2.2.2 Disease and Parasite Avoidance

This leaves the mechanism subserving core disgust, whose associated response features include a sense of oral incorporation, offensiveness, and contamination sensitivity. According to the Entanglement thesis, this mechanism was shaped by the adaptive problems raised by disease-causing pathogens and the evolutionary arms race underlying the struggle between parasites and their hosts. It evolved to provide one way to protect against infection from pathogens and parasites, namely, by avoiding them. Unlike the affect program, this mechanism is not specific to ingestion and does not respond only to potential threats to the gut. Rather, it serves to prevent coming into any sort of close physical proximity with infectious agents. This involves avoiding not only perceivable pathogens and parasites, but also places, substances, and other organisms that might be harboring them. Other theorists who have commented on this capacity have described it as "intuitive microbiology" (Pinker 1997), an "evolved response to threats of infectious disease" (Curtis et al. 2004), and "parasite avoidance" (Kurzban and Leary 2001).

Though the psychological literature contains little discussion of parasites or infectious disease (as opposed to psychiatric or neurological disease), the possibility of infection presents a nearly ubiquitous set of adaptive problems. A parasite is any organism that grows on, feeds on, or otherwise exploits the resources of another organism—its host—but contributes nothing to the host's survival in return.[3] Given that parasites drain resources without making any contribution in return, the adaptive problems they raise for potential hosts are not only ubiquitous but also fairly simple: hosts need to avoid and protect against them and be able to eliminate parasites once infected.

Accordingly, natural selection has endowed potential hosts with a range of defense mechanisms against pathogens and other parasites. Within the body, immune systems equipped with an arsenal of antibodies wage wonderfully complicated cellular-level warfare on viruses and bacteria. Skin itself is an external protective membrane that, among other things, provides a defensive barrier against parasites infiltrating the body in the first place. Many animals instinctively engage in hygienic behaviors that minimize the likelihood of infection, such as grooming, cleansing, or bathing.

That is not all, however. Natural selection has also endowed potential hosts with capacities designed to help them avoid pathogens and parasites in the first place. These capacities can monitor a wide range of potential sources of infection, and they operate by making organisms sensitive to signs of parasites in the environment, especially to the proximal cues of parasitic infection in their conspecifics (members of the same species). Such cues can be general, like the smell of organic rot and decay, or more specific, such as particular types of aberrant appearance and behavior in others. Examples of these might include especially salient irregularities in appearance such as lesions, sores, splotches of discoloration, or disruptions of bilateral symmetry. Likewise, constant itching or sneezing, profuse sweating, and retching are all familiar examples of the types of behavior for which this capacity would be on the lookout. In general, parasite-avoidance capacities are predominantly sensitive to any phenotypic abnormalities or deviations from healthy phenotypic norms.

Kurzban and Leary also describe this adaptive problem, and in so doing point out another important feature of pathogen and parasite infection:

Because parasites specialize in exploiting the particular biochemical makeup of their hosts, transmission of parasites is most likely between biologically similar organisms. So from the point of view of parasite avoidance, a good strategy is to avoid those who are most similar to oneself, namely conspecifics and members of closely related species. (Kurzban and Leary 2001, 196)

In addition to articulating why conspecifics are especially important in the dynamics of parasite transmission, they also emphasize that phenotypic abnormality can take morphological or behavioral form. In extreme cases of the latter kind, parasites can hijack an organism's behavioral control system, causing it to engage in otherwise abnormal behaviors that specifically help spread the parasite to other hosts. Infection by rabies makes a dog more aggressive, increasing the likelihood that it will bite other animals and thereby transmit the rabies virus to them; the lancet fluke infects ants and causes them to climb to the tops of blades of grass, where they are more likely to be eaten by grazing cattle or sheep, in whose stomachs the lancet fluke reproduces.[4]

Capacities for disease and parasite avoidance are likely to have other features, as well. In the case of humans, there is good reason to think that we will be instinctively sensitive to some signs of infection, or, to make the same point, that some of the cues that trigger avoidance would be innately specified in humans. This is not only because the capacity itself is likely to be evolutionarily ancient but also because some signs of the presence of parasites or infection are both species specific and universal (more on this later). Ancestral humans who avoided those cues in the past would be more likely to live long enough to produce offspring, and organisms manifesting those cues would be less likely to attract a mate.

There is also good reason to think that organisms sensitive to the dynamics of parasite *transmission*—the fact that infected substances and conspecifics can be contagious and can thus pass on their infection—would be more fit, as well. Such organisms would avoid not just the substances and conspecifics that manifested the telltale signs, but also other substances, items, and conspecifics that came in contact or proximity with those infected. Finally, the relevant selective pressures would favor a capacity that is more prone to false positives than false negatives, since there is significantly greater cost—infection and possible death—in mistaking an actual source of infection as clean than in mistakenly avoiding uncontaminated items, places, or conspecifics. "Better safe than sorry" is the appropriate guiding logic.

Given this general description of the adaptive problem and the requirements it imposes on a capacity that can effectively deal with it, it should be no surprise how widespread capacities of this sort seem to be in the animal kingdom. Evidence of parasite avoidance has been found in a variety of species, ranging from tadpoles and three-spined sticklebacks, to eastern bluebirds and red-winged blackbirds, to primates such as lemurs, baboons, and chimpanzees (see Kurzban and Leary 2001 for discussion and references). The evidence of such a capacity in humans is even more impressive, though it is not always appreciated as such and is rarely brought together in one place.

Disgust has nearly all the properties one would expect of a parasite avoidance mechanism, given the contours of the relevant adaptive problem. More specifically, the features of core disgust, especially offensiveness and sensitivity to contamination potency, fit the description almost perfectly. These constitute just the patterns of inference and generate just the types of behavior to be expected in response to carriers of infectious, potentially transmittable parasites and diseases. Thus, according to the Entanglement thesis, the other component of disgust's execution subsystem is a parasite and pathogen avoidance mechanism.

In fact, the conclusion that human parasite and pathogen avoidance is subserved by disgust is nearly inescapable when one recalls more details from the behavioral profile, including the wide range of prima facie unrelated behaviors and entities that fall in its actual domain. For instance, strong evidence exists that reliable signs of disease are universal elicitors of disgust (Curtis et al. 2004, in press). Disgust, rather than fear, underlies aversion to nonpredatory animals whose threat to humans takes a less direct form than brute bodily harm. This includes some animals that are poisonous, such as snakes and spiders, but mostly animals commonly associated with decay and disease transmission, such as rats, flies, worms, and maggots (Davey, Forster, and Mayhew 1993; Webb and Davey 1993; Ware et al. 1994).

Some of Rozin's most striking findings show how the human disgust system is prone to be activated by false positives, including such memorable instances as turd-shaped fudge, rubber vomit, and juice stirred with a sterilized cockroach (see Rozin, Hammer, et al. 1986; Rozin et al. 1989). Indeed, the disgust response is equipped—understandably, given the nature of the adaptive problem—with a bit of a hair trigger. The resulting propensity for false positives can be used to explain some of the more puzzling facts about the elicitor set. As noted in the behavioral profile, another common theme in disgust elicitors is that some types of phenotypic abnormality that do not result from parasitic infection, such as being elderly, disfigured, or handicapped, can trigger disgust nevertheless (Park et al. 2003; Faulkner et al. 2004). AIDS sufferers elicit aversion to physical contact and worries about contamination even in those who know the disease is not communicable by mere proximity or touch (Rozin et al. 1992).

Other previously puzzling features of disgust also fall into place once its role in parasite avoidance becomes clear. Together, eating and sex constitute two of the most basic evolutionary imperatives. Both behaviors are unavoidable ingredients of evolutionary success, but both involve the crossing of bodily perimeters at various points. By virtue of this, both activities leave those engaging in them highly vulnerable to infection. The upshot is that disgust's role in monitoring the boundaries of the entire body (rather than just the mouth) makes much more sense in light of its connection to infectious disease. Moreover, both feeding and procreating are activities that require those boundaries to be breached. They are highly salient to disgust both because they are universal and unavoidable and because they are two of the most potent vectors of disease transmission.

All these elements of core disgust bear the mark of disease and parasite avoidance. With this claim, the second part of the Entanglement thesis is now in place: the ultimate explanation of the features of the core disgust component of the human disgust system, as well as an explanation for many of the innate and universal elicitors of disgust, is to be found in the evolutionary logic of parasite and pathogen avoidance. For short, I will call this the *parasite mechanism*.

2.3   Descent with Modification

Evolution is characteristically conservative, and it tends to preserve, modify, and build on existing structure. Or in innocently anthropomorphic terms, Mother Nature is a tinkerer. Indeed, the human disgust system bears many marks of her tinkering. Before getting into the details of that tinkering, however, it is worth reemphasizing that, according to the Entanglement thesis, underlying disgust are two integrated but originally distinct mechanisms. One type of evidence for this claim comes from comparative research, which suggests that while each is individually present in many other species, the mechanisms and behavioral patterns they produce often remain distinct. Moreover, while both mechanisms are evolutionarily ancient, they follow different evolutionary trajectories. The poison mechanism is specific to ingestion and the gastrointestinal system, and serves to prevent the oral intake of any sort of substance that was previously harmful to the gut—whether that harm was due to poison, toxins, or whatever else might cause upheaval in the stomach. The parasite mechanism, on the other hand, is sensitive to a much wider range of factors. It serves to prevent close physical proximity to any potential sources of infection, rather than only those that might target or enter the body by way of the gastrointestinal system.

Another type of evidence that supports the Entanglement thesis is provided by the fact that the two mechanisms appear to follow different developmental schedules in the course of human ontogeny. The gape face, sensitivity to the facial expressions of caregivers, and other aspects of the affect program are present near birth, while at least one major aspect of the parasite avoidance mechanism—namely, contamination sensitivity—does not emerge until significantly later. Research suggests that children respond to the facial expressions of caregivers by the time they are a year old (Bandura 1992). While all appear to agree that contamination sensitivity has a later onset, there is no consensus about its exact schedule: some studies mark it at 4–8 years (Rozin, Hammer, et al. 1986; Rozin et al. 1985; Fallon et al. 1984), while others mark it at 2 1/2 to 3 years (Siegal and Share 1990).

According to the Entanglement thesis, these two cognitive mechanisms must have become functionally integrated with each other at some point in human evolutionary history. As such, the human disgust system appears to have been shaped in important ways by the evolutionary process of descent with modification. Roughly speaking, a trait (character, system, etc.) is shaped via descent with modification when selection pressures gradually alter its structure from one generation to the next. Traits subject to this process will slowly morph over evolutionary time, so that when they appear in different generations, instances of the trait will exhibit slight differences, but usually an underlying continuity from one generation to the next. Traits resulting from descent with modification can be found all over the evolutionary spectrum, but most recognized cases involve the modification of physical traits or morphological characters.

Disgust, by contrast, presents a case in which natural selection modified the psychological structure of human minds. Through a number of generations, two mechanisms were gradually modified, combined, and functionally fused to the point where activation of one automatically brought about activation of the other. This resulted in the formation of the cluster of elements that make up what we now recognize as the disgust response: offensiveness, contamination sensitivity, nausea, withdrawal, and a gape face. The reaction to potential carriers of parasitic infection came to involve nausea and gaping of the mouth. Alternatively, Garcia aversions and misgivings about certain sorts of cuisine can turn the offending food not just inedible but offensive and contaminating. Thus, through the modification of human cognitive architecture, the execution component depicted in our model was formed, and the unified disgust response was added to the human psychological repertoire.

2.3.1 Factors Leading to Entanglement

A natural question about the Entanglement thesis arises at this point: what factors might have been instrumental in causing these two systems to coalesce into their modern human form as they descended through earlier hominid generations? Initial answers to such a question will have something of the flavor of a Just So Story about them, but identifying and separating out specific selective pressures and other relevant factors can serve to lend plausibility to the thesis itself. No doubt such factors were many and subtle, but a few stand out as likely to have played a pivotal role. First, prior to the influence of any novel selective pressures, there was a nontrivial degree of *antecedent functional overlap* between the two mechanisms. Mitigating the respective adaptive problems associated with each mechanism required the production of aversion of some sort. As noted earlier, food is a major vector for disease transmission and is thus already likely to be salient to a parasite and pathogen avoidance mechanism. Spoiled or decaying food not only smells bad and causes gastrointestinal upheaval, but it is also more likely to carry pathogens and parasites—indeed, the pathogens that spoil the food are often the same pathogens that cause the subsequent upheaval. Thus, given the respective adaptive problems each was designed to solve, the two mechanisms were probably good candidates for functional integration to begin with.

Second, there is good reason to think that the significance of this functional overlap between the poison and parasite mechanisms was amplified by major changes in the diets of ancestral humans. Most important of these changes was an increase in their level of meat consumption, enabled by advances in hunting or its likely precursor, aggressive scavenging (Leakey 1994; cf. Sterelny, n.d.). This, in turn, brought with it an increased vulnerability to infection, from both more and novel parasites. The expansion of diet introduced more exposure to disease and parasites due to more frequent proximity to both dead animals and other scavengers. Jon Haidt makes the point nicely in the following passage:

During the evolutionary transition in which our ancestors' brains expanded greatly, so did their production of tools and weapons, and so did their consumption of meat (Leakey 1994). . . . But when early humans went for meat, including scavenging the carcasses left by other predators, they exposed themselves to a galaxy of new microbes and parasites, most of which are contagious—they spread by contact. (Haidt 2006, 186)

It is noteworthy that the expansion of diet to include more meat would not have introduced any new adaptive problems to ancestral humans. As noted earlier, contagious diseases, infections, and parasites are ubiquitous in nature, and capacities to protect against them are found in a variety of other animals. To be evolutionarily successful, early humans were likely no different. In light of this, the disease and parasite avoidance system was probably not originally *generated* by the expansion of diet to include more meat. Rather, it is more likely that a shift in emphasis was brought about in the nexus of selective pressures relating to disease and parasites. This shift subtly effected a case of descent with modification, driving the relevant avoidance mechanism (which was almost certainly present in some form by this point in evolutionary history) to play an even more pronounced role in screening potential foods and in shaping practices surrounding food consumption.[5]

Finally, another factor that likely contributed to the fusion of the two capacities and their underlying mechanisms has to do with the advantages gained by being able to *transmit information* between conspecifics. This topic will be taken up in greater detail in the next two chapters, but for now it suffices to say that in the case of humans, emotional facial expressions are not just mere symptoms or functionless by-products of some internal state, but serve to signal information to others. In the case of disgust, what has become a signal of potential for infection and contamination is a prima facie unrelated expression, the *gape*: the facial movements that accompany the expulsion of food from the mouth. Given the properties of core disgust and the elements of the disgust response identified as stemming from parasite avoidance, ancestral versions of that system probably did not have a distinctive, easily decodable component of its behavioral repertoire that could act as a recognizable signal. The gape face, however, could easily have been recruited to serve as one. As the two systems began to integrate, what started out as a functional behavioral component of the taste aversion system, the facial movements that accompany retching, took on another function, namely, that of signaling the presence of parasites and infectious disease to others. The need for perspicuous signals added to an already substantial set of mutually reinforcing selective pressures driving the two systems toward integration.

This collection of preexisting features, functional overlaps, novel selection pressures, and the need for a distinctive form of signal all support the Entanglement thesis. Indeed, the conjunction of circumstances makes a powerful case that the human parasite avoidance mechanism gradually combined with the poison mechanism, dragging their concomitant response features together in the wake.

2.3.2 Entanglement and Human Uniqueness

This positive story about how and why the two mechanisms became entangled also sheds light on why it is difficult to find anything fitting the description of human disgust in other animals: in the respects relevant to the Entanglement thesis, other species went down different evolutionary pathways than the one humans traversed. For instance, our closest living relatives in the animal kingdom, other primates, are omnivorous like us.

Primates remain mostly reliant on foraging for sustenance, however. The evolutionary account sketched in the previous section suggests that since other primates never made the shift to hunting, scavenging, and a diet high in meat, they were also never exposed to the new wave of parasites and corresponding selection pressures that would accompany such a diet. Though other primates faced the omnivore's dilemma, on the one hand, and the ubiquitous threat of pathogens, on the other, those sets of adaptive problems never came to coincide to the degree that they did for early humans. Thus the capacities designed to address those distinct problems were never forced to integrate into anything akin to the composite human disgust system. Finally (as we will see in later chapters), the developing ultrasociality and reliance of humans on culture and social learning made information especially important in ways that had no counterpart in other species.

Similar reasoning suggests why two homologous mechanisms might not have combined in purely carnivorous species, either. Many such species have a long evolutionary history of obtaining food not only through hunting fresh meat but also, during dry spells, falling back on the option of scavenging. As a result, they would long have been endowed by natural selection with a lethally toxic digestive and gastrointestinal system, the sort of ironclad gut that is much more robust than our own. Being designed and conditioned to process scavenged food, such species' digestive systems would be much better equipped to digest and deal with the types of parasites commonly found around death and decay. Humans, on the other hand, have a gastrointestinal system originally designed for foraged foods, or at least not accustomed to rotting meat or scavenging. Thus humans would need to avoid the sorts of parasites that actual scavengers could simply consume and count on their gastrointestinal system to eliminate.

2.4   Conclusion: Solving the Puzzle

This chapter began with a puzzle that arose from a tension between two views about the status of disgust when considered from the comparative vantage point. One of these, the Simple Continuity view, held that clear homologies to disgust exist in primates and other species. The other, Terror Management theory, held that disgust is a uniquely human emotion with no counterpart in other animals.

The Entanglement thesis provides the solution to this puzzle. It shows that while both views contain a kernel of truth, each is potentially misleading enough that it should be rejected. Consider the two comparative questions posed earlier. First, are there homologies of disgust in primates and other animals, as supposed by the Simple Continuity view? According to the Entanglement thesis, the answer to this question is, indeed, yes. Capacities dedicated to monitoring food intake against poisons and toxins, including mechanisms for acquiring taste aversions, are found in other mammals. There are capacities devoted to protecting against parasites and disease in other mammals as well. However, the Simple Continuity view should be rejected because it is too simple: the core mechanisms involved in disgust production remain separate and functionally distinct from each other in other species. Thus other animals, even our primate cousins, lack a single capacity that fits the full description of disgust, which contains such diverse elements as sensitivity to contamination potency, nausea, a gape face used to transmit information, a tendency toward avoidance, and a sense of offensiveness.

This leads to the second comparative question: is the emotion of disgust unique to human beings, as supposed by Terror Management theory? According to the Entanglement thesis, the answer to this question is, again, yes. Only in humans did these two mechanisms become entangled to form this particular emotion. However, those who subscribe to Terror Management theory see disgust as a specifically mouth-based rejection system. However, this is only half the story, and given the fascinating contamination effects that can be traced to the disease avoidance mechanism and the perplexing range of false positives they can generate, the least interesting half. Moreover, proponents of Terror Management theory also see a major role for disgust in helping to manage terror, which it does by helping to repress thoughts of our animal nature and mortality that would disrupt our normal, fitness-enhancing behavior. As illustrated earlier, however, in producing aversion to things like blood, feces, and organic decay, the emotion is actually providing protection from the parasites and other microbes that are likely to be present there. Thus the Entanglement thesis provides a better explanation than either the Simple Continuity view or Terror Management theory of the central features of disgust, both the common themes in the elicitor set, and especially the cluster of elements that make up the disgust response. The Entanglement thesis also supports the controversial claim that disgust is uniquely human, but provides new grounds on which to rest that claim.

In terms of the larger goal of constructing a theory of disgust, the Entanglement thesis provides another key piece of the puzzle, namely, an ultimate explanation of the execution mechanisms that underlie production of the emotion. Like the psychological model, this evolutionary story also contributes to the goal of satisfying the three constraints. More specifically, this ultimate explanation directly addresses the unity of the response desideratum:

Unity of the response   The characteristic disgust *response* comprises a number of distinct features. These features form a stable or homeostatic cluster. That is, the features occur together as a package; regardless of what triggers disgust on any particular occasion, once it is triggered, the production of one element of the cluster is regularly accompanied by the production of the others. What accounts for the clustering of this particular, idiosyncratic set of features? Why have these particular cognitive, behavioral, and physiological elements merged into a single, unified, and apparently universally human response type?

Variation of the elicitors   While the disgust response itself, along with a small set of elicitors, is a human universal, a large amount of variation exists in what is found disgusting, and so in what types of elicitors activate disgust systems. Indeed, disgust allows for variation at both the cultural and individual level. What accounts for this feature of the emotion?

Diversity of the elicitors   There is also a wide and surprisingly diverse range of elicitors that trigger disgust, ranging along one dimension from the concrete to the abstract, and along another from the brutely physical and inert to the highly social and interpersonal. What accounts for the pairing of such a diverse range of triggering conditions to this one specific type of response?

The Entanglement thesis, which is now incorporated into figure 2.1, shows that the different components of disgust, though they can be traced to distinguishable underlying mechanisms, each bearing the marks of its own evolutionary history, now form a homeostatic cluster that we recognize as a single response type. Those underlying mechanisms were driven together by natural selection until they became functionally fused. In light of the Entanglement thesis, together with the insight provided by the psychological model, I consider the unity of the response constraint to be satisfied.

The Entanglement thesis also begins addressing the desiderata concerning the variation and diversity of the elicitors, albeit in a slightly more subtle way. First and foremost, it explains why the most reliable, pan-cultural indicators of disease make good candidates to be innately specified universal elicitors of disgust. It also explains the prominence of food in the elicitor pool. Moreover, the details about how the taste aversion acquisition system works show one way that individual-level variation in disgust elicitors is produced. Most interestingly, the entanglement of these two mechanisms created a psychological system that was ideally positioned to accrue novel functions as humans became increasingly social creatures. That system was able to reliably produce a specific aversive pattern of behavior and inference. This, in turn, is just the sort of thing that a tinkering Mother Nature is liable to exploit and build on. As I discuss in chapter 3, the system was also equipped with the beginnings of a flexible elicitor detection and acquisition system. The disease and parasite avoidance mechanism was antecedently sensitive to a wide range of cues that might indicate potential for infection, having to do with places, substances, and phenotypic abnormalities in others. This contrasts markedly with the restricted set of conditions associated with the food rejection and acquired taste aversion mechanisms.

Completely satisfying the constraints concerning variation and diversity of the elicitors, however, requires looking more closely at how exactly Mother Nature exploited this new response and the flexibility of its elicitor detection system. Making sense of the elicitor pool requires a closer look at the environmental and social contexts in which early humans lived, and the novel functions that disgust accrued.

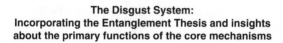

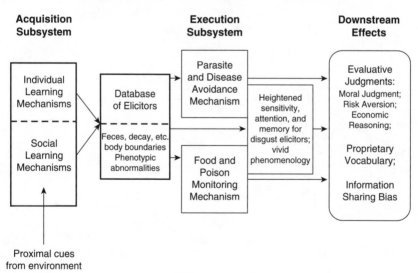

Figure 2.1
A functional-level model of interlocking mechanisms that make up the human disgust system. The arrows represent causal links between the various mechanisms.

3 Disgust's Sentimental Signaling System: Expression, Recognition, and the Transmission of Cultural Information

3.1 Introduction

Anyone who has played Texas hold 'em or seven-card draw can tell you how hard it is to keep a good poker face. It is extremely difficult to keep from broadcasting to the entire table your opinion of a hand, whether you are elated that you made a full house, disappointed that you missed a high flush by a single card, disgusted that you think your opponent pulled an inside straight, or just ambivalent about your pair of kings. From the inside, it can seem that such emotions are dying to break free and show themselves. The intensity with which poker players scrutinize each other only adds to the drama of the game, as they are always looking for each other's "tells," searching for the slightest hint in their opponents' faces, behavior, and body language, trying to discern what it says about their state of mind— and ultimately their cards. In such circumstances, which often include risky bets and large amounts of money, the amount of control it takes *not* to give away any information about what you are actually thinking or feeling, let alone to convincingly express misleading information, can be staggering. Genuine emotions seem to *want* to reveal themselves, especially in charged situations like poker games, and often at the worst possible moment. All but the most stoic and unflappable of us regularly reveal our emotions, even in spite of our best attempts to keep a lid on them.

In this respect, the example of poker makes vivid a feature of the emotions that is often taken for granted, namely, that expressing them is quite natural and nearly unavoidable. The perspective of evolutionary theory, however, turns this commonplace on its head and turns it into something quite perplexing. In fact, in the midst of a discussion of emotional facial expressions in his book *How the Mind Works* (1997), Stephen Pinker identifies this feature as "one of the longest-standing puzzles of the emotions: why we advertise them on our face" (414). When we convey our emotions through our facial expressions, we reveal to all the world some of the most prominent features of our current inner lives. Why should we do this? Surely it would be better to keep our feelings to ourselves, at least some of the time (like, say, during a poker game). But much of the expression of emotions—and, in fact, much of the recognition of emotions—appears to be largely automatic and difficult, if not impossible, to completely stop. Which makes the question all the more pressing: why are we such instinctive and unabashed emoters? For short, and as a nod to his framing of the relevant issues, I call this question Pinker's Puzzle.

A couple of candidate answers to these types of questions, solutions to Pinker's Puzzle, are currently available, some more developed than others. Moreover, there is no convincing argument that there could not be more than one solution to the puzzle, and that we advertise different emotions for different reasons. With this in mind, I take it that my concentration on disgust is not objectionable on the grounds that it is too focused or fails to generalize to other emotions. And so in what follows, I compare two different models that can be used to understand the relevant features of disgust. First, though, I begin the next section with a brief survey of the central set of facts that a correct theory should accommodate. This involves describing what we now know about the capacities, using recent cognitive scientific research to fill in details about the surprisingly complicated cognitive machinery underlying expression and recognition of disgust and the gape, its characteristic facial expression. Each of the next two sections then considers a different type of model that might help account for such facts.

The first has been widely discussed and is most commonly associated with Robert Frank (1988), who was the first to work out in detail the idea that social emotions are commitment devices. After laying out the core ideas of commitment problems and commitment devices in general, I use a couple of examples to flesh out how Frank uses commitment in his account of social emotions. I then extract from this what I call the Classic Commitment model, and consider, in broad outline, how the model would construe the relevant features of disgust. Next I turn to a second type of account, which I call the Cultural Transmission model. This model is not closely associated with a single theorist, as is the first, and is instead grounded in themes found in a growing body of literature on cultural evolution and transmission (for representative treatments, see Boyd and Richerson 1985, 2005a; Richerson and Boyd 2005; Sperber 1996; Tomasello 1999; Mesoudi et al. 2006). After once again motivating the basic outlook and central notions, I describe the kinds of psychological capacities that are thought to be important for transmitting cultural information and the sorts of features they are likely to bear. Once this is done, I consider how this model would construe disgust and what it suggests about the nature and function of its sentimental signaling system.

Finally, I argue that the Cultural Transmission model offers a far superior account of disgust expression and recognition. Not only does the Cultural Transmission model mesh better with a number of theoretical considerations, including the Entanglement thesis established in chapter 2, but I also show that it is able to make sense of a wider range of evidence than can easily be explained by the Classic Commitment model. One implication of the argument presented here is that the perspective of the Cultural Transmission model sheds light on the question of acquisition, and can thus be incorporated into the broader theory of disgust by going some way toward accounting for the variation and diversity of elicitors we find on both an individual and a cultural level.

3.2 The Expression and Recognition Facts

Pinker's formulation of the relevant issues focuses on facial expression, and for good reason: human faces are perhaps our richest nonverbal source of information about other people. While the face may be the most salient and expressive broadcaster of body language, however, it is not the only one. Disgust, along with many other emotions, is expressed through a variety of other behavioral channels. These include actions such as a quick withdrawal, other features of a sender's bearing such as orientation and posture, as well as nonverbal elements of vocal expression such as intonation and cadence, or the sound of retching. Intuitively, these can be thought of as the other elements of body language, broadly construed. In the case of disgust, many of these amount to various manifestations of a feeling of offensiveness. Like the gape face, most of these features probably did not originate to convey information to others but were behavioral elements and by-products of the disgust response that later acquired a signaling function.

That said, in much of what follows, I confine my discussion to the face and facial expression, primarily for simplicity of exposition. I take it as likely that much of what I have to say can be extended to other forms of body language, inflection, other types of sounds, and so on, but I take no hard stand on the issue (though see Susskind et al. 2008 for some evidence specific to disgust; and Hatfield 1994 for an overview of all the emotions). The face is just the most salient and expressive physical feature in humans, and the focus of the research on expression and recognition reflects this.

3.2.1 Expressing Disgust: The Gape

It will help to recall a number of facts gathered together in the behavioral profile of disgust outlined in chapter 1 that had to do with its typical forms of expression. Like many other emotions, disgust is associated with a unique and characteristic facial expression, called the gape or gape face. Indeed, the gape is part of the nomological cluster of components that make up the disgust response and is thus automatically and involuntarily produced whenever the emotion is triggered. Moreover, the gape itself can be broken down into its component parts,[1] and many of its constituent muscular movements are similar to those that precede or accompany expelling a substance from the mouth. Thus the facial expression itself is thought by many to derive from the motion of retching or vomiting, a fact that I took to be evidence for the Entanglement thesis defended in chapter 2.

Since Darwin's time (1872), the emotion of disgust itself has been thought to be pan-cultural, a human universal, and likewise the gape has been thought to be the emotion's pan-cultural, universal facial expression. It is also unsurprising, then, that on the other side of the coin, the gape has also been thought to be universally recognizable *as* the expression of disgust. Indeed, much recent research has largely been in accord with Darwin's initial speculations on these issues (see Rozin et al. 2008 for work on disgust in particular; and Ekman 1992, 2003, for a wealth of evidence about similar features in the so-called basic emotions or affect programs, which include disgust). Apart from the universal "core" of these capacities for expression and recognition, research has turned up some fascinating facts about the variability of many of these emotions as well. Indeed, variation is sensitive to details of the specific contexts in which emotions are expressed and recognized (Ruiz-Belda et al. 2003) and subtle differences have been found in how an emotion is expressed—and how easily it is recognized—that vary along cultural, gender, and even individual specific lines (Matsumoto et al. 2001; Hess and Thibault 2009; Hess et al. 2004; Barr et al. 2008). While these two lines of evidence can appear to pull in opposite directions, there is a convincing case that they are in fact compatible with each other and, taken together, reveal a pattern of local variations on themes that are themselves universal (see Mallon and Stich 2000 for details). While both the variations and the themes are interesting, in what follows, I focus mainly on the universal core of the capacities, rather than the range and extent of their variation.

While the gape appears to have its origins in the musculature of retching, it is generally agreed that today the gape is not *merely* a vestige of the motion that allows for the easy expulsion of material from the mouth (neither, of course, is it a purposeless but unavoidable concomitant to production of the emotion). Indeed, calling it an *expression* already suggests that the gape is displaying information and as such serves as a rudimentary signal. What type of message might the gape be sending? First and most obviously, it conveys to others the information that the gaper is experiencing the emotion of disgust. Emotions and inner lives are not directly perceivable by others, so outward expressions of them are significant. In this case, the gape is an external, observable indicator of one of the gaper's unobservable, internal mental states, and thus perhaps the gaper's imminent behavior.

Another set of facts can be thought of in terms of what poker players call "tells"; we reveal our disgust even when we do not know we are doing so, and even when we would rather not. Since gaping is automatic and involuntary, the expression is almost always made when one is actually disgusted. This is true across a number of different conditions. For instance, people who are only very slightly disgusted tend to gape even if the facial movements are so minimal and understated that the gaper is not aware of producing them. These *microexpressions* flash quickly across the face; they last as briefly as forty milliseconds and can remain completely below the conscious awareness of the individual producing them (and so are sometimes called "subthreshold"). So perhaps it is more edifying to say that when a person is only slightly disgusted, she "microgapes." People also reveal their disgust even when they would rather keep it to themselves. When genuinely disgusted, people tend to flash a microgape even they try to voluntarily suppress it. As nice as it would be to be able to hide it sometimes—for instance, while choking down a nasty dinner at the in-laws'—this kind of "leakage" betrays disgustedness by displaying it on the face, subtly but automatically (for extended discussions of these phenomena, see Ekman 2003; Hatfield et al. 1994).

It is a platitude that the more intensely disgusted one is, the more exaggerated one's expression of the emotion will tend to be. Research has added to this that once triggered, voluntarily exaggerating or suppressing a gape can actually serve to enhance or diminish, respectively, the intensity of the entire emotional reaction itself (Laird and Bressler 1992). Perhaps by the same mechanism, starting from an emotionally neutral state and voluntarily making a gape face can itself trigger a mild but actual episode of disgust by activating the entire coordinated suite of components that make up the emotion. In other words, due to the "plasticity of the elicitor" (Levenson 1992), gaping can produce full disgust; faking it (the gape) *becomes* making it (disgust). Another way to put this point is that rather than being unidirectional, the causal relations between the gape and the other elements of the emotion tend to go in both directions. This sort of feedback loop of influence, exhibited by other emotions as well as disgust, has been discussed using the terminology of "facial feedback."

One noteworthy upshot of these features of expressing disgust is that to the extent that the gape serves as a signal, it is a signal that is particularly difficult to fake. This difficulty stems directly from the reliable connection between production of the gape face, on the one hand, and production of the full emotion, on the other. In this case, the potential for false signaling is impeded in both directions. It is difficult to produce the signal (gape) without thereby entering the state it indicates (being disgusted). Likewise, when in the relevant state (of being disgusted), it is difficult to refrain from producing the signal that reveals it (gaping).[2]

3.2.2 Recognizing Disgust

Recognition and expression go hand in hand; they are two sides of the signaling coin. In general, a signal is only of use in conveying information if it is both discernible to others and is also recognizable *as* a signal. For a trait or behavior to play the role of a signal effectively, others must be able to detect it, identify it as a signal, and extract the relevant message or information from it. In the case of emotions, if expressing emotions is a form of sending signals, then recognizing the emotional expressions of others is a form of receiving them.

Since recognition, in this sense, is crucial to the whole enterprise of conveying information, it is unsurprising that the capacity for recognizing disgust also appears to be pan-cultural, universal, and at least partially innately structured (Ekman 2003). One piece of evidence for this is the early emergence of central elements of the capacity. Children become sensitive to facial expressions of caregivers very early in ontogeny; in the case of the gape, this occurs by the time they are twelve months old (Bandura 1992). Many take this to indicate that the core meanings of such faces do not have to be learned or explicitly taught.

More significantly, in normal mature humans, disgust recognition is also often *empathic*. Not only are people able to naturally recognize a gape *as* an expression of disgust, but doing so often involves the extra step of actually becoming disgusted oneself. This is striking. Not only is recognition of disgust automatic, but the processes involved automatically put the recognizer into a similar mental state as the person being observed. In essence, disgust recognition involves a form of mental-state imitation.

Moreover, from the point of view of cognitive architecture, that recognition is empathic implies that the capacity for disgust recognition is subserved by many of the same mechanisms that underlie production of the emotion. Several lines of evidence support the idea that recognition is empathic, and that at least some of the mechanisms underlying it do double duty in both recognizing and producing the emotion. First of all, fMRI studies link both disgust production and disgust recognition to the same neural substrate, namely, the putamen and the insula or insular cortex (Phillips et al. 1997; Wicker et al. 2003; Jabbi et al. 2008 found that reading and imagining scenarios involving disgust also activated the anterior insula). This specific neural location is noteworthy because it is different from that associated with other emotions, such as anger and fear, where the relevant brain area is the amygdala. A second form of evidence comes from a pattern of selective impairments that is familiar from other areas of cognitive science. In this case, research has found that the capacity for recognizing disgust can become impaired while other similar capabilities remain intact. Such a pattern indicates that underlying this capacity are at least some important components specific to the emotion of disgust—distinct from, for instance, components that may be common to recognition of multiple emotions (anger, fear, surprise, etc.; see Sprengelmeyer et al. 1996, 1997; Wang et al. 2003; Calder et al. 2001), and distinct from mechanisms employed in identifying individual people by their faces (Keane et al. 2002). Finally, when the capacity to recognize disgust breaks down, it exhibits a pattern of paired deficits, another important type of evidence in cognitive science. In this case, researchers have found that losing the ability to produce the emotion of disgust is correlated with losing the ability to recognize disgust, but only disgust, in others. Indeed, linking this form of evidence to the first, damage to the putamen or insula impairs both recognition and production of disgust (but only that emotion) (Calder et al. 2001; Adolphs et al. 2003).[3]

The exact character and causal sequence of the mechanisms linking production and recognition are still not fully understood, either in the case of disgust or with respect to other emotions. Candidate hypotheses differ on several issues, including the prominence of place they give to (perhaps automatic) facial mimicry of others' expressions, even of their microexpressions; the exact role, if any, of facial feedback; the role and causal priority of "hot" versus "cold" processes, that is, whether production of disgust precedes and facilitates "colder" cognitive recognition, or whether production of disgust is a result of "cold" cognitive recognition (for a discussion of these and other possibilities, see Goldman and Sripada 2005).

More generally, an impressive body of evidence indicates that this sort of empathic recognition can be not only automatic but unconscious as well, and thus one can become "infected" with another's emotions unknowingly. When this kind of "emotional contagion" occurs (Hatfield et al. 1994), a person may enter into an emotional state of the same type as the person she is interacting with, even if the infector isn't aware she is in or is expressing the emotion, and the infected isn't aware she has empathically detected the expression and come to share the emotion.[4]

3.2.3 A Sentimental Signaling System

I call the set of facts described in the previous two sections the expression and recognition facts. Taken together, they show that disgust comes equipped with what I call a *sentimental signaling system*, whose key features are gathered together here:

Expression	Recognition
• Automatic and potentially unconscious	• Automatic and potentially unconscious
• Microexpressions	• Link to putamen and insula, the same brain areas linked to disgust production
• Facial leakage	• Characteristic patterns of breakdown —Selective impairment —Paired deficits
• Facial feedback	• Empathic

The signaling system is sentimental because reliable production of the actual emotion is involved on both sides of the information-conveying enterprise. Disgust occurs during expression and the sending of signals and, due to its empathic nature, during recognition and the receiving of signals, as well. Moreover, from the point of view of signaling systems in general, the sentimental character of this one gives it several noteworthy features. As noted earlier, the signals are (doubly) difficult for the sender to fake; both false positives and false negatives are impeded. Due to their distinctiveness and location on the face, gapes are salient and easy for others to detect. Finally, since recognition is empathic, extracting the relevant information from those signals (at least at the coarse-grained level of realizing that the gaper is disgusted) is fairly easy, as well; indeed, it involves imitating the emotional state of the sender.[5]

Surely much remains unknown, many details need to be worked out, and different hypotheses about the relevant proximate mechanisms need to be teased apart and tested. But in broad strokes, the picture is coming into focus enough that those kinds of high-resolution questions may be set to the side so that a related but different and more general cluster of issues can be considered. At the center of those is a basic question: why is disgust equipped with this sentimental signaling system in the first place? Many ancillary questions can be asked as well. What is the significance of the more fine-grained expression and recognition facts about disgust that we already know? Why is this emotion equipped with such a sophisticated signaling system, and why is it *sentimental*? What information is being signaled? And to what end? What larger social dynamics are these signals involved in? What is (are) the relevant adaptive problem(s) and ultimate explanation(s) associated with the expression and recognition facts? In the next two sections, I consider a pair of models that provide very different answers to these questions.

Finally, though, note the slight shift in emphasis that a closer look at the expression and recognition facts has prompted. The chapter began by posing what may be the first and most obvious question that comes to mind, which I dubbed Pinker's Puzzle: why are we such instinctive and unabashed emoters? In focusing attention exclusively on the capacities for emoting and expression, however, this way of framing the topic of inquiry can leave out or distort important aspects of the phenomenon in question. Rather, by looking more closely at the facts about expression *and recognition* discovered by empirical research, and by construing both as equally relevant to the nature of disgust's sentimental signaling system, we gain a fuller view of the phenomenon itself and can ask a broader range of questions about it. Pinker's Puzzle still looms, but it points to only half of what needs explaining. One aim of this chapter is to find a solution to the disgust version of Pinker's Puzzle, but ideally that solution would not only explain why humans are such inveterate emoters but account for the striking facts about empathic recognition as well.

3.3   The Classic Commitment Model

A natural first place to look for an explanation of the expression and recognition facts is Robert Frank's work on social emotions (1988). Frank himself does not discuss disgust in particular, but in and of itself, this does not mean that his framework would be unable to shed light on the set of questions being considered here. The absence of disgust in Frank's discussion is not totally surprising, from a sociological point of view; for a long time, disgust was neglected by researchers who studied emotions, and much of the recent interest in the emotion, especially in the influence it has on social and moral judgments, arose after Frank's seminal book. For reasons that will be made clear as we go, the Classic Commitment model remains a sensible place to begin investigating the function of disgust's sentimental signaling system. In short, that model purports to explain, for a broad range of emotions, the very kinds of phenomena concerning expression and signaling I have raised about disgust. Rather than reinventing the wheel, it is worth considering whether or not Frank's framework can be applied to disgust without substantial modification and yield a straightforward set of answers. Ultimately I argue that this is not the case, as I am skeptical that disgust is a classic Frank-style commitment device. However, it will be instructive not only to articulate Frank's model but also to show where and how it fails to account for the expression and recognition facts. It can then be used as a contrast case to help develop and differentiate it from the competing Cultural Transmission model I argue for in sections 3.4 and 3.5.

3.3.1 Commitment Problems and Commitment Devices

At a general level, the issue of commitment usually arises in the context of strategic social interactions. A strategic social interaction is one that involves multiple agents, where each agent calculates his or her behavior at least in part by predicting what the other agents will do. This, of course, includes predicting how those other agents might react to certain actions that she herself might take.[6]

Within these sorts of strategic social contexts, a commitment is a pledge, promise, or threat to act in a certain way or take a particular course of action in a given set of circumstances, often circumstances that are likely to arise in the future. For instance, a newlywed might commit to remain faithful to a spouse, in sickness and in health, for richer and for poorer; a nation might commit itself to coming to the aid of another nation in times of duress; or a client might threaten to pursue legal action if a company sells him or her a faulty product or fails to provide an agreed-on service. A main strategic use of commitments is to alter other agents' beliefs, expectations, and incentives regarding the situation, its players, and how they will respond to different situations, thus altering those other agents' own strategic calculations and ultimately their behavior.

A brief terminological digression will help clarify the discussion to come. I will use the (admittedly somewhat awkward) phrase "impetus to act" in a way that is neutral between internal and external factors that figure into the production of behavior. Thus I mean "impetus to act" to include both incentives, which I understand as environmental factors external to an agent, and motivations or motivational structures, which are psychological states internal to an agent. I introduce this terminology and distinction for a number of reasons. One is that for a given agent, incentives and motivations may change independently of one another. For instance, an agent might retain his same internal motivational structure while his external environment changes; the shift in the external environment could result in different incentives and thus produce different actions, despite an unchanged motivational structure. Likewise, an agent may remain in an unchanging external environment, with incentives that remain the same, but undergo a shift in his or her motivations, resulting in different kinds of actions in the face of the same incentives. Second, the terminology provides the resources to capture what different forms of commitment—namely, what have been called objective and subjective commitment (Nesse 2001b)—have in common, and thus why they both properly count as commitment. Separating impetuses to act into external incentives and internal motivations, in turn, allows me to mark and talk about the differences between the commitments that are objective and those that are subjective.

The main problems that arise for the strategic use of commitments in social contexts are tied to the intertwined issues of credibility, on the one hand, and shifting circumstances and impetuses to act, on the other. A *primary agent*—what I will call the agent attempting to employ some form of commitment in a strategic interaction—will often have trouble convincing other agents that he or she will honor her pledge or follow through on her threat, that she will keep her commitment to act as promised, should the relevant circumstances arise. The issue of credibility is directly linked to the fact that oftentimes, those very circumstances, should they arise, thereby alter the impetuses to act of the primary agent in such a way that the promised course of action would no longer seem be the optimal or rational one, from the primary agent's point of view, when it comes time to act. This threatens to unravel the entire rationale behind making commitments in the first place, however. If other agents are sensitive to this possibility of shifting scenarios and impetuses to act, they will have good grounds not to take the initial commitment seriously in the first place; in and of itself, it will not be credible. This, in turn, would undermine the commitment as an effective tool in influencing the behavior of others and would defeat the primary agent's purpose in making it.

A *commitment device* is a mechanism that helps solve such problems by performing a number of related functions. Again, at a general level, commitment devices perform three main tasks:

1. Influence the behavior of the primary agent
2. Make the primary agent's threats and promises credible
3. Strategically influence the behavior of other agents

Commitment devices do their first task, influencing the behavior of the primary agent, by manipulating incentives or motivations in a way that makes the primary agent more likely to take the promised course of action when the time comes. This task is important because commitment problems are generated when the pledged course of action is one that, given her initial, unaltered incentives or motivations, the primary agent would not otherwise take. Commitment devices often help induce the promised behavior by somehow restricting the range of actions or options available to the primary agent or by altering her impetuses to act. Some commitment devices (associated with so-called objective commitments) alter the environment, often in ways that change the incentives under which the primary agent acts, while others (associated with so-called subjective commitments) reorganize her internal motivational structure in such a way that makes her behavior insensitive to certain incentives or countervailing considerations related to the situation. In many cases, the primary agent gives up certain options by abdicating control over some aspect of her behavior or by making herself impervious to countervailing circumstances that might come up and influence that behavior. The behavior of primary agents in the grip of such commitment devices is no longer under direct or immediate control; they have, in a sense, gone ballistic.

Commitment devices do their second task, making threats and promises credible, by producing reliable signals (or exploiting some reliable signaling system) that advertise that the first task has been or will be done. Effectively conveying this information ideally serves to convince others that the primary agent has or will have the appropriate set of incentives or motivations or that she is strategically restricted in the appropriate way. This persuades other agents that the primary agent is much more likely to take the promised course of action when the time comes, which in turn influences the other agents' subsequent strategic calculations.

The final task of a commitment device is to strategically influence the behavior of others. Although this is in many ways the most fundamental function of commitment devices, they perform it indirectly, by changing other agents' beliefs, expectations, and incentives. More specifically, the point is to alter other agents' beliefs and expectations about how the primary agent will act in given circumstances and in response to actions taken by others within the strategic context, and thus alter those other agents' calculations regarding how best to interact and engage with her.[7]

3.3.2 Social Emotions as Commitment Devices

In his influential book *Passions within Reason*, Robert Frank (1988) argues against a long tradition of thought that sees the emotions as a source of irrationality. He holds instead that many emotions, particularly social emotions that primarily influence and regulate interactions between people, are in fact commitment devices. Once they are understood within the context of the commitment problems they help solve, not only do many features of social emotions make more sense, but it also becomes clear that their functioning and the types of behavior they generate are often perfectly rational.[8]

Frank's basic idea can be illustrated by considering a couple of compelling examples, such as the emotions of romantic love and anger. Consider Larry, who is deeply and vocally in love with his new spouse and shows it in the proverbial million different little ways. In this account, in addition to many other things it does, Larry's love also serves as a sort of guarantor for his partner, ensuring that he will remain faithful and refrain from any extramarital shenanigans, devote time and resources to child rearing, and be a steadfast mate and partner in general. His love reshapes his motivational structure, making it more likely that he will keep all these commitments to his wife, even if raising a child turns out to be extremely burdensome and time consuming, even while he is away on a business trip and subject to the enticements of a sultry and very discreet seductress, or more generally, even if something "objectively" better comes along. Larry's love, together with the reliable signals indicating that it is genuine, also ideally serves to convince Larry's spouse that he will honor his promises in the face of such temptations, and hence convinces her to trust him and in turn commit herself in a similar way.

Another example is provided by anger. Imagine Allison, the office hothead, whose trademark fits of rage are well known among her peers and colleagues, who is often easily and visibly angered, and liable to fly off the handle at the slightest provocation. According to Frank's account, Allison's susceptibility to anger makes her more likely to retaliate against those who break promises to her, and provides her with the impetus to follow through on threats she has made. In short, her hotheadedness makes her extremely vindictive in general and thus willing to pursue vengeance against those who have slighted her, even at the expense of substantial resources of time and energy. Indeed, her anger drives her to punish those who have failed her even when, considered in isolation, such an undertaking appears irrationally costly and, to a coolheaded observer, it would seem to be to her advantage to just let it go. Since Allison's colleagues and acquaintances are well aware of her unmanageable tendencies, however, they are also more likely to take her threats seriously and less likely to break promises to her or cross her in general.

This view holds that social emotions such as these function as commitment devices because they are able to effectively perform the three tasks listed earlier. According to Frank's account, they accomplish the first task of influencing the behavior of the primary agent by triggering a set of psychological changes within her. What is altered by these social emotions is not any external or material set of incentives, but the primary agent's internal motivational structure. These reorganized motivational states then provide the impetuses for the primary agent to take the threatened or promised course of action.[9] Novel motivations produced by the emotions can be so strong that they are difficult for the primary agent to supersede or override, even in the face of countervailing considerations or external incentives to take some other course of action. Thus those passions can drive her to act in a way that, given her initial unaltered motivations, she would not have acted on otherwise. This is well illustrated with the examples of Larry and Allison. Larry, since he is so deeply in love with his wife, easily resists the advances of a luscious supermodel he meets at a hotel bar. Allison, brimming over with anger, undertakes a vicious retaliation when an underling goes over her head in making a business decision, knowing full well that doing so puts her at professional risk.

According to Frank's account, social emotions do the second task of making threats and promises credible mainly via a variety of emotional expressions. The expressions of the primary agent advertise that she is susceptible to or experiencing the relevant emotion, and thus harbors the sorts of dispositions and motivations associated with it.

These expressions signal to others that the primary agent is disposed to keep the kind of commitment associated with the specific emotion. Larry's professions of love signal that he will keep his pledge to remain a faithful spouse. Similarly, Allison's hotheadedness lets everyone know that she is the sort of person who follows through on her threats and pursues vengeance even at high cost to herself.

These threats and promises to act in certain ways are credible due to the reliable connection between the two components of the emotions involved: the internal, unobservable dispositions and motivational structures they produce, on the one hand, and the external, observable expressions that reveal them and signal their presence, on the other. The reliability of this connection is important in blocking against the possibility of strategic deception, and is thus crucial in effectively convincing others that the primary agent is in fact "passionate" in the advertised way, rather than faking it for Machiavellian reasons.

By performing the first two tasks, social emotions are thereby able to fulfill their third and fundamental aim of strategically influencing the behavior of others. In this view, because other agents are able to recognize the emotional expressions of the primary agent and take them as credible, they will also take the passions they reveal to be genuine. Thus those other agents will adjust their beliefs and expectations about how the primary agent will act, that is, whether or not she will keep her threats and promises, based on her emotional expressions and passionate character. Such adjustments will in turn alter those other agents' incentives concerning how to strategically interact with the primary agent. Some types of emotions, like romantic love, can make others more likely to trust the primary agent or help convince them to enter into strategic and cooperative ventures with her. Others types of emotions, like anger, can make other agents less likely to renege or break promises to that primary agent or even make them wary of entering into strategic or cooperative interactions with her in the first place.

3.3.3 The Classic Commitment Model and Disgust

It is now possible to step back and extract a general picture provided by Frank's work on the social emotions and to pose a few questions. What work does the framework do? What issues does it speak to? To the extent that it is a theory, what is it a theory *of*? What does it purport to explain, and what resources does it provide to do the explanatory work?

In what follows, I use the Classic Commitment model (CCM) to capture the particular perspective and set of explanatory resources provided by Frank as a whole, rather than any specific hypotheses that can be generated from that perspective. The CCM, however, can help shed light on a number of different topics about social emotions. As mentioned earlier, Frank (1988) is mainly concerned with exploring how social emotions interact with issues of rationality and irrationality. The main thrust of his argument is that while agents in the grip of passions appear to be acting irrationally, especially when those actions are considered in isolation, such an impression is mistaken. Rather, such actions and the emotions that drive them are better seen as components of more complex strategies. When the larger strategic context is taken into account and the roles of the individual emotions are better understood, it becomes clear that both the emotions and the resultant actions make rational sense.

Aside from the particular dialectic purposes Frank uses it for, the general model and the perspective it affords provides an account of the nature of the social emotions themselves. Each is a commitment device that performs the three tasks described earlier in some domain or in response to some range of commitment problems. Of equal importance is the CCM's account of the larger social milieu in which those emotions operate. It sees them as performing their functions within the context of strategic interactions that generate commitment problems. Using the lens of commitment, the CCM explains how the social emotions smoothly (and rationally) *fit* into the sorts of social dynamics in which they are involved.

At a more specific level, the CCM also provides an explanation of certain properties of social emotions that can initially seem quite perplexing. Most importantly, its account of the significance of emotional expressions suggests an elegant solution to Pinker's Puzzle. By identifying social emotions as commitment devices, the CCM sees that emotional expressions need to provide credible signals about the likely strategic behavior of primary agents, and that *believable* advertisement is close to the core of their being able to function effectively as guarantors and deterrents. The CCM predicts that the production and expression of social emotions will be tightly bound together and that revealing one's passions to others is nearly the point of having them. It also holds that if social emotions are to perform their function successfully, others must be able to recognize the emotional expressions of the primary agent as such and adjust their own beliefs, expectations, and strategic calculations accordingly.

In addition to shedding light on the nature of social emotions at the level of social interaction, as well as on the details of the structure of the psychological mechanisms underlying those emotions, the CCM also suggests an account of why the passions evolved in the first place. By placing the passions within the social context that it does, the CCM links them to the issues of coordination, cooperation, and reciprocity that have recently loomed large in evolutionary theory. In suggesting that the challenges posed by these issues generated the sorts of pressures that selected for the social emotions, the CCM points toward an ultimate explanation for the emotions themselves, as well as the more specific psychological facts about their expression and recognition. Frank is not the only theorist who has adapted such an evolutionary perspective. Many have explored the emotions using a point of view informed by evolutionary theory, often attempting to understand the role that social emotions can play in, for instance, sustaining cooperation via reciprocal altruism (Trivers 2002; Humphreys 1976; Byrne and Whiten 1988; see also Cosmides and Tooby 1992, 1996), or, focusing on the other side of the same coin, how the possibility of deception has shaped social emotions and their expression (Griffiths 2003, 2004). For obvious reasons, this family of explanations of *cooperation*, which sees it as being sustained by complicated patterns of reciprocity, patterns that are in turn supported by the social emotions, has been called the "heart on your sleeve hypothesis" (Boyd and Richerson 2005b). By dubbing the framework extracted from Frank's work the *Classic* Commitment model, I mean to limit it to the claims that the emotions to which it properly applies evolved to function as commitment devices in the sense described earlier, and that the cooperative dynamics in which they are involved can be explained by appeal to patterns of reciprocity, rather than various alternatives like kin altruism, cultural group selection, and so on (see again Boyd and Richerson 2005b; as well as Henrich and Henrich 2007).

Initially, then, the CCM appears to be quite well suited to speak to the questions raised about the particular emotion of disgust. Its tool kit of explanatory resources is certainly designed to explain many of the same kinds of phenomena described in section 3.2. It offers a plausible candidate solution to the disgust version of Pinker's Puzzle about why we so blatantly advertise our disgust with the gape face (and other forms of disgust expression). By locating it within the particular variety of reciprocity-driven social dynamics it does, the CCM identifies a general role for disgust's signaling system, suggests why the information being signaled might be significant, and even provides an account of why the mechanisms underlying expression make the signals themselves so difficult to fake. Broadly speaking, the CCM would place disgust within the context of commitment problems and would construe the emotion as, or at least as playing the role of, a classic commitment device. Furthermore, it would hold that gape faces signal information to others in an attempt to alter their behavior in strategic interactions and that the reliable link between the expression and production of disgust makes the type of commitment signaled by the gape credible. Finally, the CCM suggests an ultimate explanation of disgust and its sentimental signaling system, which is centered on the issues of reciprocity, cooperation, and deception.

Does the initial impression stand up to examination, though? The Classic Commitment model may be appropriate for many emotions, but does it in fact apply to disgust? Though it looks initially promising, I argue that the CCM is a poor fit for disgust and that there is a much better account of disgust's sentimental signaling system. To make a case for that claim, however, I need to have that other model on hand. In the next section, I set the Classic Commitment model aside to sketch what I call the Cultural Transmission model, and show how this alternative provides a much better account for the relevant facts about disgust.

3.4   The Cultural Transmission Model

Recent work on culture and cultural transmission provides another, different perspective on the expression and recognition facts. As mentioned previously, this approach is not closely associated with any one theorist, and in describing what I call the *Cultural Transmission model* (CTM), I draw on themes found throughout this growing literature (for representative overviews, see Boyd and Richerson 1985, 2005a; Richerson and Boyd 2005; Sperber 1996; Tomasello 1999; Mesoudi et al. 2006). Whereas Frank explicitly focused on the social emotions and their expressive components (but offered little commentary about the specific emotion of disgust), there is little systematic discussion of emotion expression or recognition in the literature on cultural transmission. Once again, this absence does not mean that the perspective and conceptual apparatus found in that literature should not or cannot be used to address the questions about the expression and recognition facts. Indeed, after articulating the Cultural Transmission model, I ultimately argue that it provides a superior account of disgust's sentimental signaling system.

This section is organized similarly to the previous one. I first motivate and unpack some of the key notions used to think about culture and cultural transmission, and explain how they are related to each other. Then I describe the types of psychological capacities that are thought to be important components of our ability to use cultural information. Finally, I briefly comment on how the CTM might be applied to other areas of research in cognitive science, including work on the emotions.

3.4.1   Culture and Transmission

The core idea behind the Cultural Transmission model is much simpler than that of the Classic Commitment model. The idea is that humans learn a great deal of what they know from each other. Much of what we believe, value, and want, as well as many of the ways we behave, the tools we use, and the strategies we use to attain our goals, are originally picked up from other humans. We do not have to figure everything out on our own, nor are we born into the world with our entire cognitive and behavioral repertoire innately structured in our brains or coded in our genes. This idea may be pure common sense, but taken as a starting point, the perspective it affords has been used to generate more specific and interesting research questions, as well as a more refined theoretical vocabulary with which to ask and answer them.

First and most central is the notion of culture itself. Robert Boyd and Peter Richerson nicely articulate the informational conception of culture that is at the heart of much of the relevant work, which I take to be operative in the CTM: "Culture is information capable of affecting individuals' behavior that they acquire from other members of their species through teaching, imitation, and other forms of social transmission." They go on to unpack how "information" is to be understood and how it relates to terms found in the vernacular:

By *information* we mean any kind of mental state, conscious or not, that is acquired or modified by social learning and affects behavior. We will use everyday words like *idea, knowledge, belief, value, skill,* and *attitude* to describe this information, but we do not mean that such socially acquired information is always consciously available, nor that it necessarily corresponds to folk psychological categories. (Richerson and Boyd 2005, 5)

To say that a belief, value, attitude, or bit of technology is cultural is not to say anything about its content. Cultural information can take the form of beliefs about the local environment or other individuals, a preference for Duke Ellington's big-band compositions over Wagner's operas, a norm dictating which side of the road to drive on, the skills and know-how needed to properly field dress a moose, or information about virtually anything else. Information is cultural, in this sense, by virtue of how it is come by— it is any information that is learned or picked up from others. The most salient contrast classes are information that is transmitted genetically, on the one hand, or information, beliefs, skills, and so on that an individual learns or figures out on his or her own, on the other.

Equally important to the CTM is the notion of transmission, which is used to capture the ways and means by which cultural information is actually passed from one individual to the next. The term "transmission" is often used in a fairly general sense, but we can separate the components of transmission of information into two sides. On the one hand, there is broadcasting, when an individual sends information. On the other hand, there is reception, when an individual receives or acquires information. Culture can be transmitted, in this sense, in a number of different directions, depending on the relationship between the sender and the receiver. For instance, when it is passed between peers and across the members of a population within a single generation—for example, from friend to friend or from colleague to colleague—culture is transmitted *horizontally*. When it is passed from parents to their biological offspring—for example, from mother to daughter or from father to son—it transmitted *vertically*. Finally, when information is more diffusely passed on from one generation to the next along pathways that are not directly vertical, it is transmitted *obliquely*.

Given this general picture, one level of questions can be posed about the dynamics of transmission and about the fates of particular types of information, or different kinds of *cultural variants*, as they are sometimes called. How are they distributed throughout a given population at a snapshot in time? By what means and how quickly do they spread when introduced into new populations? Are some more likely to be transmitted and to survive in new generations than others? If so, why? What are the most important factors that determine which cultural variants are more likely or less likely to be passed along, to spread, and to survive in later generations?

Similarly, we can ask a host of questions, clearly related to these but pitched at another level of analysis, about the conditions that allow the transmission of cultural information in the first place. How do humans engineer their epistemic environments to facilitate the transmission of cultural variants? How is cultural information transmitted from one person to another—what sorts of capacities do individual humans have that are most important in allowing them to transmit culture?

Different research strategies might be used to provide answers to such questions, depending on which of these sorts of questions they choose to concentrate. Since my concern is on disgust and its sentimental signaling system, the most natural point of entry is to focus on questions directed at the nature and design of the psychological capacities that allow the transmission of culture.

3.4.2   The Psychology of Cultural Transmission

Some of the most important capacities for cultural transmission are relatively obvious. For instance, the capacity for mind reading—that is, understanding others in terms of mental states like beliefs, desires, intentions, goals, and so on—is most likely an important component of the ability to learn from them. Likewise, the capacity for language, broadly construed, is likely to be a tremendously important piece of the puzzle. What other types of capacities would the CTM lead us to expect to find in the human psychological repertoire? It is unlikely that a single kind of psychological capacity is responsible for transmitting the full range of cultural information, but nothing like a completed taxonomy of the sorts of cognitive mechanisms, and the types of subcategories of cultural information they deal with, has yet been settled on. However, the two-sided character of information transmission points to what will likely be an important fault line in the types of psychological faculties that carry it out. Some mechanisms will be operative in what we might think of as teaching: these facilitate the transmission of culture by influencing the sending of information. Others will be operative in what we might think of as learning or acquisition: these facilitate the transmission of culture by influencing the receiving of information.

3.4.2.1 Capacities That Facilitate the Sending of Cultural Information

Perhaps the first thing to say about this class of capabilities is that relative to its counterpart class (which I discuss in the next section), not much systematic work has been done, and so not much is known about the range of relevant capacities or the details of their operation. One exception to this, however, is a particular capacity that has been a focal point for quite some time: the capacity for language *production* (as opposed to acquisition or comprehension). Obviously, speaking (and writing, for that matter) is one way for an individual to broadcast, that is, to send forth to others information about a wide range of subject matters. Certain putative features of the capacity for language production appear to help facilitate the learning of language in small children, as well. For instance, parents speaking to children in the early stages of language development will often employ a characteristic intonation pattern, sometimes called "motherese" or less technically "baby talk," which may help the child understand the utterance, or at least helps signal to the child that he or she is being addressed and should pay attention to the speaker (see, e.g., Cooper and Aslin 1990; Brand et al. 2002).

Other researchers have taken a perspective broader than one that focuses just on language and have investigated the propensity of humans to engage in what they call *natural pedagogy* (Csibra and Gergely 2006, 2009). In addition to offering a novel reinterpretation of much of the data initially gathered to shed light on the nature of our mind-reading capacities, researchers working on natural pedagogy have looked more closely at a range of propensities that humans exhibit when teaching each others—teaching them various skills, for instance, or teaching them knowledge about the surrounding environment, and so on (Gergely 2007; Gergely et al. 2007). These include not just intonation and cadence when speaking but complementary features like preferential attention on the part of learners for the sources of ostensive signals, often triggered by eye contact made by the teacher. They have often found that learners have referential expectations and interpretive biases that appear to be specifically *about* the intentions and ostensive actions of those they are learning from (Csibra and Gergely 2009). Other researchers have adopted a similar perspective on many elements of social cognition but use the intriguing and suggestive terminology of "herding in humans" (Ramsey et al. 2009).

Following the lead of the natural pedagogy researchers, one could construe much of the research on the production of body language (e.g., Hatfield et al. 1994, as discussed in sec. 3.2), be it in the form of posture, facial expression, or body language in general, under the general heading of "cultural transmission," as well. The sorts of psychological capacities associated with body language and facial expression, and the particular features of the cognitive mechanisms that underlie those capacities, could be understood as primarily serving to transmit cultural information—not just information about the internal state of the individual sender, or information about commitment designed to influence the dynamics of strategic interaction, but information about the surrounding physical environment as well. We use the emotional expressions of other people as a source of information about the world around us. In effect, I argue that this is how the data on disgust expression are best interpreted.

3.4.2.2 Capacities That Facilitate the Receiving of Cultural Information

More attention has been paid to the psychology of the other side of the enterprise of transmitting culture, namely, on the sorts of capacities that facilitate the receiving of information. Some of these capacities can be used in the transmission of information about a wide range of subject matters. Again, research on the language capacity provides insight into the structure and function of a pair of subcomponents relevant here, namely, the mechanisms that subserve language acquisition, on the one hand, and language comprehension, on the other. Albeit in different ways, both of these mechanisms allow various kinds of social learning; picking up information from others, rather than having it encoded in genes or having to figure it out for oneself, via individual learning, problem solving, or simple trial and error.

Another important form of social learning, and thus of cultural transmission, centers on imitation: humans learn from others by observing, retaining, and replicating their behavior. Indeed, theorists of cultural transmission have begun to explore more deeply the relation between humans' facility with and reliance on culture, on the one hand, and the fact that we are instinctual imitators, on the other. Imitation or mimicry is one way of extracting information from the behavior of others and often leads to similar behavior. But more cognitively advanced forms of imitation could also lead to imitators entering more directly into mental states that are type similar to the mental states of the models they are imitating. For instance, while some theorists emphasize the connection between imitation, on the one hand, and empathy and emotion, on the other (Hatfield et al. 1994), most cash out imitation in terms of theory of mind (Tomasello et al. 1993; Tomasello 1999). Indeed, research on mind reading has increasingly come to see an important role for some form of mental imitation and simulation (see, e.g., Goldman 2006; Gordon 1986; cf. Stich and Nichols 1993; Nichols and Stich 2004).

The relationship between imitation, learning, and cultural transmission is still not completely understood, however. Comparative research has begun exploring the range of capacities for imitation found in humans and other species. One of the goals of this line of research is to determine how sophisticated and robust different forms of the ability to imitate can be. It also attempts to determine which forms of imitation, if any, are necessary or sufficient not just for social learning and the development of culture, but also for sustaining a body of cultural information—what kind of imitation is required for a group not only to retain information from one generation to the next but also to be able to add to the cultural repertoire, creating a body of culture that snowballs, and whose content increases as it is passed along through the years (Heyes 1993; Whiten et al. 2009; Boyd and Richerson 1996; chap. 4 of this volume; see also Caldwell and Millen 2008 for a discussion of the import of cumulative culture and ways in which experimental techniques can be used to study it).

Another class of capacities for receiving culture involves mechanisms dedicated to acquiring information about some restricted subject matter, capacities that are domain specific. In an excellent discussion, Fessler and Machery (forthcoming) systematize much recent thought about the conditions under which such mechanisms, which they dub *domain-specific cultural information acquisition mechanisms*, should be expected to have evolved. They provide some context for the discussion by first pointing out that social learners face two fairly general problems: the abundance of information contained in the entirety of the social environment in which they develop, on the one hand, and the poverty of the stimuli associated with specific adaptively important domains, on the other. With respect to the problem of the abundance of information, Fessler and Machery point out that any given learning environment is rich with all kinds of information, but only a fraction of that information is significant. Domain-specific acquisition devices, they argue, provide the innate structure and constraints that allow learners to distinguish the important aspects of their social environment, at a particular time in their ontogeny, from the aspects that are irrelevant. Such mechanisms also allow learners not just to distinguish but also to properly prioritize what needs to be attended to and learned, and so can influence what is salient to the learner at different periods in development. With respect to the problem of the poverty of stimuli, Fessler and Machery make a familiar point that the utterances and actions of other agents, from whom learners are acquiring cultural information, often make explicit only a small fraction of what motivates those actions and utterances. They go on to argue that without domain-specific acquisition mechanisms, learners would be unable to extract the amount and type of information required to survive (or, from a theorist's point of view, needed to account for the capacities that they end up with). This includes not just information about objects, entities, or cues in the relevant domain, but how others apply what they know about, and generate responses to, those objects, entities, or cues. It is to overcome these general problems, they argue, that humans come equipped with domain-specific cultural information acquisition mechanisms.

Fessler and Machery go on to argue that for an acquisition mechanism of this sort to have evolved, the associated domain must satisfy three conditions. The first is what I will call *universal adaptive import*. To satisfy this condition, "the domain must have been of substantial and relatively uniform importance to biological fitness across the diverse socioecological circumstances that characterized ancestral human populations" (Fessler and Machery, forthcoming, 19). They go on to unpack the evolutionary rationale behind the condition: "This will have provided the steady selection pressure necessary for the evolution of a complex adaptation" (ibid.). The second condition is *domain-relevant ecological variation*: "The domain needs to involve content that will have varied significantly across said [socioecological] circumstances" (ibid.). Once again, Fessler and Machery articulate the evolutionary reasoning behind this condition, claiming that such variation in what is relevant from one environment to the next "precludes the evolution of extensive innate knowledge" (ibid.). In relying on information that is socially learned, rather than innately specified, such a mechanism "maximally exploits culture's ability to effectively compile information of parochial relevance" (ibid.). Finally, the third condition is *unavailability of other acquisition options*. While the considerations represented in the second condition preclude the information about the domain from being completely innately specified, the considerations represented in this third condition preclude information about the domain from being gained through, for instance, trial-and-error learning, individual problem solving or information gathering, or direct observation. It is in cases where acquiring information via such routes would have been too costly—because it would be potentially fatal or would simply be impossible, given the time constraints on individual lifetimes or conditions of ancestral living situations—that we should expect the information about these domains to be transmitted through culture, and for individuals to bring dedicated cognitive mechanisms to bear on the task of acquiring it.

3.4.2.3 Transmission Biases

Finally, research has begun to show how features of the capacities that facilitate social transmission can have systematic influence on the distribution and transmission dynamics of that information. These sorts of *transmission biases* often stem from the character of the cognitive mechanisms that underlie the capacities in question, including the specific cues in the environment that trigger them, and how they process the information to which they are sensitive. Such transmission biases can also take several forms. For instance, as mentioned earlier, theorists see an important role for imitation in the transmission of culture. There is widespread agreement, however, that humans are not equal-opportunity mimics. Rather, individuals are somewhat selective in whom they choose to imitate; the propensity to imitate is supplemented with a number of instinctual biases. Preliminary evidence supports this claim, which is predicted by theory and incorporated into empirically plausible mathematical models of cultural transmission (Boyd and Richerson 1985; McElreath et al. 2005). I will call members of one important family of biases *context biases*. Context biases predispose people to find compelling, and thus imitate, certain behaviors and attitudes based on who else in the relevant social domain has adopted them. They are called context biases because they are sensitive to the social context in which transmission takes place, but are relatively blind to the content of the cultural variants they help propagate. Within this family, two kinds of biases stand out. Biases of the first kind induce imitators to embrace variants adopted by prestigious members of the relevant social domain, and are thus called *prestige* biases (Henrich and Gil-White 2001). *Conformity* biases, on the other hand, induce imitators to adopt the cultural variants that are most common among their peers (or some blend of the variants that are most common; see McElreath et al. 2005 for experimental evidence on conformity, and for discussion of blending, see Boyd and Richerson 2000a, 2000b). By influencing which behaviors and attitudes will be most imitated, context biases can influence the dynamics of transmission and produce measurable effects on the population-level distribution of cultural variants as well. Research has shown that such biases can influence how cultural variants will spread in a population or how they will fare over the course of several generations (Boyd and Richerson 1985, 2005; Richerson and Boyd 2005).

Transmission of cultural information can be influenced by human psychology in other ways, as well. What I will call *content biases* make up another variety of biases important to the CTM. Whereas prestige and conformity biases are sensitive to social context and influence which model an individual selects to imitate, content biases are sensitive to the more intrinsic features of cultural variants themselves. These incline people to find more compelling, and thus adopt, certain cultural variants based (roughly) on their content. In some cases, imitators will subject different cultural variants to cost-benefit analyses before deciding which to adopt (Richerson and Boyd 2005). In others, cultural variants with some types of content will simply "fit" the machinery of the human mind better than others, because some bits of information are more easily processed by the mechanisms that underlie human cognition (Sperber 1996).

Like other types of transmission bias, content biases influence the dynamics of cultural transmission and thus the population-level distribution of cultural variants. For example, content biases in individuals' capacities for cultural transmission are liable to make cultural variants with content that fits them more likely to be socially transmitted than others, which in turn increases the frequency of those cultural variants throughout a population. Recent work on religion and religious cognition suggests that underlying much surface variation in religious beliefs across cultures are some common themes in their content. Nearly all religions have beliefs about gods and other supernatural agents, and attendant beliefs with certain contents about those supernatural agents—that they have minds, intentions and beliefs about humans, and so on. Not coincidently, religious beliefs of this sort are more likely to be found more intuitive or compelling than others and are thus much more likely to be passed along and spread throughout a population (Boyer 2001; Atran 2002; cf. Barrett 2000). Because they are thought of as a matter of fit between bits of information and psychological structure, biases for different kinds of content might be generated by different mechanisms in the human mental repertoire. In other words, no one system or feature of human psychology is responsible for these kinds of content biases in cultural transmission. One bias might be generated by features of the human conceptual system, another by features of the mechanisms underlying mind reading, yet another by the mechanisms underlying racial classification, and so on.

3.4.3 Putting the Cultural Transmission Model to Work

As with the CCM, it is now possible to step back and attempt to extract a general picture provided by this work on culture and the social transmission of information. Again we can pose a set of questions: What work does the framework do? What issues does it speak to? To the extent that it is a theory, what is it a theory *of*? What does it purport to explain, and what resources does it provide to do the explanatory work?

The discussion in the previous sections gathers together ideas from a number of overlapping research programs. While each program may be involved in different dialectics and each may emphasize different aspects of the phenomena of culture, they all share some common ground. At the heart of that common ground is simply the insight that culture, and the ability to use cultural information, is a central and enormously important feature of human nature. As such, we should expect that the requirements and constraints placed on us by the need to detect, acquire, and use socially transmitted information have shaped our psychology in rather profound ways. What I mean to capture, at least initially, with the Cultural Transmission model is an approach, a broad, high-level perspective on a range of issues that this core insight allows.

This is still a bit thin on details, of course, but the last section pointed to examples of several more detailed proposals (see also chap. 4). Moreover, the general perspective provided by the CTM can help organize and understand what is already known about other individual psychological capacities by placing that knowledge against the background of social learning and an appreciation of the sorts of abilities required to take advantage of culturally transmitted information. It is worth noting that this is quite a different theoretical framework with which to interpret nitty-gritty facts about the functioning and significance of individual-level cognitive mechanisms than the framework supplied by the Classic Commitment model. The CCM sees such fine-grained facts through the lens of the problems surroundings commitments and the broader context of cooperation, reciprocity, and deception in which they arise. The CTM, on the other hand, frames questions about individual-level cognitive mechanisms in terms of teaching, social learning, and information transmission, and their associated questions. Some of the more specific issues are pointed to in Fessler and Machery's discussion, and include the problems that arise for the achievable acquisition of important cultural information, for the high-fidelity transmission of that information, and for the use and reliability of parochial information in specific domains.

As should be evident, another way in which the CTM differs from the CCM is that it is not organized around questions that stem from the emotions in particular and so makes few explicit or direct claims about them. Unlike the CCM, for example, it provides no immediate suggestions about the nature or rationality of the emotions, or what broad category of function the social emotions might be performing.[10] However, if we take the emotion of disgust as a jumping-off point, with an eye toward the expression and recognition facts, the outlines of a picture become discernible. The perspective of the CTM suggests that, broadly speaking, disgust's sentimental signaling system primarily serves to socially transmit information. In this view, the facts about expression shed light on a psychological capacity for sending cultural information, while facts about recognition shed light on a complementary capacity for receiving cultural information. By identifying this kind of broad role for disgust's sentimental signaling system, the CTM provides a different starting point from which to construct explanations of the more specific features of that system.

3.5 Disgust and the Case for the Cultural Transmission Model

Applying the CTM to the emotion of disgust involves building on claims made in chapter 2. Given the primary functions that disgust performs, it is far from surprising that the emotion comes equipped with mechanisms that facilitate social transmission of information relevant to the associated adaptive problems. In addition to these theoretically motivated considerations, I also discuss some preliminary evidence indicating how disgust systematically influences the transmission dynamics of cultural information. I conclude that the CTM provides a far superior account of the expression and recognition facts than the CCM does.

3.5.1 The Entanglement Thesis and Disgust's Sentimental Signaling System

Perhaps the best place to begin making the case that the CTM can provide a superior account of disgust's sentimental signaling system is with the nature of disgust itself. Recall that in the previous chapter, I argued for the Entanglement thesis, which holds that disgust was created when a mechanism dedicated to monitoring food intake and protecting against poisons functionally fused with a mechanism dedicated to monitoring for potential signs of disease and protecting against parasites. The full disgust response is a piecemeal conglomeration of elements from each of these. While the emotion does not perform them in the most elegant or efficient manner, it still appears to perform each of these primary functions in mature, modern humans, serving both to keep them from ingesting potentially poisonous substances through the mouth and to prevent them from coming into close physical proximity with substances or entities likely to be contaminated or infectious.

Now recall Fessler and Machery's three conditions for the evolution of domain-specific cultural-information acquisition mechanisms: universal adaptive import, domain-relevant ecological variation, and the unavailability of other acquisition options. It is clear that given the twin primary domains of poisons and parasites, disgust satisfies each of these conditions. With respect to universal adaptive import, eating is crucial for survival, of course, but knowing what not to eat and refraining from consuming anything poisonous are of the utmost importance. This problem is exacerbated by the fact that humans are both omnivores and generalists; that is, humans can eat both meats and plants, and the range of what we can extract nutrition from within each of those categories is relatively unrestricted. Likewise, the adaptive import of avoiding diseases and anything that may potentially infect us with them is self-evident and universal. So clearly there are good grounds on which to expect disgust to come equipped with some innately specified structure to help with the acquisition of information regarding these two adaptive problems.

Disgust satisfies the condition of domain-relevant ecological variation on both scores, as well. Human diets vary—and would have varied ancestrally—greatly from niche to niche and habitat to habitat, depending on what was available for consumption in those differing habitats. Likewise, what is potentially contaminating and infectious can vary from one habitat to the next, as can the relevant cues in the perceivable environment that indicate the presence of parasites or pathogens. Thus there are good grounds to expect disgust to come equipped with mechanisms allowing the easy acquisition of parochial information concerning the relevant details about poisons and parasites in the local environment.

Finally, by virtue of the unforgiving nature of its associated adaptive problems, disgust satisfies the third condition of the unavailability of other acquisition options. In both of the emotion's primary domains, relying *solely* on information gathered via individual learning or trial and error would quite clearly be too costly.[11] Indeed, attempting to individually determine whether or not a substance is poisonous, or whether or not some entity, object, or place is contaminated or harboring infectious parasites, could easily cost the ultimate price: one's life. Once again there are good grounds to expect that disgust comes equipped with mechanisms that allow for easy *social* learning of information relevant to poisons and parasites. Fessler and Machery end their discussion of domain-specific cultural-information acquisition mechanisms by speculating on the sorts of learning domains that might meet their three conditions, and explicitly mention both diet and disease avoidance.[12] Taking their discussion and the Entanglement thesis together, then, I conclude that there are strong theoretically based reasons to expect the human disgust system to include mechanisms dedicated to the social acquisition of disgust elicitors.

Returning to the recognition facts of disgust, I further submit that we not only have good grounds to *expect* the human disgust system to include such mechanisms but already know quite a bit about those mechanisms, when the facts are understood from the perspective provided by the CTM. Perhaps the most interesting features of disgust recognition, from the point of view of the CTM, are that it can be unconscious and automatic, and that it is often empathic. Given the importance and nature of the adaptive problems involved, these features help ensure the fidelity of a stream of information that is crucial to survival. When one individual recognizes that another is disgusted, the first individual is automatically put on alert. The type of "better safe than sorry" built into the hair trigger of disgust seems to be operative in the emotion's sentimental signaling system, as well. Automatic empathic recognition helps ensure that the information provided by conspecifics to deal with disgust's primary adaptive problems is effective.

There is still much to learn about the role of disgust recognition in receiving cultural information. For instance, does the empathic recognition of facial expressions play a more diachronic role, analogous to that played by the capacities underlying language acquisition, wherein an individual's disgust system is calibrated within a developmental window, and children acquire disgust elicitors they will possess for most of their lives? Or does it play a more synchronic role, more analogous to that played by the capacities for language comprehension, wherein the gape is primarily useful for quickly signaling information about potentially disgusting entities or substances in the immediate environment? Or, perhaps, can empathic recognition facilitate information transmission in both ways? With respect to the former, young humans are extremely dependent on their caregivers, and the period of dependence extends far into children's lives. It is likely that part of what children rely on their parents and caregivers for is information about what to eat and what not to eat, and what might be infectious or contaminating. That disgust recognition is automatic and empathic may also help ensure that young children receive the relevant information and react to it accordingly without having to be explicitly taught. Indeed, it is noteworthy, given the central role that imitation plays in the literature from which the CTM was drawn, that disgust recognition is basically a form of automated imitation, where receivers mimic senders and naturally enter into a type-similar mental state as those they are observing.

What about the other side of the information transmission coin? Recall a point made in the previous chapter. There, I raised a question concerning the sorts of selection pressures that could have driven the poison and the parasite mechanisms to become entangled with each other, to the point of forming what we now recognize as a single emotion. I discussed three factors likely to have been important, the first two being antecedent functional overlap of the poison and parasite mechanisms, and the expansion of the human diet to include a much greater amount of meat. The final factor I pointed to is directly related to the CTM and the expression and recognition facts that have been center stage in this chapter. It has to do with the advantages gained from being able to transmit information socially, from one individual to another, and the need for an easily recognizable signal to carry that information.

Consider the components of the disgust response that can be traced to the problem of parasites and disease avoidance: quick withdrawal, feelings of offensiveness, and sensitivity to the possibilities of contamination. When we consider these characteristics in the context of information transmission, one thing that stands out is that this set does not include a distinctive, easily decodable component that could act as a straightforwardly recognizable signal. Moreover, it does not include a characteristic facial expression. This is striking, because, as mentioned in the discussion of the expression facts about disgust, the face and facial expression serve in humans as the richest and most salient source of nonverbal information. The gape face, however, could easily have been recruited to serve as one. As the two systems began to integrate, what started out as a functional behavioral component of the taste aversion system, the facial movements that accompany retching, took on another function, namely, that of signaling the presence of parasites and infectious disease to others.[13] The need for such a distinctive facial expression to help transmit adaptively crucial but ecologically variable information about parasites and infectious diseases could easily have provided yet another element to an already substantial set of mutually reinforcing selective pressures that helped push the poison and parasite mechanisms toward the sort of functional integration we see in modern disgust.[14]

More importantly, from the point of view of the concerns of this chapter, the gape face and the cognitive mechanisms that produce it can be understood to perform an important role in broadcasting adaptively important cultural information about the surrounding environment. Of special interest is how appreciation of this point, in conjunction with the particular adaptive problems raised by food consumption and infectious diseases and parasites, offers a novel solution to the disgust version of Pinker's Puzzle. Recall that the gape is a particularly hard signal to fake, because false signaling is inhibited in two ways: making the gape induces the full disgust response, and gapes are produced automatically, so that individuals broadcast their disgust via microexpressions, facial leakage, and other subtleties of body language even when they actively attempt to suppress or hide the emotion. Now let us pose a form of Pinker's question: why do we nearly unavoidably advertise our disgust to others on our faces?

One type of answer is suggested by considering emotions in the context of reciprocity, cooperation, and deception, but very different answers are suggested by considering the question within the context of the problems associated with the omnivore's dilemma, disease avoidance, and the different facets of social living. On the one hand, when the issue is food consumption and potential poisons, the gape allows caregivers to signal to their charges what not to eat. Since those charges are often genetic relatives like offspring or grandchildren, being able to transmit information about what foods to avoid would straightforwardly help boost one's inclusive fitness. On the other hand, when the issue is infections and parasites, which are potentially contagious and contaminating, individuals have a vested interest in ensuring that *everyone* in their social group also remains disease free. Indeed, it is in everyone's *self-interest* to "sound the alarm" whenever a potentially infectious or contaminating substance or entity is detected. In this context, there is little or no benefit in being deceptive about, or withholding information concerning, contagious diseases or easily communicable microbes. Indeed, allowing anyone in one's social group to become infected with a contagious disease or parasite, whether or not that individual is kin or is a good reciprocator, is self-defeating: it increases the chances that one will eventually become infected oneself. This suggests a novel but extremely plausible reason why individuals so automatically and unavoidably advertise their disgust on their faces: because it is (and was) very much in their own, individual best interests to do so.

3.5.2 Some Evidence for the CTM

In addition to the sorts of theoretical considerations just discussed, and the novel light they cast on the expression and recognition facts, there are other bits of evidence that disgust's sentimental signaling system is best understood as a mechanism for transmitting and receiving cultural information. First of all, idiosyncrasies in particular instances of gape faces have been shown to convey more discriminated information about the offending entity. Rozin et al. (1994) found that individual components of the gape face, such as the nose wrinkle, tongue extrusion, and raised upper lip, can variously be exaggerated or deemphasized depending on whether the primary source of disgust smells bad, looks disgusting, and so forth. Thus the facial expression itself can be calibrated to send more nuanced information about the state of the world the sender is reacting to. This shows that the gape is not merely a signal but can be a fairly subtle one.

Several studies discussed in chapter 1 show how disgust can influence cultural transmission, both orthogonally and vertically. With respect to vertical transmission, Heath et al. (2001) began a study with the insight that people are more likely to tell others about things that disgust them. In other words, they are more likely to pass along cultural items that are associated with disgust. The researchers used the Internet to track the spread of urban legends through a population and found that subjects were more likely to pass along an urban legend that was disgusting than one that was not. Moreover, the more disgusting a story was, the more likely people were to pass it along, and the more likely it was to appear on urban legend Web sites. With respect to orthogonal transmission, Nichols (2002b) looked at popular etiquette manuals used over the last few centuries and found that etiquette norms prohibiting behaviors that are likely to trigger disgust were more likely to be passed down and survive through generations than those that are not. In both of these cases, it seems that disgust provides a content bias that influences the transmission of cultural variants.

Finally, and less directly, from a population-level point of view, the distribution of disgust elicitors realizes a familiar pattern of within-group similarity and between-group differences (Haidt et al. 1994; Haidt et al. 1997; W. Miller 1997). This pattern suggests that there is an important role for social learning and acquisition in what disgusts individual people. In other words, disgust elicitors are not all innately specified, nor are they all acquired via individual learning. Moreover, this type of evidence is also compatible with the claim that the transmission of information about disgustingness is influenced by social context, and that acquisition of disgust elicitors is subject to conformity biases. Though this claim sounds plausible, I do not know of any direct experimental evidence that supports it. Nor do I know of any evidence supporting the equally plausible claim that transmission of disgust elicitors is influenced by prestige biases as well— that individuals are likely to adopt the disgust elicitors of the prestigious members of their communities or social groups. It would be surprising if, on closer examination, researchers failed to turn up evidence for either of these claims.

3.5.3   The CCM, the CTM, and Disgust

In closing the case for the CTM, it will be useful to briefly contrast it with what I have set up as its foil, the CCM. Table 3.1 attempts to make clear what each model would say about disgust on a number of issues. Both the Classic Commitment model and the Cultural Transmission model provide high-level frameworks through which the more fine-grained facts about expression and recognition that psychologists and cognitive neuroscientists have been uncovering can be interpreted. Indeed, it is worth emphasizing that the CTM and the CCM provide very different theoretical contexts and resources with which to make sense of the specifics of disgust's sentimental signaling system. The most convincing reasons for accepting the CTM, I submit, involve the dovetailing of the theoretical considerations central to the CTM and the theoretical claims about the nature of disgust and its primary functions. However, further support can be garnered by pointing out that the CCM is simply unable to comfortably accommodate certain key features of disgust's sentimental signaling system. Perhaps the most prominent of these is the fact that disgust recognition is often not just automatic but *empathic*. From the point of view of commitment, there is no reason why recognizing that another is "passionate" in a way that makes her signals of commitment credible should involve this sort of mental mimicry. The CTM would also hold that disgust is a classic commitment device by nature, but unlike emotions such as anger or love, it is far from clear how disgust is supposed to be influencing the dynamics of reciprocity.[15] Moreover, I have argued that there are much more convincing arguments showing the primary functions of disgust to involve protecting against poisons and parasites, rather than securing commitments of any sort. Again, the CTM certainly does not provide the last word on the workings of disgust or its expression and recognition, but it does provide a perspective and a set of conceptual tools for generating more specific questions and testable hypotheses.

3.5.4   Acquisition and Variation

Application of the CTM yields insight into how the expression and recognition facts about disgust's sentimental signaling system fit into the broader theory of disgust. Recall that one of the constraints imposed on that theory had to do with the variation in what people find disgusting:

Table 3.1
Why does disgust have its sentimental signaling system? CCM and CTM give very different answers.

	Classic Commitment Model	Cultural Transmission Model
General set of adaptive problems the signaling system primarily deals with	Cooperation Reciprocity Deception and reputation	Food consumption and poison avoidance Parasite and disease avoidance Each problem being further exacerbated by a variety of factors, i.e., expansion of human diet, migration into new niches, habitats, climates, etc.
Import of the signals; what the information and signaling system is fundamentally about	Navigating the hazards of the social environment Dynamics of strategic behavior Motivational profile of the individual primary agent, and whether she will keep commitments	Navigating the hazards of the physical world Potentially parochial information about the physical environment What is and isn't edible in the local habitat What is potentially infectious and disease transmitting in the local habitat
Account of reliable causal link between emotion production and expression	Advertising is very nearly the point of the emotion's existence Credible signaling is crucial to effectively influencing the strategic calculations of others, ultimately changing their beliefs and behaviors	Signal important information about what not to eat Signal to others to avoid sources of contamination Sound the alarm: nature of group living and infectious disease Vested individual interest in making sure others in the social group don't get infected
Account of capacities for easy recognition	Recognize signal as signal, extract relevant information Detect signs of commitment in others Make appropriate strategic calculations about interacting with them	Recognize signal as signal, extract relevant information Ensure fidelity of important information, making sure it gets transmitted to everyone, easily
Account of why recognition is empathic	None	Ensures others react accordingly Automatic imitation instantly puts receivers on alert
Dynamics of deception	Classic dynamics of reciprocity and defection Push and pull between advantages of deception and the need for credible signals for commitment devices to be effective	Deception would usually be self-defeating Individuals have a vested interest in letting all members of the group know about potential sources of contagious disease

Variation of the elicitors While the disgust response itself, along with a small set of elicitors, is a human universal, there is also a large amount of variation in what is found disgusting, and so in what types of elicitors activate individual disgust systems. Indeed, disgust allows for variation at both the cultural and individual levels. What accounts for this feature of the emotion?

In this broader context, my main claim in this chapter is that disgust's sentimental signaling system is a crucial part of disgust's acquisition system. Thus, the mechanisms underlying expression and recognition of the emotion are in fact some of the most important mechanisms subserving the social transmission and acquisition of disgust elicitors. Appeal to these mechanisms, in turn, will be crucial in explaining the variation in what people find disgusting, since it is these mechanisms that allow people to pick up information about what is disgusting from their peers, parents, and other members of their community. Different communities find different things disgusting, and these sorts of mechanisms of social acquisition are operative in transmitting those different sets of elicitors to their members.

Part of the utility of the cognitive model presented at the end of chapter 1 (and depicted, with some modifications, hereafter) lies in the way it allows the formulation of fairly precise questions about disgust. These include questions about variation. For example, I find both medium-rare rib-eye steaks and Philadelphia rolls delicious; others find both of them disgusting. One might wonder: How does a vegetarian, say, come to be disgusted by rare steaks? How has my high school friend come to love pork rinds and deep-fried Twinkies but find the sushi that he has never tasted revolting? Are some elicitors innate, so that one doesn't have to learn to be disgusted by, say, the smell of organic decay? Did individual experiences, perhaps a visit to a slaughterhouse during childhood, lead her to become disgusted by beef? Has my high school friend been too long subject to the unsavory social influence of his provincial, unhealthy coworkers? Or, in a less food-based example, if a person is disgusted by conservative positions on homosexuality and abortion, is this because she acquired those elicitors from her liberal parents and peers?

The model allows such questions to be put in a form that is not only more tractable but also more focused on their psychological dimension—rather than on who is right in the case of disagreements, for instance. In the picturesque language made vivid by the model, one might ask of any particular person and any specific elicitor, "How has *that* elicitor got into *that* person's disgust box?" The data compiled in the behavioral profile suggested that some things are universally disgusting, for instance, a variety of bodily fluids, corpses, and reliable indicators of infection. The account of the evolutionary history and primary functions of mechanisms in the disgust execution subsystem, encapsulated in the Entanglement thesis and defended in the previous chapter, provides further reason to think that many of these universal elicitors of disgust are innately specified, part of the species-typical psychological endowment of modern humans.

The model can also accommodate the truism that different people are disgusted by different things. It indicates that there are likely to be domain-specific learning mechanisms that allow for both individual and social acquisition of disgust elicitors. In this chapter, I have argued that the research on the humanly universal capacities to express and recognize emotions can be brought to bear on questions about the social acquisition of disgust elicitors, as well as other related issues, including the social dynamics that disgust might influence. Along with the need to be sensitive to the broad range of cues that may indicate the presence of parasites and infectious diseases, its sentimental signaling system contributes to the *flexibility* of the disgust acquisition system.

Another factor contributing to its flexibility lies in the fact that a number of additional mechanisms can also deliver a new elicitor to the disgust database. These include several mechanisms that underlie individual acquisition. One specific mechanism of individual, "one-shot" learning was mentioned in chapter 2, which implements a "once bitten, twice shy" rule to narrow down culinary options. While this mechanism itself is innate, it provides one route, albeit a highly restricted one, by which organisms can acquire aversions to foods that have caused gastrointestinal stress.[16]

Other routes of acquisition are less restricted. Processes as simple as classical and operant conditioning might lead to the acquisition of a new disgust elicitor. Rozin points out that intense experiences can lead individuals to become disgusted by substances that did not disgust them previously. He uses the example of a visit to a slaughterhouse, which might be so gruesome that one is forever after repulsed by beef. Theorists of other persuasions might point out that a traumatic incident occurring during toilet training could also have unanticipated but far-reaching effects on an individual's disgust system. Rozin also speculates that new elicitors can be acquired more circuitously with the help of language, as when one is swayed by passionate testimony or convinced by rational argumentation of the immorality or disgustingness of a practice such as eating meat or smoking (Rozin 1997). Fessler et al. (2003) lend some indirect empirical support to this speculation when they conclude, based on a Web-based self-report survey of nearly one thousand adults, that "moral vegetarians' disgust reactions to meat are caused by, rather than the cause of, their moral beliefs." In other words, in many cases of moral vegetarianism, something other than an antecedent revulsion to meat—perhaps propositional reasoning or effective rhetoric—is instrumental in becoming disgusted by meat.

Another noteworthy route of individual acquisition involves recognition of family members. In cases of this sort, disgust appears to operate in conjunction with a kin recognition system to help prevent incest. The adaptive problem here is familiar: inbreeding leads to a decrease in genetic diversity and allows for the expression of recessive genes, which in turn diminishes the health and fitness of inbred offspring. Westermarck (1891/1921) originally posited that disgust played an important role in human incest avoidance, and subsequent research has, in broad strokes, vindicated his conjecture. Experimental data establish the hypothesis that the emotion of disgust plays a crucial role (Lieberman, Tooby, and Cosmides 2003; Fessler and Navarrete 2004). Furthermore, some unusual marriage arrangements from various cultures serve as natural experiments bearing on this issue and provide startling insight into the role played by the mechanism of kin recognition. For example, marriage rates between boys and girls brought up in close personal proximity with one another—that is, children unrelated but raised as if they were siblings—are inordinately low. In one case, Shepher (1983) shows that marriage among Israeli kibbutz age mates is extremely rare. In another, Wolf (1995) shows that Taiwanese minor marriages were extremely unsuccessful. In both cases, marriages were arranged while the eventual bride and groom were still young. Moreover, once the pairing was arranged, the family of the eventual groom would adopt the eventual bride, usually between a few months to three years of age. The couples were raised together from that point on, with the understanding that they were to be married once they reached the appropriate age. However, the success rates of these marriages were extremely low. Why? These examples are taken to show the kin recognition mechanism misfiring and giving false positives: the eventual spouse is encoded, roughly, as a sibling. The pattern of failed marriages illuminates the principles that govern the kin mechanism, showing how it is automatically calibrated during a developmental window early in life. When it identifies a sibling—or in the unique social arrangement just described, *misidentifies* a future spouse as a sibling—it also generates a type of disgust elicitor. The kin mechanism recruits disgust to block potential sexual attraction later in life between what are sometimes called crèche mates.[17]

3.6 Conclusion

In this chapter, I have brought together a variety of evidence about the expression and recognition of disgust and argued that together they paint

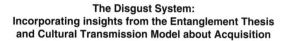

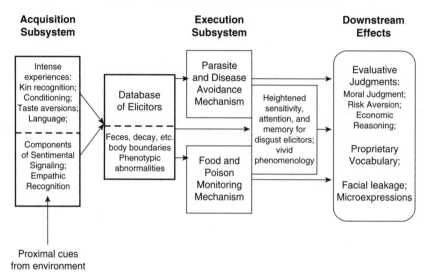

Figure 3.1
A functional-level model of interlocking mechanisms that make up the human disgust system. The arrows represent causal links between the various mechanisms.

a picture of disgust's sentimental signaling system. I then went on to consider two models that cast that signaling system in very different types of roles and thus suggest different rationales for specific features of expression and recognition. Based on considerations drawn from both the Cultural Transmission model and the Entanglement thesis, I argued that disgust is best understood as being equipped with capacities that allow the transmission and acquisition of important but ecologically variable adaptive information that cannot be entirely innately specified and is too costly to be acquired solely by other means. I conclude that the mechanisms subserving expression and recognition are important components of these capacities—that disgust's sentimental signaling system is a crucial part of disgust's acquisition system. Together with a variety of other routes of acquisition associated with taste aversions, kin recognition, and so on, this suite of mechanisms is responsible for the flexibility of disgust's acquisition system and the variation, and hence disagreement, that it allows.

4 Disgust and Moral Psychology: Tribal Instincts and the Co-opt Thesis

4.1 Introduction

What is the relationship between disgust and morality? Although both this chapter and the next attempt to say something about this relationship, I do not pretend to provide an exhaustive answer. Indeed, the question can feel not just difficult but intractable largely because, as stated, it is ambiguous and so can be interpreted in a number of ways. One might be interested, for example, in whether and how disgust can illuminate issues in moral theory that traditionally fall within the domain of metaethics (Mackie 1977; McDowell 1985, 1987; Blackburn 1994; D'Arms and Jacobson 2000, 2005; Knapp 2003; Nichols 2004; Gert 2005). Such issues often center on the relationship between the disgust response and the property of disgustingness, and whether and how this relationship can best be used as a simplified model to help understand the relationship that holds between our moral capacities and putative moral properties like goodness, virtuousness, and wrongness. Many of these discussions explore the metaphysical issues indirectly by first investigating the similarities between moral discourse and the way we talk and argue about disgust and disgustingness. In what follows, I do not have much to say about these types of questions (though see Kelly, n.d.).

On the other hand, one might be curious about a cluster of prescriptive issues that fall within the domain of normative and applied ethics, and focus on questions about how and whether feelings of disgust should enter into our moral deliberations, how they should be weighted in our considered moral judgments, how they should influence legal theory, and how they should be handled by the legal system and other institutions. Such questions, which primarily have to do with justification rather than description or explanation, have been discussed explicitly by several authors in recent years (W. Miller 1997; Kass 1997, 2002; Nussbaum 2004a,b), and I address their debate directly in the next chapter.

Finally, one might be interested in a cluster of descriptive and explanatory issues concerning the emotion of disgust and the way it can—and, as a matter of fact, often does—interact with aspects of human life associated with morality, such as judgment, the cognition of rules and norms, the motivation to act morally and to punish those who do not, and so forth. These issues are the focus of this chapter. As will become evident, many questions remain open when it comes to understanding the psychological and evolutionary details about disgust's involvement with morality. Moreover, the theory developed in previous chapters suggests that disgust primarily evolved to deal with adaptive problems that have little to do with highfalutin matters like right and wrong, the good life, virtuousness, and the like. Nevertheless, empirical work in anthropology and cognitive science has shown that disgust has indeed come to play an important and systematic role in human moral psychology as well. In addition to its primary roles of protecting humans from poisons and parasites, therefore, the emotion must have acquired auxiliary functions connected to morality. Clarifying the character of these functions and the way disgust performs them is my aim in this chapter, and doing so will complete the overarching theory of disgust whose construction is a principal aim of the book.

Understanding the roles that disgust has been co-opted to play in morality, broadly construed, requires understanding those roles on their own terms first. To this end, section 2 is devoted to developing the tribal instincts hypothesis. I first sketch the general contours of gene-culture coevolution, which inspired and provides context for the tribal instincts hypothesis, then go on to discuss recent empirical work relevant to the hypothesis. Returning to disgust in section 3, I argue that disgust acquired its sociomoral valence when it was caught up in the selective pressures that shaped human tribal instincts. The Co-opt thesis advanced here holds that in the face of those adaptive pressures, disgust was recruited to perform several novel functions and became implicated in the psychological systems underlying cognition of social norms and ethnic boundary markers. Finally, in section 4 I take up some of the questions about so-called moral disgust and argue that the Co-opt thesis shows that some of the more puzzling and troublesome features of putatively moral judgments influenced by disgust are best understood as by-products, generated by a cognitive system that originally evolved to deal with one set of adaptive problems, and its imperfect fit with the domains where it has also been pressed into service.

4.2 Developing the Tribal Instincts Hypothesis

Gene-culture coevolution (GCC) theorists seek to understand culture, biology, cultural evolution, and biological evolution all within a single overarching framework. Obviously this is no small task. As one might expect, the GCC literature is fascinatingly complex, and the number of topics on which it touches is enormous (see Henrich and McElreath 2007 for a brief overview, and Richerson and Boyd 2005 for an accessible book-length treatment). To pick a line through this work, then, I will be guided by the ultimate goal of clarifying the relationship between disgust and morality and describing the roles that the emotion plays in human tribal instincts. First, I sketch the basic outlook and key principles of the theory, with an eye to elucidating its picture of the interactions between innate, genetically specified information and the phenotypic characteristics it specifies, on the one hand, and the reliance on and dynamics surrounding the social transmission of cultural information, on the other. Then I spell out the more specific idea that one result of our species' immersion in culture has been that humans are now innately disposed to see their social world in tribal terms and to react accordingly. In unpacking what, exactly, this idea amounts to, I discuss the importance of social norms and ethnic boundary markers and the impact of their increased importance on the evolution of human cognitive architecture.

4.2.1 Gene-Culture Coevolution

This discussion of gene-culture coevolution need not begin from scratch, since much of GCC overlaps with and extends the ideas gathered together in the Cultural Transmission model described in chapter 3. Indeed, many of the ideas put forth there were drawn from the literature on gene-culture coevolution. There is more to GCC than I discussed in the last chapter, however, and the perspective of GCC can be used to reimagine the surrounding conceptual landscape in illuminating ways. For instance, one of the foundational ideas of GCC is that genetic information and cultural information can be seen as constituting two distinct *inheritance systems*— it is sometimes called "dual inheritance theory." Each system allows the transmission of information from one generation to the next. Genetic information is, of course, encoded in genes and transmitted biologically. Alternatively, cultural information is information stored primarily in brains[1] and transmitted—passed from one generation to the next, as well as between members of the same generation—via many forms of teaching and social learning. Moreover, GCC holds that each inheritance system is subject to evolutionary forces, and that different kinds of selective pressures influence biological and cultural evolution respectively, thus shaping the contents of each system over time. Perhaps most significantly, GCC also sees the genetic inheritance system and the cultural inheritance system as each exerting systematic long-term influence on the operation and evolution of the other.

This leads to another of the foundational insights of GCC. The increased reliance of our species on socially acquired information, in contrast with information transmitted genetically, radically altered the selective pressures that acted on early humans, and the complex interactions between the two inheritance systems have profoundly influenced human evolution. The novel selective pressures that were unleashed had their most pronounced impact on human psychology and cognitive architecture. A collaborative effort of several GCC theorists nicely articulates this idea:

> Our framework, however, emphasizes the additional possibility that adaptation to rapidly shifting evolutionary environments may have favored evolved psychological mechanisms that were specialized for various forms of learning, particularly complex forms of imitation (Richerson & Boyd 2000; Tomasello 1999). We call the action of these mechanisms cultural learning. The idea is that, at a certain point in our cognitive evolution, the fidelity and frequency of cultural learning increased to the point that culturally transmitted ideas, technological know-how, ethical norms, and social strategies began to cumulate, adaptively, over generations. Once this cumulative threshold is passed, selection pressures for social learning or imitation, and the requisite cognitive abilities, take off. A species crossing this threshold becomes increasingly reliant on sophisticated social learning (Boyd & Richerson 1996). The fact that humans in all societies depend upon locally adaptive, complex behaviors and knowledge that no individual could learn individually (through direct experience) in a lifetime, motivates such a theory. (Henrich et al. 2005, 842)

This deserves to be spelled out in more detail. Once again, GCC sees culture in general as a repository of information that can be passed from one generation to the next. Once certain conditions are met and a critical mass of culture is reached, the volume of information itself begins to increase from one generation to the next.[2] The repository of information is gradually modified, refined, and expanded by members of subsequent generations, so that it contains the accumulated wisdom of many generations. Additionally, as the size of the cultural inheritance system balloons, cultural items must increasingly compete with each other to survive. As some cultural items prove more useful or compelling than others, they are more likely to be passed along and thus represented in the inheritance system in later generations. In this way, the contents of the entire snowballing body of information becomes subject to various forms of selection, some of which stem from what is useful, others from what is compelling, or how they interact with the components of human psychology that deal with them (see the discussion of transmission biases in sec. 3.4.2.3). GCC theorists have developed an array of sophisticated game-theoretic models and computer simulations to study the properties of cultural evolution under a variety of empirically plausible conditions, which incorporate reasonable assumptions about human psychology (see Boyd and Richerson 1985, 2005a). Exciting and elegant as this research is, much of it is not immediately relevant, and so, in general outline, this sketch will suffice to illustrate the recipe for the evolution of culture.

The presence of this growing body of culture, along with its increasing importance to survival and success, also generates a unique set of pressures on the human beings who use it; the reliance on culture places new demands on human minds.[3] These demands act as adaptive pressures that select for psychological capacities allowing individuals to easily *access, use,* and *transmit* what is stored in that pool of cultural information. Put another way, once the body of cultural information is large enough and reliance on it becomes sufficiently high, the coevolutionary threshold or tipping point is crossed, and a feedback loop is generated. On one side of this feedback loop, features of the innate, genetically specified psychological mechanisms that allow acquisition, use, and transmission exert influence on the evolution of the body of cultural information. On the other side, important statistical regularities in the contents of the cultural inheritance system exert influence on the evolution of the psychological capacities required to use culture and culturally transmitted information. This *core coevolutionary feedback loop* at the heart of GCC provides an extremely general picture of the ways in which the features of individual-level cognitive mechanisms and population-level cultural processes can mutually influence each other over the course of evolutionary time. It is represented in figure 4.1.

As this figure indicates, one of the key implications of GCC is that, due to its crucial role in mediating between individuals and the repository of cultural information on which they so heavily rely, human psychology is caught right in the middle of the major evolutionary forces of gene-culture coevolution.

This core feedback loop can be expected to have changed human psychological structure and the social dynamics it supports in a number of ways—and there are likely some that have not yet been anticipated—but only a few of them have begun to be explored in much detail (as least under this description). Hopefully, this rough sketch of the flourishing

Gene Culture Coevolution and Cognitive Architecture

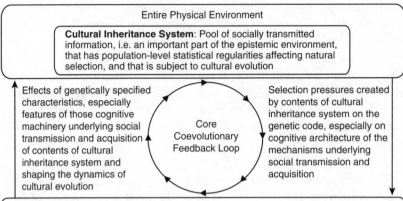

Entire Physical Environment

Cultural Inheritance System: Pool of socially transmitted information, i.e. an important part of the epistemic environment, that has population-level statistical regularities affecting natural selection, and that is subject to cultural evolution

Effects of genetically specified characteristics, especially features of those cognitive machinery underlying social transmission and acquisition of contents of cultural inheritance system and shaping the dynamics of cultural evolution

Core Coevolutionary Feedback Loop

Selection pressures created by contents of cultural inheritance system on the genetic code, especially on cognitive architecture of the mechanisms underlying social transmission and acquisition

Genetic Inheritance System: Genetic information about, among other things, the innate cognitive architecture of mechanisms whose functions are to track, acquire, use, and transmit information in the cultural inheritance system

Figure 4.1
Innate, genetically specified cognitive mechanisms allow humans to access and manipulate information in the cultural repository. By virtue of mediating between the two inheritance systems, psychology is central to the study of cultural evolution, and the study of cultural evolution is just as important to psychology, especially in understanding the features of human psychology that make us distinct.

GCC literature gives an indication of how the novel perspective it affords on human evolution is bristling with insights and implications.

4.2.2   Tribal Instincts and Cognitive Architecture
Gene-culture coevolutionary theorists often take population-level dynamics and the evolution of culture as their starting point, and many of their efforts are focused at that level. The tribal instincts hypothesis, however, is a component of GCC that is best interpreted as a claim fundamentally concerned with human psychology and cognitive architecture. It maintains that one important consequence of the enfolding of cultural and natural selective pressures has been the evolution of a set of tribal social "instincts" that are unique to humans. These are sensitive to particular types of cultural information, namely, types of information that structure and facilitate living within the context of small-scale societies, groups that can be thought of as "tribes."[4] These instincts also lead to distinctive kinds of inferences, motivations, and behaviors that are appropriate to tribal living. Given this collection of hypothesized features, talk of tribal instincts is best

interpreted in terms of dedicated cognitive mechanisms, which process the information and cues to which they are sensitive in characteristic ways, and give rise to typical inferences, motivations, and behaviors.

Understood this way, the tribal instincts hypothesis can be a source of more fine-grained psychological hypotheses about the proximate mechanisms underlying social interaction and can help cast new light on what is already known.[5] The tribal instincts hypothesis is concerned with ultimate explanations, as well. A major source of motivation for this hypothesis is the claim that the complexities of human cooperative behavior, especially our propensity for living in tribal-sized groups, outstrip what can be explained by appeal to kinship or reciprocity alone, the usual suspects of evolutionary explanations of cooperation (Richerson and Boyd 1998, 1999, 2001; Richerson et al. 2003; Boyd and Richerson 2005b, 2006). GCC holds that what is sometimes called human *ultrasociality* is greatly facilitated by the fact that human social interactions are regulated by complex systems of norms, and that humans are able to recognize and selectively interact with members of their own tribe or ethnic group, who abide by the same set of norms. The tribal instincts hypothesis holds that (a) dedicated cognitive mechanisms underlie different features of these abilities, and (b) any viable ultimate explanation of those cognitive mechanisms and the role they play in social cognition will crucially involve selective pressures generated by the core coevolutionary feedback loop. Again, in the words of Boyd and Richerson:

We believe that the human capacity to live in large-scale forms of tribal social organization evolved through a coevolutionary ratchet generated by the interaction of genes and culture. Rudimentary cooperative institutions favored genotypes that were better able to live in more cooperative groups. (Richerson, Boyd, and Henrich 2003, 387)

Pressures generated by the core coevolutionary feedback loop favored individuals able to easily pick up culturally transmitted information—including, specifically, information that facilitated living in tribal-sized groups.[6]

Since much of the work in gene-culture coevolution theory tends to focus on population-level phenomena rather than on the fine-grained features of psychological structure, GCC theorists are right to admit that nothing terribly precise about the underlying cognitive machinery can be derived directly from the tribal instincts hypothesis. As Boyd and Richerson put it, "The division of labor between innate and culturally acquired elements is poorly understood, and theory gives little guidance about the nature of the synergies and trade-offs that must regulate the evolution of our psychology" (2005a, 264). The tribal instincts hypothesis, however, can provide a valuable theoretical supplement to the work done in experimental and comparative psychology, cultural and evolutionary anthropology, and even archaeology (see, e.g., Shennan 2002). The coevolutionary perspective does have some broad implications for the types of cognitive mechanisms we should expect humans to come equipped with, given the selective histories that shaped them. Clearly articulating the adaptive problems those mechanisms evolved to solve can give us a better sense of what they would look like, how they might function, and what they might be doing. In the following sections, I tease apart and focus on two different aspects of human cognition that the tribal instincts hypothesis suggests will be especially important.

4.2.2.1 Social Norms

Discussion of social norms spans many disciplines within the humanities and social sciences, and the term "norm" itself can have different nuances in the hands of different researchers. However, most would agree to a rough first approximation that characterizes social norms as rules regulating behavior and governing social interactions. GCC in particular sees norms as playing a crucial role in allowing humans to successfully live and cooperate in tribal sized groups. Norms also contribute to the unique ability of humans to thrive in a wide range of habitats and climates (for more on the importance of social norms in coevolutionary theory, see Boyd and Richerson 2005a; Richerson and Boyd 1998, 1999; Henrich and Henrich 2007).

Since psychological work relevant to social norms is scattered, I focus on an account that attempts to synthesize some of that work, and that was much inspired by the GCC perspective. In what can be read as a development of one strand of the tribal instincts hypothesis, Sripada and Stich (2007) argue that the escalating importance of norms led to the evolution of a set of innate, dedicated cognitive mechanisms underlying *norm psychology* in human beings.[7] In motivating their model of those proximate mechanisms, they emphasize many population-level properties of norms, including the fact that norms are ubiquitous and important in all known cultures, often possessing a type of existence and normativity independent of any social institution. Sripada and Stich are also impressed by the fact that systems of social norms are stabilized in large part by punishment (see Boyd and Richerson 1992), and that, viewed from a population-level perspective, the distribution of particular norms realizes a pattern of within-group similarity, but between-group variation. While nearly all (nonpathological) members of a cultural group—despite any differences in their biological heritage—acquire the set of norms that prevails in the group in which they grow up, many differences exist between the sets of norms that prevail from one cultural group to the next.

In addition to these group-level properties, norms can also be understood in terms of the influence they exert on the individuals who acquire them. Such effects are more directly relevant to the psychological focus of the tribal instincts hypothesis and are more the focus of Sripada and Stich's model. They maintain that the pattern of within-group similarity and cross-cultural variation suggests that, by and large, norms are learned from the social environment. Their model thus posits a set of mechanisms dedicated to socially *acquiring* norms from others.[8] Corresponding to the properties of independent normativity and punishment-supported stability mentioned earlier are the motivating effects that norms have on the individuals who have acquired them. Sripada and Stich assemble evidence suggesting that once an individual has acquired a norm, she is thereby intrinsically motivated both to *comply* with that norm and to *punish*, or at least direct punitive attitudes toward, those who violate it. The model thus posits another set of execution mechanisms that produce those paired motivations.

Together with a database for storing norms that an individual has acquired, the interlocking set of mechanisms dedicated to acquisition and execution makes up the norm psychology, according to this theory. While those mechanisms are posited as being innate and universal, many of the norms themselves, according to Sripada and Stich, are not innate but learned. (Indeed, the model remains neutral about whether *any* norms are innately specified.) Rather, the evidence suggests that there is room for considerable variation in the *sorts* of rules that can be acquired, in terms of the types of behaviors that they govern, which behaviors are permitted, required, or forbidden, as well as the types of people to whom they apply. Indeed, the model allows that different norms can apply to different groups of people; some may apply to everyone, while some may apply only to narrowly circumscribed categories of people, such as children, adult women, unmarried men, members of one's own tribe, and so on. The model also allows that particular norms can differ greatly with respect to the sort of punishment that should be directed at violators of that particular norm.

While the architecture posited by this model has the resources to explain some systematic cross-cultural regularities in the psychology of social norms (the ubiquity of norms themselves, their independent normativity, the associated motivation to punish violators, etc.), it also allows for a high degree of diversity across tribes and cultures. More broadly speaking, the GCC perspective that inspired it can accommodate and begin to explain diversity in norms. One of the main advantages associated with culturally transmitted norms is the behavioral flexibility that they afford. Different sets of norms can produce different patterns of behaviors, each of which can be locally adaptive to a different environment. In light of this, it is not surprising that different cultural groups or tribes are governed by quite different *systems* of norms, or what can be thought of as distinct moral codes.[9] Norm diversity can further be explained by appeal to the possibility of multiple stable equilibriums: in some conditions, even in very similar environments, there may be a number of different possible systems of norms on which a group might settle. Where multiple stable equilibriums are available, the system of norms associated with each equilibrium point can be internally stable and can produce relatively adaptive collective behavior in that environment (see Boyd and Richerson 1992; Henrich et al. 2005; Sripada 2005, 2007).

Sripada and Stich's proposal takes the form of a general framework, and as they point out, many more specific questions remain open. These include questions about the prevalence and nature of constraints on the types of norm (individuated by their content) that can be acquired, the proximal cues in the environment to which the acquisition and execution mechanisms are sensitive, and the representational format of the norms themselves. More detailed psychological research on norms and associated cognitive architecture is just getting started in earnest (though see Nichols and Mallon 2006; Mallon and Nichols 2010; Kelly and Stich 2007). One question that has drawn much attention recently is the role of emotions in the psychology of norms and in moral judgments more generally (Haidt 2001, 2006; Greene and Haidt 2002; Nichols 2004; Prinz 2008; Nado et al. 2009). However the details may turn out, what seems beyond question is that in some way or another, the mechanisms associated with the psychological norm system often interact and work in conjunction with emotions and other psychological systems.

As for the ultimate origins of the psychological norm system, many suggestions have been made, but no systematic explanation has been widely accepted yet. The tribal instincts hypothesis promises to loom large in any plausible story, however, so any viable explanation will need to appeal to the core coevolutionary feedback loop. Indeed, the GCC perspective has inspired many of the most promising ideas concerning the evolution of our distinctive capacity to cognize norms. Different proposals emphasize the centrality of punishment (Sripada 2005; see also Carpenter et al. 2004; Fehr and Gachter 2002; Fehr and Fischbacher 2004); the role of cultural group selection (Henrich 2004; Boyd and Richerson 2005a, 2005b); the adaptive flexibility of the cultural inheritance system relative to the genetic inheritance system, and the power of norms to fine-tune behaviors so that they are locally adaptive, given the contingencies of different environments (Henrich and McElreath 2003; Richerson and Boyd 2005); and the power of a system of mutually shared norms to stabilize and coordinate interactions in large groups (Sripada 2007; Machery and Mallon 2010; also see Boyd and Richerson 1992 for a discussion of punishment and stabilization). At this point, it is not clear how these proposals are related to each other—which are mutually incompatible, which might be complementary, and so on. What is clear, however, is that each is intriguing in its own right, and further investigation promises to yield valuable insight into this part of human nature.

4.2.2.2   Ethnic Boundaries
A second important strand of the tribal instincts hypothesis begins with the idea that human sociality is further enhanced if actors can make informed decisions about the individuals with whom they might interact. Such decisions will be better informed, for instance, if people can readily identify others with whom they share similar social norms: "Symbolically marked groups arise and are maintained because dress, dialect, and other markers allow people to identify in-group members" (Boyd and Richerson 2005a, 99). Here again, GCC provides an illuminating perspective on the nature of the adaptive problems generated by the need to discriminate among potential interactants, as well as the nature of the strategies and cognitive mechanisms that help solve, or at least mitigate, the difficulties raised by those problems.

The potential adaptive value of symbolic markings is perhaps less obvious than that of social norms. Discussions of ethnic boundary markers often begin with the observation that humans in nearly all known regions and time periods have divided themselves into something resembling ethnicities. That is, humans organize themselves into groups with which they identify, and whose members mark themselves with arbitrary symbols of various sorts (McElreath et al. 2003; Henrich and McElreath 2003; see also Barth 1969). Such a striking fact deserves an explanation.

Gene-culture coevolutionary theory holds that that ethnic marking is fundamentally linked to social norms. Ethnic symbols allow members of the same tribe (or "ethnie," as they are sometimes called) to identify and selectively interact with each other. This is significant because members of the same tribe share a large set of beliefs, values, and, most importantly, social norms.[10] Sharing the same norms, in turn, facilitates *coordination* in the social interactions that are governed by them: actors will have similar and complementary expectations about the "proper" form of the interactions, practices, and customs in which they might mutually engage. Coordinated interactions, in which the norms and expectations of the actors are aligned, will go more smoothly, to the relative benefit of all parties involved. Alternatively, actors who do not share norms will often be at odds with each other, or at least will find that their expectations are not aligned, and as a result their behaviors will fail to mesh. This will obviously disrupt the interaction in question, to the relative detriment of all interactants involved. Note that as described, one party will not benefit at the expense of another by "defecting" in these cases; rather, all participants will be negatively affected by such failures of coordination.[11]

Thus, according to this view, one important function served by arbitrary ethnic symbols is to help maximize coordinated interactions. They do this by providing an external, physical, and observable indicator of an underlying set of internal, psychological, and unobservable dispositions, namely, the beliefs, values, and clusters of social norms endemic to one particular tribe rather than another. The visibility of such symbols, of course, provides easily accessible information that helps all parties selectively engage in coordinated interactions while avoiding those that promise to be uncoordinated and difficult. Since those symbols mark a set of psychological differences between members of one ethnic group and the next, they are often called *ethnic boundary markers* (McElreath et al. 2003).

A noteworthy feature of this account of the function of ethnic markings is that as such, it does not directly appeal to cooperation and altruism (cf. Kurzban et al. 2001). By emphasizing coordination rather than cooperation, it has some leeway to sidestep (or at least downplay) many of the problems associated with freeloaders and defectors, including those linked to costly and false signaling. On the one hand, this account maintains that ethnic boundary markers *do* allow actors to be selective about whom they interact with. On the other hand, those markings need not purport to provide information about where to direct *altruistic* impulses, or which potential interactants are likely to *reciprocate* such impulses in cooperative ventures. Such a scenario would be unstable for familiar reasons. If a set of arbitrary, easily observable ethnic markings advertised indiscriminate cooperative tendencies toward individuals bearing the same markings, then defectors and freeloaders could easily infiltrate a tribe of cooperators by adopting the relevant set of markings, and then reaping the benefits of others' altruistic behaviors without ever reciprocating, and thus without ever paying the cost.

Rather, in facilitating *coordination*, ethnic boundary markers can help maximize a feature of interactions that benefits *all* parties. Thus, unlike other signaling strategies more directly related to cooperation and defection, the information signaled by ethnic boundary markers provides no immediate opportunity for one actor to asymmetrically exploit another, without thereby diminishing her own returns. According to this first approximation of the underlying social dynamics, then, there is little incentive to display false signals by adopting the ethnic markers of an unfamiliar tribe—it would be self-defeating.[12]

In terms of tribal instincts and human psychology, this account of the role and significance of ethnic boundaries suggests that humans will be sensitive to, and have dispositions associated with, ethnic boundaries and the types of symbols that mark them. Indeed, in describing a model of the evolution of ethnic boundary markers, Henrich and McElreath make explicit the link to the core coevolutionary feedback loop that helped create tribal instincts:

The model makes predictions about both evolved psychological propensities and sociological patterns, and explicitly links them. *Ethnic marking* arises as a side effect of other psychological mechanisms—which themselves have solid individual-level selective advantages—that happen to generate behaviorally distinct groups. The strategy of using *arbitrary symbolic markers to choose interactants then evolves because of features of the culturally evolved environment.* Cultural transmission mechanisms may create statistically reliable regularities in the selective environments faced by genes. Thus, explaining many important aspects of human psychology and behavior will require examining how genes under the influence of natural selection responded to the regularities produced by culture. This means that understanding the behavior of a highly cultural species like humans will sometimes demand a culture-gene coevolutionary approach. (Henrich and McElreath 2003, 133; italics mine)

These considerations suggest that in addition to a norm psychology, human tribal instincts will also include an evolved *ethnic psychology*.

The tribal instincts hypothesis and the GCC perspective can provide valuable guidance in the investigation of the architecture of human ethnic psychology. For example, together they imply that the importance of identifying and classifying ethnic actors as such generated selective pressures for mechanisms that were especially sensitive to ethnic boundary markers. In developing this idea, Gil-White (2001) suggests that the ethnic psychological system borrows some of the same mechanisms that underlie folk biological categorization and the representation of species. He appeals to evidence (Medin and Atran 1999) suggesting that these mechanisms initially arose to process information about biological entities and so already had "solid individual-level selective advantages" of the type described by Henrich and McElreath (2003). According to Gil-White's proposal, those mechanisms were then put to further use performing some of the functions associated with ethnic categorization. Gil-White further argues that folk biological capacities provided a fit candidate to be recruited to this purpose: they antecedently applied to living organisms, and they also antecedently produced inductive generalizations about unobservable properties of those organisms based on their observable properties. Similarly, in the domain of ethnic categorization to which they were being recruited, such capacities would need to be able to make inferences about unobservable behavioral dispositions and social norms on the basis of visible ethnic boundary markers.

One virtue of this proposal is that it allows for the explanation of some of the more idiosyncratic features of ethnic cognition. Since inferences about both species and ethnies are, according to this account, subserved by the same mechanisms, unobservable attributes *in addition* to behavioral dispositions and social norms are ascribed to actors based on their ethnic categorization. Indeed, evidence suggests that ethnic actors are "essentialized"; subjects tend to cognize ethnic groups *as if* they shared many properties with biological species, and the character of inferences made about ethnic actors suggests that the intuitive conditions for inclusion in an ethnic group include possession of an unseen, inner "essence." Attribution of such an essence is often based on certain observable features, but not always: the ethnic system conceives of it as being transferred biologically from parent to child, suggesting that inferences about such essences are sometimes made independently of any observable signs (Gil-White 2001; see also Gelman 2003 for a discussion of similar intuitive essentialism in other domains). Many of these inferences are clearly false in the case of ethnic actors, but they are easily explained by this proposal: they are by-products carried over from the original function of the folk biological mechanisms into the new domain of ethnic identification and categorization.[13]

Whether more research vindicates the details of this account of an ethnic recognition mechanism, it is unquestionably correct in its implication that ethnic boundary markers and symbolic markings are salient to human actors. Another truism about symbolic markers and boundaries is that they are often motivating and emotionally charged. Gil-White's proposal has little to say about this aspect of ethnic psychology, however. More specifically, while it explains features of the identification and categorization of ethnic actors, the proposal remains silent on the types of motivation and emotional reaction characteristically produced by in-group and out-group members, respectively. Some experimental work has been done investigating in-group biases (Tajfel et al. 1971; Turner 1984; see also Richerson and Boyd 1998), but there is still much to learn about the biases or motivations associated with ethnies in particular, as opposed to other types of in-groups, and the perspective of GCC can help better understand what is known.

In addition to being sensitive to and inclined toward in-group members, humans can also be sensitive to but disinclined toward out-group members. The darker side of in-group preference and tribal solidarity is xenophobia and prejudice. The tribal instincts hypothesis locates these phenomena in an evolutionary context and, in doing so, puts a peculiar twist on them. Recall that from the point of view of coordination, interactions with members of other ethnies are likely to go less smoothly than interactions with members of one's own tribe. Because of this, interactions between members of different tribes who do not share social norms will be relatively costly to *all* parties. This, in turn, suggests that certain forms of ethnocentrism, though often repugnant and largely at odds with moral codes founded on equality and egalitarianism, could very well be adaptive (Bowles and Gintis 1998, 2001; see also Gil-White, n.d., for more discussion). Ethnocentric attitudes and instincts to avoid members of other tribes, triggered by their different or unusual ethnic markers, would decrease the number of uncoordinated and inefficient interactions—again, to the relative benefit of all, so the line of thought goes.

This suggests that the ethnic psychological system will include cognitive mechanisms that produce motivations to interact with those bearing the markers of their own tribe and avoid those from other groups. The same mechanisms could be responsible for many aspects of ethnocentrism and bias against out-group members. Indeed, the prevalence of ethnocentric attitudes and out-group biases cannot be seriously disputed. Recent experimental work also supports common sense in finding that such mental states are often emotionally charged. Cottrell and Neuberg (2005) give preliminary evidence that links different emotions to the prejudicial attitudes directed at different out-groups. Some of the most striking experimental work also strongly suggests that ethnocentric and out-group biases can take both implicit and explicit form. That research also shows that in their implicit form, many such mental states are easy to acquire, difficult to eradicate or reverse once acquired, and require effort and attention to suppress (Greenwald et al. 1998; Nosek et al. 2007; Lane et al. 2007; see also Kelly, Machery, and Mallon 2010 for discussion with an emphasis on race). There does not seem to be much contact between research on implicit attitudes and the higher-level theoretical orientation of gene-culture coevolutionary theory yet, so it remains to be seen what the tribal instincts hypothesis might add to this exciting area of experimental work.

4.3   The Co-opt Thesis: Tribal Instincts and Disgust

Having sketched out GCC and the tribal instincts hypothesis in their own terms, I now turn back to the emotion of disgust. The discussion will take for granted what has been established in previous chapters, including the Entanglement thesis and the rejection of the Classic Commitment model in favor of the Cultural Transmission model. Several relevant points can be made up front. First, neither of the mechanisms at the heart of the disgust execution system is primarily devoted to monitoring the vicissitudes of coordinated or cooperative interactions; nor did either originate to deal with the Machiavellian move–countermove of strategic social interactions between conspecifics. At the same time, social life and the behavior of others, more broadly construed, would indeed be salient to the workings of the disgust system. Recall that according to the Entanglement thesis advanced in chapter 2, one of the two mechanisms that make up the heart of the disgust execution subsystem evolved to protect against poisons, and the other evolved to monitor for parasites, infectious diseases, and the wide range of cues that might indicate the presence of such contagious entities. As made clear in previous chapters, other conspecifics and their behavior would certainly be relevant to the performance of both of these functions. I also argued, in chapter 3, that disgust is equipped with a sentimental signaling system allowing the social transmission of important but parochial adaptive information about both poisons and parasites from one individual to another. This system, and the importance of socially acquired information about the specific poisons and parasites in the local habitat, also served to make humans sensitive to others' expressions of disgust, and thus helped shape an acquisition system that was highly flexible. This combination of features left the emotion susceptible to accruing new auxiliary functions, particularly in the social domain. Indeed, I argue that disgust was recruited to play a number of roles associated with the tribal instincts discussed in sections 4.2.2.1 and 4.2.2.2.

4.3.1   New Adaptive Problems and Novel Functions

Recall that at its most general level, the GCC framework describes how a body of social information can be sustained by groups of humans and accessed and transmitted from one human to another. Moreover, it shows how reliance on such a body of social information created new adaptive problems and selective pressures, which in turn further shaped the cognitive architecture of human psychology. These helped form a new set of tribal instincts, according to the strand of GCC theory I focused on earlier. The novel adaptive environment, filled with radically new selective pressures generated by the core coevolutionary feedback loop, also created a set of conditions wherein novel functions could be performed by more ancient cognitive mechanisms, which had originally evolved for completely unrelated purposes. In other words, culture itself created a scenario in which old cognitive mechanisms are likely to be co-opted to new purposes.

The term "co-opt" is used here to capture the process wherein a preexisting trait or mechanism acquires a new function in response to novel or shifting selection pressures from its environment.[14] The preexisting trait might itself be an adaptation, shaped by natural selection to perform some original function, or it might initially have been a functionless by-product (the proverbial spandrel; see Gould and Lewontin 1979). If, however, it was an adaptation, it is possible that the new function could replace the old. On the other hand, it is also possible that the old function could continue to be performed alongside the new one without impaired efficacy to either. In such a case, an auxiliary function is added to the primary function of the trait or mechanism, thus rendering it *multifunctional*.[15] Unlike the process of descent with modification described in chapter 2, co-opting need not involve substantial alteration of the structure of the trait or mechanism. Rather, the emphasis is on changes in the environment and thus on the role that the trait or system is playing. The structure of the trait itself often, at least initially, remains the same, while the new selection pressures alter the relevant adaptive landscape, resulting in the trait accruing a new function. (Once co-opted, of course, selective pressures associated with its new role may further refine the trait.) As in the case of descent with modification, most commonly discussed examples involve the co-opting of physical traits or characters. A common example is insect wings, which initially evolved to preserve warmth but gained the function of enabling flight once they were large enough. Nothing in principle, however, prevents psychological attributes from being subject to the same process or, for that matter, from being co-opted more than once.

This segues nicely into the Co-opt thesis, which maintains that the disgust system was recruited in just this way and so acquired auxiliary functions associated with tribal living. For a number of reasons, the emotion was an ideal candidate to be co-opted, especially to perform new roles that involve regulating social interactions. In general, the two core mechanisms of the disgust execution subsystem take advantage of available social information to better perform their *primary* functions of protecting against infection and regulating food intake. In the face of new selective pressures generated by the core coevolutionary feedback loop, other characteristics of the different mechanisms that make up the disgust system gained new significance. On the one hand, there are the features of the disgust system associated with *detecting* and *acquiring* elicitors. Since conspecifics are centrally important to issues of disease and parasite avoidance, disgust was already in the business of monitoring others and their behavior. While the system is innately sensitive to phenotypic abnormalities, there is some latitude in what "abnormal" amounts to, with the innate structure taking the form, perhaps, of an open-ended set of initial guidelines that is revised, refined, or augmented with information gleaned from the local social environment or from others via the sentimental signaling system. In addition, disgust is capable of exhibiting great diversity and variation, and as I argued in previous chapters, an important part of the explanation for this lies in the flexibility of its acquisition system. Such flexibility also makes for an emotion easily activated by new types of cues and thus well suited to be co-opted to perform new roles.

On the other hand, the disgust system produces a *response* that is fairly consistent across elicitors and types of domains. This is significant from an evolutionary point of view, since natural selection is sensitive to stable statistical regularities and correlations of the sort that hold between the elements of the disgust response. Indeed, its rigidity makes the disgust response a reliably elicited pattern of thought, motivation, and behavior, the sort of prominent behavioral regularity that is visible to natural selection. Metaphorically speaking, the execution component of the disgust system represented a standing option, and the response it generated became a type of motivation and behavior that was available when new functions arose that needed performing, or new adaptive problems arose that required solving. Taken together, the emotion of disgust consisted of a rigid, reliable type of motivation and behavior, paired with an open-ended database of elicitors and a flexible acquisition system, enhanced with a sentimental signaling system available for the transmission of cultural information. As new adaptive problems arose, these features, and the mix of rigidity and flexibility they offered, made the disgust system well positioned to be co-opted to new purposes, including purposes that had little or nothing to do with food intake or disease avoidance.

When considered next to each other, (a) the conditions created by the core coevolutionary feedback loop and (b) the nature of the disgust system seem an almost ideal match for each other: the feedback loop generates a variety of new adaptive problems, involving especially social interactions, and the disgust system lends itself to being co-opted to deal with new adaptive problems, especially those involving social interactions. Moreover, the sentimental signaling system would have been extremely useful to a species becoming more reliant on socially transmitted cultural information. Given this perfect storm of converging factors, it is not at all surprising that disgust has become as multifunctional as the Co-opt thesis maintains that it has. While continuing to perform its primary functions, it accrued auxiliary ones generated by the novel conditions into which early humans were thrust. As such, the Co-opt thesis maintains that disgust has become deeply involved with human tribal instincts, indeed, with both aspects discussed earlier.

4.3.2   Disgust and Social Norms

The tribal instincts hypothesis helps identify and clarify some of the specific roles disgust has been recruited to play. From a psychological point of view, the disgust system can interact with the mechanisms that make up the norm psychology in a number of ways. For example, Sripada and Stich's account of the norm system emphasizes motivations to comply with norms and motivations to punish those who violate them. As noted earlier, the precise role of emotion in moral judgment is still a matter of debate, but few if any theorists maintain that emotions exert no influence at all. If Sripada and Stich are correct about the paired motivations associated with acquired social norms, their proposal provides a pair of clearly specified roles that different emotions might play. Different emotions might provide the motivation to comply with different norms, or even different classes of norms, in the form of either an impetus to actually comply or an impetus to judge that the norm should be followed. Alternatively, different emotions might provide the motivation for punishment, in the form of either an impetus to actually punish or an impetus to judge that transgressors of the norm are wrong and should be punished.[16]

Disgust was available to fill each of these roles and has come to fill one or the other or both for certain types of norms. For instance, norms regulating behaviors that involve intrinsically disgusting entities, such as the proper disposal of corpses or bodily wastes, or activities that are antecedently salient to the disgust system, such as dining practices or issues of sexual propriety, are probably most likely to engage the disgust system for motivational purposes. This could be the case for both compliance and punishment motivations. For instance, disgust could provide the motivation to *comply* with a norm that says to never eat food with the left hand, which is reserved for body maintenance: the action itself would become aversive, and one would be motivated to avoid doing it. Disgust could also provide the motivation to *punish* those who violate the norm; violators would be ostracized, avoided, considered dirty and contaminated, even gaped at. Additionally, as described in previous chapters, the norms governing incest have been shown to recruit disgust, and it does not require a stretch of the imagination to see how the emotion is involved in both the compliance and punitive aspects of such norms: it is repulsive even to imagine oneself violating such norms, and hearing stories about others who have committed incest can induce disgust, as well (see Fessler and Navarrete 2004 for discussion of disgust and third-party incest). In addition, some suggestive work in psychology demonstrates how breaking certain kinds of norms, or even merely *considering* violating those norms, or remembering a transgression that one has committed in the past, can trigger a disgustlike reaction, followed by a felt need to engage in (perhaps symbolic) cleansing or purification (Tetlock et al. 2000; Zhong and Liljenquist 2006; see also Jones and Fitness 2008 for a discussion of disgust and norm transgression).

Norms involved with disgust can also help fine-tune the emotion in important ways, helping it to perform its primary functions. For instance, food taboos, broadly construed, provide a clear case in which the universal features of disgust work in conjunction with culturally specific information encoded in social norms that calibrate those universal features. From an evolutionary point of view, especially one supplemented with the resources of GCC, norms governing the practices surrounding diet stand out as a class of social norms of singular importance. For a wide-ranging and omnivorous species such as humans, the problem of locating, obtaining, and preparing nutritional resources takes many different forms, as habitats in, for example, sub-Saharan Africa, the Arctic Circle, and the Amazon rain forest all provide vastly different sets of dietary possibilities. A set of culturally transmitted, tribally specific, locally adaptive food taboos that have been built up over time is of prime value in navigating those possibilities. Moreover, such norms help coordinate the collective efforts directed at location, procurement, and preparation. Many of these could refine and augment the rough guidelines provided innately by the disgust system. The need for this type of behavioral fine-tuning in the case of food consumption, as well as other locally adaptive practices that are directly linked to diet and nutrition—hunting strategies, foraging strategies, food preparation strategies, and so on—was paramount. Indeed, it could very well have provided one of the most fundamental and significant pressures shaping the evolution of the norm psychological system itself. In light of these types of considerations, the co-opting of disgust to help guide these types of locally prescribed behaviors is far from surprising.

Another class of norms that appear to be heavily involved with the emotion of disgust has been called *purity norms* (Shweder et al. 1997; Haidt et al. 1997; Vasquez et al. 2001). These govern issues that are often described in terms of purity but are not thought to primarily protect the physical body from contamination and defilement. Instead they are intuitively understood to help with what might be thought of as "spiritual hygiene": purity norms keep the soul clean and unpolluted. They are also distinct from other types of norms, such as harm norms or fairness norms, in that violations of purity norms do not usually result in any direct physical harm to other persons, or in the unjust or unequal treatment of other persons. Rather, purity norms, which are central to the moral codes of many traditional or religious cultures, are said to regulate the domain of divinity. In such cultures, transgressors of purity norms are thought to be defiling their selves or very souls, either by showing disrespect toward God or the gods, or by violating the sacred, divine order. Purity norms are present but more peripheral in the moral codes of secular cultures, where they are often justified differently, usually by appeal to the so-called natural order. Consequently, transgressions of purity norms in secular societies are often thought of as unnatural acts or crimes against nature.

According to Shweder and his colleagues (1997), purity norms can govern a range of issues, including what foods can be eaten, who is fit and unfit to prepare them, and how foods must be cleaned or treated before they can be eaten. Purity norms also address the specifics of which sexual activities are permissible and what is forbidden, deviant, or "dirty"; allowable and inappropriate sleeping arrangements involving the members of nuclear and extended families; what sorts of clothes can and cannot be worn at different times or in specific places and settings, especially in temples and other sacred locations, or during religious rituals; how a range of organic matter, such as corpses, blood, feces, and so on, should properly be dealt with to avoid the risk of pollution; and which other social groups one can interact with, as well as how and when it is permissible to interact with them, and how to avoid becoming tainted by members of "lower" groups. The subject matter of the issues governed by such norms shows a fairly clear affinity with the subject matter regulated by disgust, and the defining contrast between purity, on the one hand, and dirt and contamination, on the other, further implicates the emotion. The Co-opt thesis holds that disgust will provide the motivation for individuals to comply with purity norms that they have acquired, and that disgust also shapes the punitive motivations that are directed at violators. Initial experimental evidence has begun to flesh out this picture in more detail (Rozin et al. 1999).

The interaction between disgust and the psychological system dealing with social norms can shed light on other ways the emotion is influenced by both nature and nurture. For instance, appeal to norms might explain how the central elements of the response can be elaborated in culturally specific ways. The disgust response is rigid enough that its central elements, including, most prominently, a reflexlike withdrawal, a gape (even if in the form of a microexpression), a sense of offensiveness, and a sense of contamination, will be exhibited to some degree whenever disgust is triggered, regardless of other circumstances like the nature of the elicitor, the other psychological systems that are activated in conjunction with disgust, or even the individual and cultural idiosyncrasies of the person experiencing the emotion. However, culturally specific norms that use disgust might include more detailed information about the locally correct way to express the various elements of that response. While the clustered components will be produced in some form, social norms may help refine their expression, providing guidance on when suppression is appropriate or when exaggeration is more fitting, which features of the response should be embellished, and how, et cetera. These more finely honed displays can easily differ in specifics from culture to culture, but they will broadly instantiate a pattern of variations on the universal themes provided by the basic disgust response.[17]

Finally, the disgust system can also influence the population-level distribution of social norms themselves by providing content biases on their social transmission. Recall that in the case of content biases, as opposed to context biases, intrinsic features of some cultural variants, rather than the social context in which they are transmitted, make them more or less likely to be adopted and passed along than others. Disgust is implicated in a specific instance of a content bias: agents are more likely to adopt and pass along cultural variants associated with disgust universals like phenotypic abnormalities, body fluids, decay, and so on, because those cultural variants are made salient by the disgust system they activate. This content bias has been shown to affect the fitness of etiquette rules (Nichols 2002b, 2004) and the relatively restricted class of norms made up of food taboos that regulate the meat (Fessler and Navarrete 2003b). It has been suggested that disgust can affect the cultural evolution of entire moral codes, as well, by influencing which of several locally stable equilibria a developing norm cluster settles on (Shweder et al. 1997; Rozin et al. 1999).[18]

4.3.3 Disgust and Ethnic Boundaries

Surprisingly, the perhaps most remarkable connection between disgust and sociality was one of the last to receive systematic attention from experimentalists. Many commentators have previously noted that disgust plays some role in marking and sustaining boundaries between groups, but other than bemoaning this fact, researchers have achieved little in the way of clarification or explanation. Here, again, gene-culture coevolutionary theory and the tribal instincts hypothesis provide valuable insight and theoretical context. Consider again food taboos and norms regulating eating practices: different tribes, situated in different environments, will settle on different diets and clusters of food taboos. On the one hand, behaviors related to cuisine—what food one will eat, what one refuses to eat, how one procures and prepares that food—provide a clear, observable source of information about the types of food taboos one adheres to. This information is about something quite basic to survival, but eating practices also inevitably contain and display information about group membership, and thus about the other types of social norms one accepts. In short, many facets of cuisine come to act as ethnic boundary markers.

On the other hand, disgust is intrinsically linked to cuisine by virtue of one of its primary functions, regulating food intake. Given the tight connection between cuisine and ethnic boundary markers, it would have been a small step for the disgust system to be co-opted to play other important roles in human ethnic psychology. For instance, visible aspects of the disgust response like the gape face can themselves act as ethnic boundary markers, especially when elicited by particular types of food.[19] If I turn my nose up at a revolting deep-fried Twinkie, my companions at the state fair might regard me with suspicion, conclude I am a fancy-pants outsider who thinks he is too good for their favorite dessert and rural lifestyle, and keep their distance. Alternatively, if I fail to contain my disgust at a sophisticated colleague's dinner of snails, seaweed, and uncooked fish, she might wonder about my uncultured palette, conclude I am a hick fresh in from the provinces, and keep her distance. The point being that people show their colors when they reveal what they are willing or unwilling to eat, and perhaps especially when they reveal what they find, or do not find, disgusting. These behaviors mark whether one is a member of one particular group or another. This idea fits with GCC and the tribal instincts hypothesis, as well as casual observation and common sense, but psychological experiments exploring its implications are still scarce (though see Rozin and Siegal 2003).[20]

Disgust has been co-opted to play more insidious roles in the psychology of ethnic boundaries and group membership as well. It is the emotion, or one of the prominent emotions (fear being another), of ethnocentrism, xenophobia, and prejudice. The tribal instincts hypothesis predicts that as keeping track of group membership increased in social and adaptive importance, selective pressures would have favored the creation and recruitment of cognitive mechanisms dedicated to monitoring and providing motivation appropriate to ethnic boundaries and the symbols that mark them. As described earlier in the chapter, Gil-White has offered an account of one mechanism that subserves classification of and inferences about ethnic actors, which hypothesizes that the mechanism initially evolved to guide inferences about species but was co-opted to be sensitive to ethnic boundary markers and categorize ethnic actors as such. That proposal says little about the motivations and evaluations associated with human ethnic psychology, however. The Co-opt thesis helps fill this lacuna. It holds that in the domains monitored by the ethnic psychological system, disgust is sometimes the emotion recruited to fill these roles and can thus be instrumental in shaping and sustaining ethnocentrism, xenophobia, and many forms of out-group biases and discrimination. Boyd and Richerson express the idea succinctly:

Groups of people who share distinctive moral norms, particularly norms that govern social interactions, quite likely become ethnically marked. This suggests that *ethnocentric judgments easily arise* because "we the people" behave properly, while those "others" behave improperly, *doing disgusting, immoral things*, and showing no remorse for it, either. (Boyd and Richerson 2005a, 101; italics mine)

Here again, the idea that disgust can influence these types of attitudes fits with both theory and casual observation, but researchers have only begun to gather experimental data supporting such an idea. Nevertheless what they have discovered thus far is comfortably compatible with the Co-opt thesis. For instance, heightened disgust sensitivity has been found to correlate with xenophobic attitudes; people who are more easily disgusted were less positive about out-groups and were more likely to associate them with danger (Faulkner et al. 2004; see also Navarrete and Fessler 2006 for similar results). Other work found that activities, and their perpetrators, that involve breaking a core norm or disregarding a central and defining value of the cultural in-group are often considered not just wrong but disgusting by members of that tribe (Haidt et al. 1997; see also sec. 1.2.2.2 for elaboration). In terms of ethnic boundary markers, flouting a core social norm or defining value of the tribe, as opposed to a trivial norm, is another way ethnic actors might show their colors. In-group members may thus see a substantive transgression of this sort not merely as an isolated transgression of a particular norm but also as a repudiation of the entire tribe, what it stands for, and the set of values that bind it together. Likewise, such violators can be seen not just as mere transgressors but also as threats or impostors of the worst kind. They are thus shunned and worthy of disgust.

In addition, proponents of the idea that disgust can play this type of role in human ethnic psychology often point to well-known instances where one group is subjugated, demeaned, and dehumanized by another. The most infamous recent example of this is the Nazi stance toward Jews before and during World War II. Other examples of extreme prejudice include the treatment of, and biases directed against, members of the bottom castes in the traditional Indian caste system or, more generally and much less excessively, the dim attitude taken by an upper class toward a lower class (see Taylor 2007). Common to all these cases is that the subjugating group often uses the idiom of disgust in characterizing the lower group, portraying them as uncivilized, barbaric, animalistic, and dirty (W. Miller 1997; see also Smith 2007). Rhetoric of this sort can be sadly effective, as this language not only expresses disgust but can *invoke* it in listeners and readers, as well. Once in play, the effect of disgust can be particularly pernicious because of the powerful but subliminal—perhaps powerful *because* subliminal—influence it can have on behaviors and judgments (Wheatley and Haidt 2005; Murphy et al. [2000]; see also Haidt 2001). In addition, neuroimaging research has recently begun to fill in some of the relevant details. Not only has it confirmed the link between the most intense forms of prejudice and the brain areas associated with disgust, but it also confirms the correlation between disgust and dehumanization: only in cases of prejudice where disgust was the accompanying emotion did the higher brain areas associated with agency and interaction with other people (the medial prefrontal cortex, or mPFC) fail to activate (Harris and Fiske 2006). In other words, when an out-group member is disgusting, he or she is often not even cognized as a *person*.

4.4 Moral Disgust

My goal in this chapter is to set out some descriptive and explanatory claims concerning the relation between disgust and morality. The Co-opt thesis I have been developing holds that disgust acquired several novel functions in regulating social interactions, related to social norms and ethnic boundary markers. Taking the Co-opt thesis as established, it would not seem to be much of a stretch to simply conclude that I now have an account of *moral disgust* on hand. This inference needs to be handled with care, however, for the term "moral" and the term "disgust" each raise their own difficulties in this context. I will consider the problems of each in turn and then go on to make explicit a theme that has been an undercurrent throughout this and previous chapters, showing how the Co-opt thesis casts many of the most striking findings about so-called moral disgust as by-products.

4.4.1 Demarcating the Domain of Morality

The expression "moral disgust" at least suggests that the domain or definition of morality can be delineated clearly and that disgust sometimes operates comfortably within its purview. Unfortunately, it remains far from clear what might determine, or how we should adjudicate, what properly falls within the domain of the moral. Is a norm that prohibits menstruating women from entering the kitchen a moral norm, or might it be for some cultures? If disgust is the emotion that produces the compliance and punitive motivations associated with either norm, would this thereby count as moral disgust? One way to delineate the domain of the moral, and thus to decide such questions, might be to subject the concept of morality to the type of analysis in which philosophers often engage, reflecting on typical uses, elaborating those reflections into explicit accounts of the necessary and sufficient conditions for the concept's application, and testing those accounts against a range of hypothetical cases, with an eye for where each explicit account parts ways with intuitions about proper use of the concept. This sort of armchair conceptual analysis might also be supplemented with the empirical methods of experimental philosophy (Knobe and Nichols 2008; Knobe 2007). No consensus about the concept of morality has yet been reached by philosophers using this method in its pure form (see Nado et al. 2009 for discussion and references), but experimental philosophy may help make progress (Stich et al. in prep.).

Another way to distinguish morality from other domains would be to treat it as a natural kind and proceed by using the methods of cognitive anthropology and experimental psychology to demarcate norms that govern moral matters from, for instance, religious edicts, conventional rules, prudential guidelines, or issues beyond the reach of morality that are located within a personal domain of autonomy. Researchers working on the so-called moral–conventional distinction can be interpreted as taking this tack. The developmental psychologists who pioneered this research claim to have found systematic, cross-culturally stable differences in moral norms and conventional norms and the ways in which transgressions of each respective type of norm are cognized. In their view, moral norms are those having to do with harm, justice, welfare, and rights, and people judge moral norms to apply generally, rather than holding only in a particular culture or situation. People also judge moral norms to apply independently of any authority figure or institution; unlike conventional norms, a moral norm cannot be rescinded or altered by the pronouncement of someone in charge. Furthermore, transgressions of moral norms are typically judged to be more serious than transgressions of conventional norms (Nucci 2001; Turiel 1983). If correct, this would be an excellent candidate for a psychological natural kind and, with some philosophical effort, could be parlayed into an account of the extensions of terms like "moral," "morality," "moral norm," and perhaps even "moral disgust."

There is reason to think that the impressive amounts of data gathered in support of this view paint a misleading picture, however. Rather, my colleagues and I have argued at length elsewhere that the appearance of a sharply demarcated, cross-culturally robust divide between moral and conventional norms, so characterized, is an artifact, an illusion produced by the very circumscribed set of norms and transgressions used in the relevant experiments (Kelly et al. 2007; Kelly and Stich 2007; see also Stich et al. 2009). It remains to be seen whether or not other attempts that use the methods of psychology to determine which norms are, properly speaking, moral norms will be fruitful (see also the exchange between Stich and Prinz in Murphy and Bishop 2009).

Finally, it is possible that which individual social norms, judgments, and perhaps even particular psychological systems should ultimately be classified as "moral" may not be a matter that can be discovered at all. Perhaps there is simply no uniform concept or psychological natural kind in the neighborhood of the term. Instead different cultures might employ different, culturally local forms of normative regulation and are each able to decide what sorts of activities fall within the scope of which sorts of regulation (see Machery and Mallon 2010 for some discussion along these lines; cf. Shweder et al. 1997).

This issue may ultimately prove tractable, but as long as it remains unresolved, the difficulty will manifest in the more specific case of demarcating episodes of moral disgust from the rest. That disgust exhibits as much variability at the individual and cultural levels as it does only makes this instance of the problem more difficult. In addition, many of the roles that disgust plays in regulating social interactions, especially those associated with ethnocentrism, xenophobia, and prejudice against other groups, and, to a lesser extent, divinity and purity, may not easily fit in some conceptions of morality at all, especially those in the tradition of John Stuart Mill that tend to emphasize autonomy, individual rights, equality, and egalitarianism (see Haidt and Joseph 2007; Haidt and Hersh 2001; Haidt et al. 1993). This sort of tension and the discomfort it is liable to create are nicely expressed by one prominent social theorist:

> The possibility of community is also weakened, in the long term, by the democratic principle of equality. If the strongest communities are bound together by certain moral laws that define wrong and right for its members, these same moral laws also define that community's inside and an outside as well. And if those moral laws are to have any meaning, those excluded from the community by virtue of their unwillingness to accept them must have a different worth or moral status from the community's members. But democratic societies constantly tend to move from simple tolerance of all alternative ways of life, to an assertion of their essential equality. They resist moralisms that impugn the worth or validity of certain alternatives, and therefore oppose the kind of exclusivity engendered by strong and cohesive communities. (Fukuyama 1992, 323)

This can be quite disorienting, and perhaps one more source of the sense of paradox some theorists have felt about disgust. By the lights of one locally pervasive, explicitly avowed moral code familiar to many of us in the West, one of the most prominent functions that disgust has come to play in our putative moral psychology is to support decidedly *immoral* attitudes.

I have drawn attention to this issue mainly to make explicit that I intend to remain agnostic on it in what follows. I take it that disgust does play several important roles in what is generally investigated under the heading of moral psychology, especially having to do with social norms and group membership, and social interactions and judgments associated with those. I also take it that disgust's prominence and influence can vary from one culture to the next. However, there is not yet any account of how to *precisely* demarcate the domain of morality, so there is not yet any way to separate out instances of genuinely *moral* disgust from others, or whether the role one culture reserves for disgust is genuinely moral while the role reserved by another culture is not. Since nothing I have to say here depends on having such a clearly defined distinction on hand, I can remain hopeful that the current state of ignorance will soon be resolved, but need not wait for it to happen (see chapter 5 for a different angle on a similar issue).

4.4.2 Actual Disgust or Mere Metaphor?
Another kind of worry is raised by a handful of researchers who are skeptical about whether disgust is ever genuinely operative in the social domain. Instead they hold out the possibility that while things like feces and spoiled

meat are true elicitors of the emotion, talk of disgust in conjunction with social and moral issues is merely metaphorical (Nabi 2002; Bloom 2004; see also Haidt et al. 1997 and Danovitch and Bloom 2009 for discussions of related worries). Failure to appreciate this, they claim, could infect and invalidate research on the emotions and distort psychologists' and philosophers' understanding of the machinery of human moral psychology. Indeed, if proponents of this "mere metaphor" view are correct, then what often goes by the name of moral disgust is not *really* disgust at all.

While I disagree with this view, is worth being clear at the outset what I take the disagreement to be about. For instance, all parties seem to agree that the carry-over effects of "extraneous" disgust have been experimentally established at this point. Recall from chapter 1 (sec. 1.2.1.3) that activation of the disgust system can have measurable downstream effects on cognition and evaluation of various sorts, including putative moral judgments. Occurrent disgust can make negative assessments more severe, even when what activated the disgust system (fart spray, a dirty desk and overflowing garbage can, a clip from *Trainspotting*) was distinct from the object of assessment. These effects are striking, to be sure, but for my purposes here, the relevant point is that the experiments demonstrating them straightforwardly assume that the participants (in the disgust conditions) are genuinely, rather than metaphorically, disgusted. Thus, I take this to be a fairly uncontroversial sense in which putatively moral judgments are influenced by actual disgust.

This is not what proponents of the mere metaphor view are denying, though. The psychologist Paul Bloom expresses the line of thought behind that view eloquently. After surveying examples of people who claimed to be "disgusted" by things like the high price of spaghetti or the president's tax plan, he reports that his findings seem to indicate that

disgust can be highly abstract and intellectual. But I am skeptical. My hunch is that in these statements "disgust" is a metaphor. Saying that we are disgusted by a tax plan is like saying that we are thirsty for knowledge or lusting after a new car. After all, if you actually observe people's faces and actions during heated political or academic discourse, you will witness a lot of anger, even hate, but rarely, if ever, the facial or emotive signs of disgust. To say that this is a metaphor is not to dismiss it as unimportant. It is a pervasive metaphor, and one of considerable power. (Bloom 2004, 172–173)

Bloom is suggesting that while concrete things like messy trash and nasty smells can activate a person's disgust system, merely abstract and intellectual things like tax policies and exorbitant pasta prices cannot, even if that person considers those policies and prices immoral. Morally outraged people may claim to be disgusted by such intangibles, but they are merely speaking metaphorically; their disgust systems are not actually activated by those things. If this interpretation of the point of contention is correct, then my disagreement with proponents of the mere metaphor view is most charitably understood as being about what can and cannot activate the disgust system, and thus produce a genuine disgust response; the issue concerns the range of disgust *elicitors*.[21]

That said, Bloom's discussion strikes me as unconvincing on two accounts. First, casually observing the faces of people engaged in argument is a far from ideal way to determine if their disgust is implicitly influencing them, operating at a subthreshold or subliminal level. Even if they are disgusted, debaters could be suppressing the overt expression of their disgust for the sake of decorum and so could be flashing difficult-to-detect microexpressions. Or maybe not; but the research on expression makes clear that this is certainly a possibility. Obviously it is hard to say anything convincing one way or the other, and all can agree that trading anecdotes and interpretations of them would not be the best way to move this discussion forward.

Luckily, recent experimental work actually does look at disgust facial expressions in an attempt to address the status of moral disgust. Chapman et al. (2009) use electromyography (EMG) technology to monitor the facial expressions of participants presented with disgust elicitors of various sorts. To induce social or moral disgust, participants were given unfair offers while playing the ultimatum game that is a staple of experimental economics. Chapman and colleagues found that participants' facial expressions were similar across all the different types of elicitors, including the "moral disgust" condition involving the unfair offering. This, together with the fact that all the facial expressions included elements of muscular activation associated with oral and nasal expulsion, provides further evidence that disgust is in important respects uniform across domains, and so against the "mere metaphor" view of its operation in the social and moral domains (as Rozin et al. [2009] point out in a commentary on Chapman's article).

Returning to Bloom's worries, my second reason for finding his argument unconvincing is that if calling it "merely metaphorical" in instances like the ones he describes amounts to the claim that people's disgust systems are not really activated, then he loses the most plausible explanation of that idiom's "considerable power." In my view, the power of disgust-based rhetoric lies largely in its ability to subtly invoke and direct the emotion itself. As emphasized in chapter 3, there is good reason to think that expressions of disgust do, indeed, result in the (perhaps subliminal) activation of the disgust system, in both the speaker and the listener. Other work has shown that even subliminal disgust can have dramatic effects—exert "considerable power"—on judgments (e.g., Murphy et al. 2000; Wheatley and Haidt 2005).

Neurological evidence may also eventually help adjudicate this disagreement. What is known now is rather preliminary, but not incompatible with the view I favor. Two groups of researchers used fMRI technology to investigate patterns of neural activity in response to stimuli associated with disgust across a number of different domains, from lowly and uncontroversial triggers like descriptions of someone eating a scab or someone throwing up, to more abstract and controversial elicitors that Schaich Borg et al. (2008) characterize as coming from the "sociomoral" domain, and Moll et al. (2005) describe as liable to provoke "indignation." Each study finds a similar pattern of neural activation: that "elicitors from different domains recruited both overlapping and distinct brain regions," in the words of Moll et al. (68), or that "pathogen-related and sociomoral acts entrain many common as well as unique brain networks," in the words of Schaich Borg et al. (1529). One conclusion that Schaich Borg and colleagues draw from their findings is that disgust "is not a unified psychological or neurological phenomenon" (1529; see Simpson et al. 2006 for similar conclusions based on self-report data).

I think another interpretation of the data, suggested by the Co-opt thesis, is more plausible. Rather than revealing psychological disunity, the pattern of evidence shows a single psychological system, disgust, working *in conjunction with* different cognitive systems in each of the different cases. The Co-opt thesis holds that disgust need not work in isolation but has been recruited by other psychological systems, for example, those related to incest avoidance, social norms, and ethnic boundaries and group membership. According to this picture, the disgust system is not fragmented so much as it is a single, unified system that is *redeployed* multiple times, in multiple domains, and in combination with several other systems. Interpreted in this way, the extant neurological data are comfortably compatible with the Co-opt thesis. Indeed, the Co-opt thesis helps make sense of the data: it should be expected that disgust would collaborate with different parts of the mind as it performs its different auxiliary functions. In addition to the case for the view of disgust that I have been building in this chapter, there are reasons to think that this sort of recruitment and redeployment of psychological mechanisms is common in cognitive and neural organization more generally. Relevant arguments and evidence are assembled in a series of papers on what Michael Anderson calls the "massive redeployment hypothesis" (Anderson 2006, 2007a,b,c).

These neurological data on disgust are certainly not univocal or decisive on their own. There is no need to consider them on their own, however. There are now a wealth of theoretical considerations, encapsulated in the Entanglement thesis, Cultural Transmission model, and Co-opt thesis, to go with the behavioral evidence marshaled in support of them and canvassed here and in previous chapters. In particular, manifestations of the sense of offensiveness and sensitivity to contamination—the inferential signature of disgust—found in many experiments on focusing on moral judgment are particularly telling evidence of the operation of the disgust system, and thus the influence of genuine disgust, in my view (see Kelly, in press). In light of all of this, I conclude that the "mere metaphor" view is incorrect. At the least, the burden of proof now lies on those who claim that the extension of disgust beyond its primary domains of poisons and parasites is never more than metaphorical.

4.4.3   The Co-opt Thesis and Cognitive By-products

The defense of the view that so-called moral disgust is, often, genuine disgust provides a nice segue into a final point I want to make explicit, which has been a leitmotif throughout much of the earlier discussion. On the view I have been developing, Co-opt thesis presupposes the Entanglement thesis defended in chapter 2 and holds that once it is swept up in the social dynamics and selection pressures generated by the core coevolutionary feedback loop, a cognitive system that initially evolved to deal with poisons and parasites acquired several novel functions associated with regulating social interactions. Reflecting on this view can, in turn, help illuminate the way in which disgust informs social and moral matters, and shapes the putatively moral judgments and motivations it does affect.

Recall that according to the Entanglement thesis, when the food rejection mechanism and parasite avoidance mechanism fused, they also created a system whose character made it highly susceptible to being co-opted to perform other functions, including especially functions pertaining to issues in the domain of so-called moral disgust associated with social coordination and interpersonal judgment. Part of this susceptibility was due to a kind of "upstream" flexibility in the emotion: successfully protecting against poisons and parasites requires a hair trigger that is easily activated by a relatively wide array of cues. This, in turn, makes it easier for the emotion to be recruited to perform new functions. Another part of the susceptibility, however, was due to the "downstream" rigidity of the disgust response, which remains relatively consistent across these new domains. I made the point in chapter 1 (1.2.1.2) that evidence shows how disgust is elicitor neutral in important ways and that the nomological cluster of core elements that makes up the disgust response remains largely invariant across different kinds of elicitors. Perhaps most striking is that regardless of the specific character of the cue that triggers it on any particular occasion, the disgust system produces a characteristic inferential signature that involves a sense of oral incorporation, a sense of offensiveness, and sensitivity to contamination. Because of this characteristic signature, anything that triggers the disgust response will have disgustingness projected onto it and will be thought about and treated *as if* it were mildly revolting, offensive, and contaminating.

This has important implications for thinking about the operation of disgust in the social and moral domains. On the one hand, the Entanglement thesis holds that the two mechanisms at the heart of the emotion were shaped by the adaptive problems created by poisons and parasites. Many elements of the disgust response make perfect sense in light of these adaptive problems; the response is fairly well fitted to its *primary* functions. On the other hand, the Co-opt thesis implies that the disgust response is not ideally fitted or optimally matched to the *auxiliary* functions that it went on to acquire. Instead, in filling those new roles, the full nomological cluster of elements that make up the response were brought to bear on the new domains in which disgust came to operate. The behavior and attitudes associated with disgust in these new domains are influenced by those elements, particularly its characteristic inferential signature. As a result, disgust operating in its auxiliary roles can lead to behaviors and attitudes that are in some sense effective—disgust may be effective in providing the motivation to avoid violating a norm or interacting with someone from another tribe— but it can also shape those behaviors and attitudes in ways that make them idiosyncratic, inefficient or outright irrational.

Evolutionary theorists often call explanations like this *by-product hypotheses*. By-product hypotheses are often advanced to explain a puzzling but systematic (rather than random) deviation from optimal performance of an activity or function. The less-than-optimal performance is explained by appeal to the influence of some trait or system that is performing not its original function but a new one. The systematic deviations are then explained as by-products of the imperfect fit between the trait or system and the new function it has been co-opted to perform or activity it is involved with. Finally, the exact character of the systematic deviation is explained by appeal to specific features that the co-opted trait or system retained from its original function and brought to bear on its new one. For example, humans evolved from ancestral species that mainly walked around on all fours. Human spines, in turn, are descended from spines that initially evolved for quadrupedal locomotion. Once our ancestors began walking upright on two legs, the spine retained much of its original structure; Mother Nature is, after all, a tinkerer. As such, our spines made the transition from functioning to support quadrupedal locomotion to functioning to support bipedal locomotion, but they are far from optimally designed or perfectly efficient for it. Thus many modern humans suffer from characteristic types of spinal stress and chronic back pain.[22]

In the case of disgust, social norms that co-opt the emotion recruit a kind of aversion, probably useful in motivating agents to avoid the types of activities proscribed by those norms, or motivating them to avoid or shun transgressors. As a by-product, however, such norms and motivations will also be infused with the other elements that accompany the disgust response, including a sense of offensiveness, contamination, and feelings of revulsion. Thus the by-product hypothesis can provide a preliminary explanation of some of the idiosyncratic and seemingly irrational aspects associated with disgust-involving norms, most notably concerns with sanctity and defilement, unnaturalness, contamination, and moral taint associated with many purity norms; the inclination to cleanse oneself, either literally or symbolically, after violating certain types of norms; and the extremities of the attitudes directed toward other transgressors (see Kelly, in press). The Co-opt thesis, together with the Entanglement thesis, illuminates the source of these aspects of norms and the social and moral judgments linked to them. In revealing them as by-products stemming from an imperfect fit between the response and its novel role, this view also suggests that these aspects are often mere projections.

Likewise with the role that disgust plays in ethnic cognition: sensitivities to group membership might co-opt disgust to provide a powerful type of motivation, causing agents to avoid interactions with members of other tribes. As in the case of social norms, recruitment of the disgust system entails recruitment of the entire cluster of elements making up the response. Some of those elements made disgust an excellent candidate for the purposes at hand—when members of other tribes trigger disgust, an actor is thereby strongly motivated to *avoid* them. But as noted previously, disgust elicitors evoke the entire cluster of components that make up the disgust response, including the propensity to think about and treat those elicitors as if they were offensive and contaminating even when they are not. In instances where disgust underlies prejudices and ethnocentric attitudes, then, actors will not only avoid members of those tribes but will be more likely to project offensiveness and contamination potency onto them as well, and will thus judge them to be offensive, contaminating, unpleasant—in a word, disgusting. Those with different values and norms, members of other tribes that do things differently and give priority to different moral principles, will be thought of not just as different but as tainted, contaminating, immoral, and somehow less or lower than one's own tribe—animal or subhuman. The Co-opt thesis and Entanglement thesis trace these aspects of ethnic cognition to disgust's primary functions, revealing them as by-products stemming from a mismatch between the emotion and this set of auxiliary functions that it has also been recruited to perform. Once again, in illuminating their source, this view shows that in these cases, feelings of offensiveness and contamination (and their cognates), even when vivid, are often misplaced.

4.5 Conclusion

The burden of this chapter was to begin illuminating the relationship between disgust and morality from a descriptive and explanatory perspective. The Co-opt thesis defended here shows, in broad outline, how disgust might have become involved in the putative domain of morality, and thus discharges that burden. The larger framework of gene-culture coevolutionary theory provided a useful background for developing the tribal instincts hypothesis, for making sense of much of the experimental data gathered by moral psychologists, and for integrating the insights won from different approaches to studying the emotion. Moreover, the Co-opt thesis, together with the Entanglement thesis, allowed the formulation of a by-product hypothesis that is able to explain many of the more puzzling features of so-called moral disgust.

This chapter also brings to a close one of the overarching projects of this book, namely, the construction of an integrated theory of disgust. The one desideratum that had not yet been fully satisfied was the following:

Diversity of the elicitors There is also a wide and surprisingly diverse range of elicitors that trigger disgust, ranging along one dimension from the concrete to the abstract, and along another from the brutely physical and inert to the highly social and interpersonal. What accounts for the pairing of such a diverse range of triggering conditions to this one specific type of response?

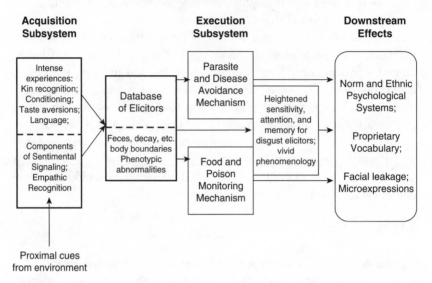

Figure 4.2
A functional-level model of interlocking mechanisms that make up the human disgust system. This depiction of the model incorporates the insights of the Entanglement thesis, the Cultural Transmission model, and the Co-opt thesis.

Together with the discussion of disgust's sentimental signaling system in the last chapter, the Co-opt thesis defended in this chapter satisfies this constraint on the theory. As humans became increasingly social and more reliant on cultural information, the selective pressures generated by the core coevolutionary feedback loop created a novel set of adaptive problems relating to social interactions. I have argued that owing to a number of its properties, including the fixed and ready-to-go behavioral pattern, on the one hand, and flexible acquisition system, on the other, disgust was recruited to help deal with a number of those new adaptive problems, including, perhaps most importantly, those associated with our tribal social instincts. In dealing with poisons and parasites, as well as certain kinds of social norms and ethnic boundaries, disgust became sensitive to a much more diverse range of elicitors. Ultimately it was shaped into the impressively multifunctional psychological system that is now a key part of modern human nature. The final incarnation of the cognitive model, incorporating all these insights, is represented in figure 4.2.

5 Disgust and Normative Ethics: The Irrelevance of Repugnance and Dangers of Moralization

5.1 Introduction

Like the last chapter, this one examines the relationship between disgust and morality, but it focuses on a different facet. Here I begin by considering two diametrically opposed views on the moral significance of what is sometimes called the "yuck factor." Say your response to an activity or social practice is simply: "yuck"; you find it simply and unequivocally disgusting. What follows? Is that a good enough reason to think the practice is morally wrong or problematic?

I use the debate over the correct answer to this question to motivate its main issues and core points of contention. Proponents of the two opposing camps typically hold extremely different views of the nature of the emotion, and their different normative conclusions rest on their opposing views. To stake out my own position in the normative debate, then, I briefly review the most important elements of my view of disgust, which, since it is mainly expressed by the Entanglement thesis and Co-opt thesis argued for in earlier chapters, I call the E&C view. I show how the E&C view is far superior to both of its competitors and argue that it provides new foundations for a powerful and sweeping form of skepticism about the roles disgust should play in moral reflection, deliberation, justification, and beyond. After separating out and elaborating on several different implications of this view, I conclude with some comments on the general form of the reasoning behind it and what it suggests about naturalism in ethics.

5.2 Should Disgust Be Involved in Morality? Advocates and Skeptics

The cluster of issues concerning disgust that has come to the fore in normative and applied ethics centers on the question of what role the emotion of disgust should play in morality, broadly construed. The issues here are not those of description or explanation but ones of justification; not of what *is* the case but of what *should* be. Should disgust influence our considered moral judgments? If so, how should we account for feelings of disgust in various ethical evaluations, deliberations, and decisions? What sort of weight, import, or credit should we assign to such feelings? How should our legal system and other institutions best deal with the emotion? Alternatively, is disgust ever the morally proper response to a transgression, attitude, or practice? Is it morally problematic to elicit and direct people's propensity to be disgusted, if we do so in the service of legitimate, ethical ends?

At one end of the spectrum of positions available in this debate are what I call *disgust advocates*. As the name suggests, advocates hold that disgust is an important tool in human moral psychology. Leon Kass, perhaps the most prominent advocate, appeals to disgust—what he calls "repugnance"—as a basis for his influential argument against human cloning and (to a lesser extent) stem cell research. Other advocates, some of whom I discuss in section 5.4, have made similar appeals to disgust in, for instance, discussions about the identification and definition of obscenity, and have employed similar lines of reasoning to argue against abortion, pornography, homosexuality, and same-sex marriage. The core idea behind this form of disgust advocacy is that the emotion is well suited to guide our assessment of a variety of activities and social practices.

Most of these types of arguments appeal, tacitly or otherwise, to a particular view of the nature of disgust itself. This view, which I call the *Deep Wisdom theory*, construes disgust as a morally attuned emotion that provides valuable insight into the "naturalness" or, more importantly, "unnaturalness" of certain activities and social practices. Advocates who follow the Deep Wisdom theory see disgust as a supra-rational source of information, a sensitivity that outstrips reason's ability to articulate and perhaps even discern certain types of properties or ethically important boundaries. Kass expresses this view in a paper titled "The Wisdom of Repugnance" (1997) and extends it in his book (2002), maintaining that "in crucial cases . . . repugnance is the emotional expression of deep wisdom, beyond reason's power fully to articulate it" (Kass 1997; cf. W. Miller 1997). He goes on:

In this age in which everything is held to be permissible so long as it is freely done, and in which our bodies are regarded as mere instruments of our autonomous rational will, repugnance may be the only voice left that speaks up to defend the core of our humanity. Shallow are the souls that have forgotten how to shudder. (Kass 1997)

Hence, by virtue of the nature of disgust as depicted by Deep Wisdom theory, disgust advocates hold that the deliverances of the emotion have a kind of *moral authority*, which should be respected and given its proper weight in ethical, legal, and institutional deliberation, and ultimately in moral assessment in general.

On the other end of the spectrum are what I call *disgust skeptics*. As this name suggests, skeptics are dubious of the influence the emotion can have on judgment and deliberation. They accordingly argue that feelings of disgust should be discounted in more considered deliberations about morality and that the influence of the emotion in legal decisions and other social institutions should be minimized. Most prominent among disgust skeptics is Martha Nussbaum (2004a), who has argued against the relevance of the emotion to a variety of issues, including not only those just mentioned, but also questions about culpability and the proper severity of justified punishment for transgressions driven by feelings of disgust. She holds, rather, that "I did it because I was repulsed" type defenses should not be allowed to mitigate responsibility for a crime or lessen the penalty or sentence that should be issued for it.

Like their opponents, disgust skeptics' arguments appeal to a particular view of the nature of disgust itself, but one that is very different from that favored by advocates. This view, which, following the literature, I call the Terror Management theory, construes disgust as an emotion that now primarily serves to repress thoughts about our eventual, unavoidable deaths.[1] In keeping us from confronting the implications of the fact that we must someday die, disgust helps to guard against the obviously maladaptive anxiety, terror, and potential paralysis that might be induced by contemplating such grim realities. Doing this, however, puts us at odds with our own physical bodies. Those bodies, and the various fluids, wastes, and functions associated with their operation and maintenance as organic systems, serve as constant, inescapable reminders of our animality and thus our mortality. As such, according to Terror Management theory, our bodies are primary and prominent objects of disgust. The emotion is thus a source of conflict: in protecting us from existential terror, disgust ends up casting our very bodies as unsavory and thus pushes us to hide from what we are, from our own humanity. Disgust becomes involved with issues commonly associated with social life and morality, according to this view, when people mistakenly project these uncomfortable feelings and anxieties outward, onto groups of people, activities, or social practices that they have come to associate with those anxieties. In short, feelings of disgust are ultimately an expression of unease about death that often stem from a deep-seated but unreasonable repugnance towards organic bodies and, because of the conflict they engender, those feelings are easily displaced elsewhere and projected onto others.

Based on these sorts of considerations, Nussbaum (2004b) argues for the separation of disgust and morality:

Does disgust, then, contain a wisdom that steers law in the right direction? Surely the moral progress of society can be measured by the degree to which it separates disgust from danger and indignation, basing laws and social rules on substantive harm, rather than on the symbolic relationship an object bears to our anxieties.

By virtue of the nature of disgust as depicted by the Terror Management theory, skeptics hold that the deliverances of the emotion should be regarded as suspect, and that it is a mistake to assign them any kind of special moral authority. Rather, feelings of disgust should be discounted in, and perhaps even viewed as counterproductive to, our ethical and legal deliberations, and moral assessments in general.

In this debate, my sympathies lie with disgust skepticism, and I agree that the emotion deserves no privileged status in ethical thought and should be regarded with deep suspicion in the moral domain. However, I find the arguments offered in favor of the position unconvincing, because I find the view of disgust on which those arguments rest highly implausible. Indeed, I find both the Deep Wisdom theory and the Terror Management theory equally unpersuasive. In the next section, then, I articulate the relevant aspects of my own view of the nature of disgust and the role it plays in the social and putatively moral domain.

5.3   The Nature of Disgust: The E&C View

Beginning with the pioneering work of the psychologist Paul Rozin (see Rozin et al. 2000 for review), empirical work on disgust has greatly increased in the last twenty years, and researchers from different fields have gathered a wealth of data on the emotion. These data are best accommodated by what I call the E&C view, since this view of the nature of disgust rests on both the Entanglement thesis and the Co-opt thesis. The first holds that disgust is a composite emotion whose two main components originally evolved to protect against poisons and parasites, respectively. The second holds that once formed, disgust was co-opted to also play a number of roles in regulating the increasingly complex system of human social interactions. In acquiring these new functions, however, disgust retained many of the features that allow it to effectively protect against poisons and parasites, rendering an imperfect fit between the emotion and the social issues on which it has been brought to bear.

A quick caveat: the alert reader will notice that this section (5.3) is, in effect, a highly compressed recapitulation of the one long argument developed throughout the earlier chapters of the book, especially chapters 2 and 4. I have been selective here, highlighting the elements of the E&C view that are most relevant to the argument I make in the following section (5.4). Those who are not persuaded by, or simply interested in more details about, the following discussion are directed to previous chapters for the case in full.

5.3.1 The Entanglement Thesis

The case for the Entanglement thesis begins by considering in detail the character of the disgust response itself. When an individual is disgusted by something, the elicited response comprises a number of coordinated but distinguishable features, including affective, behavioral, and cognitive elements. For instance, it is marked by the familiar feeling of nausea, a variety of aversion generated largely by the gastrointestinal system, which gives rise to powerful oral and gut-based feelings (which Rozin has called a "sense of oral incorporation"). The characteristic (and universal) facial expression of disgust is the gape, which, in especially intense episodes, can become the full act of retching from which it derives. Another behavioral component of the response is a behavioral tendency to make a quick, reflexlike withdrawal motion, a bodily recoil from the offending entity.

The response includes a more cognitive inferential signature as well, central to which are more sustained senses of offensiveness and contamination. Once marked as disgusting, an entity is thought of as soiled, tainted, or dirty. It is considered repugnant, as is both physical and symbolic contact with it; indeed, mere proximity to the disgusting entity is hardly tolerable. Disgusting entities tend to command attention, but even thinking about them is unpleasant. In addition to this form of offensiveness, disgusting items have the ability to transmit their disgustingness to other entities, usually by way of perceived physical or symbolic contact. Once thus contaminated, those entities are also considered disgusting and elicit the full disgust response. As a result of these features of the response, disgust is often accompanied by a motivation to cleanse or purify oneself (see Hejmadi et al. 2004).

The emotion possesses a few more noteworthy elements. First, the response is on a hair trigger; the disgust system is easily set into motion. Second, activation can happen quickly and automatically; one does not have to deliberate or engage in any explicit reasoning to become fully disgusted. Indeed, it can be involuntary, as well: one cannot simply decide to not be disgusted by something, and the response can be triggered *despite* what one knows explicitly. For instance, you may love fudge, and know full well that what is being offered to you for dessert is indeed a piece of fudge, but if it is shaped like a turd, the thought of eating it can disgust you nevertheless. Third, while elements of the response are themselves distinguishable, they function as an integrated whole. Finally, the emotion is in a sense ballistic: once activated, it runs its course, generating the full, coordinated package of affective, behavioral, and cognitive components, and influencing downstream cognitive activity in typical ways, regardless of the actual character of the eliciting entity. In light of these features of the response, once something triggers disgust, the underlying cognitive system causes an agent to think about and treat the offending entity *as if* it were revolting, dirty, impure, and contaminating, whether or not it really is, or whether or not those assessments or inferences are endorsed by the person, or whether or not they are in any way reflectively justifiable.

The Entanglement thesis explains these facts by claiming that at the heart of the system that we now recognize as disgust is a pair of cognitive mechanisms with distinct evolutionary histories and trajectories, which have become functionally entangled with each other. One of those, which I call the poison mechanism for short, initially evolved to monitor food intake and protect the gut against potentially toxic, poisonous, or otherwise harmful substances and entities that might be ingested through the mouth and taken into the gastrointestinal system. This adaptive problem was particularly acute for early humans, who were both omnivores and generalists. They also inhabited a large number of habitats, which presented different food opportunities and nutritional resources. Moreover, advances in hunting techniques led to a diet that was much more meat intensive than that of their hominid predecessors.

Many components of the basic disgust response are easily traced to this mechanism and its associated adaptive problem. The gape face, which now functions as an expression and signal, derived from, and involves many of the same muscle groups operative in, the act of retching or expelling substances from the mouth. Nausea, the feeling of aversion associated with disgust, is produced in large part by components of the gastrointestinal system, giving rise to the strong oral and gut-based feelings associated with the emotion. (Indeed, the neural seat of disgust, the insular cortex, has been linked to gastrointestinal functions and has been called the "gustatory cortex.")

Entangled with the poison mechanism at the core of disgust is what I call the parasite mechanism. As its name suggests, this mechanism initially evolved to protect the entire body from parasites of all sorts, including microbes and disease-carrying agents. It guards against these sorts of threats by causing the organism to avoid close physical proximity to infectious agents and, perhaps more importantly, anything that is likely to harbor them. Since most parasites are not directly perceivable, because they either take up internal residence in their hosts or are simply too small to be detected by the naked human eye, this mechanism is also sensitive to a wide range of cues that reliably indicate their presence, including signs of contamination or infection in other organisms. The possible routes of disease transmission include but far outstrip ingestible substances, and accordingly the parasite mechanism, and thus disgust, must monitor and be sensitive to a far larger domain of cues.

Many components of the basic disgust response can easily be traced to this mechanism and its associated adaptive problem, as well. The quick physical recoil is a first step in putting distance between oneself and something that might be potentially infectious, and the avoidance motivation and sense of offensiveness help maintain that distance. The motivation to cleanse and purify oneself after having come into close proximity with a disgusting entity is clearly fitted to the dangers surrounding parasites and diseases, and the sensitivity to contamination is a rational reaction to the vicissitudes of contagion and disease transmission. Since indicators of parasitic infection are many and diverse, disgust is sensitive to a wide range of cues, thus expanding the domain of the cognitive mechanism and laying the groundwork for a much more flexible system for acquiring new disgust elicitors. Finally, that disgust is easily activated and operates automatically, without the need for volition or deliberation, represents a "better safe than sorry" logic that is built into the cognitive system itself. While this feature reflects the potentially fatal nature of the adaptive problem, the Entanglement thesis provides the resources to see that many instances of disgust (juice stirred with a brand-new comb or a sterilized cockroach, a laundered sweater that once belonged to someone with tuberculosis) are in fact false positives.

5.3.2 The Co-opt Thesis

Opposite the disgust response is the diverse array of things that trigger it. Some of these triggers are clearly linked to the twin primary functions of protecting against poisons and parasites. For instance, some of the most likely candidates for being universal, innate elicitors of disgust are associated with infection and vectors of disease transmission: bodily fluids, organic waste and decay, insects and other types of creepy crawlies like slugs and rats, sexual contact, and reliable indicators of infection in conspecifics such as sores, discolorations, and other types of phenotypic abnormalities (though what counts as "abnormal" in this sense is fairly open-ended and can be calibrated by learning and social influence). Disgust is also closely associated with adulterated food like spoiled meat or moldy bread, though in many cases perfectly edible foods become disgusting, though the specifics of what foods are found disgusting (escargot, deep-fried Twinkies, sushi, bloody steaks) can vary at both an individual and cultural level.

On the other hand, certain types of elicitors of disgust look a bit more puzzling from the point of view of the Entanglement thesis. More specifically, disgust has been shown to play a large and important, though sometimes nearly subliminal, role in human social interactions (Haidt et al. 1997; Rozin et al. 2000). Certain activities and the people who engage in them can become disgusting, as can entire groups of people, the values and norms that bind them together, and the symbols that indicate membership in the group itself. For instance, in the United States, devoted Democrats might find distinctively Republican policies, values, and iconography disgusting, and vice versa. As with cuisine, a great deal of variation often exists from one group to the next about which activities, norms, and groups of people are in fact disgusting, but for any particular person, they are usually the activities, norms, and identifiable members of *other* groups. (Indeed, distinctive cuisines themselves are often markers of group membership.) These considerations, together with the pattern of within-group similarities and between-group differences, suggest that such instances of disgust are not all simple false positives but something more systematic and significant.

The Co-opt thesis supplements the Entanglement thesis to explain these facts. It holds that once formed, the disgust response acquired a number of auxiliary functions in addition to protecting against poisons and parasites. The cognitive system was co-opted, recruited to also play a number of roles in regulating social interactions. More specifically, it became systematically involved in the cognition of social norms and group boundary markers.

There is an increasingly convincing case to be made that social norms are a crucial ingredient in humans' ability to cooperate on a large scale (Boyd and Richerson 2005a; Richerson and Boyd 2005; Henrich and Henrich 2007). Moreover, many theorists have argued that humans are equipped with dedicated cognitive machinery associated with social norms (Nichols and Mallon 2006; Sripada and Stich 2007; Mallon and Nichols 2010), and that emotions play an important role in generating the typical motivations and behaviors associated with those norms (Nichols 2004; Prinz 2008; cf. Haidt 2001). Indeed, research has shown that disgust is the relevant emotion in certain types of norms, including table etiquette rules (Nichols 2002), meat taboos (Fessler and Navarrete 2003b), and incest taboos (Lieberman et al. 2003; Fessler and Navarrete 2004). Cultural psychologists have also identified an important class of norms that are linked to and follow the logic of disgust (Shweder et al. 1997; Rozin et al. 1999). These so-called purity norms are thought to be distinct from, for instance, harm norms or fairness norms in the sense that typically no one is directly physically harmed or obviously subject to an injustice when a purity norm is violated. Instead purity norms express and govern other aspects of a culture's way of life by prescribing acceptable foods and the proper way to prepare them, regulating sexual activity, ordering rituals, codifying appropriate clothing in specific settings (especially perhaps ceremonial contexts), and stipulating suitable ways to deal with corpses, blood, bodily waste, and other organic materials. Details of purity norms and the proper forms of life they delineate differ from culture to culture, of course. Whatever the specifics, though, they are generally thought of as guidelines for protecting the purity of the body and often the soul, and the issues they regulate are often cast in terms of sanctity and defilement; transgressors are considered morally tainted, spiritually polluted, or unnatural. Purity norms are central to the moral codes of many traditional or religious cultures, where a transgressor is taken to be disrespecting the sacredness of the deity, offending God or the gods, or violating the divine order. While purity norms do not enjoy the same prominence of place, they are not completely absent from more secular cultures. There such transgressions are often cast as crimes against nature or violations of the natural order.

Alongside work on social norms, the social sciences have a long tradition emphasizing the importance of symbolically marked groups (Barth 1969). Indeed, recent work has suggested that humans are inherently sensitive to the relevant markings (McElreath et al. 2003; Henrich and McElreath 2003; see also Gil-White 2001). Some of that work investigates the types of biases that underlie in-group favoritism and ethnocentrism, while some looks at negative biases against out-groups. Perhaps unsurprisingly, disgust has been linked to the most extreme cases of prejudice and xenophobia toward other groups. Indeed, researchers have found that different emotions are associated with the subtly different forms of prejudice that one group directs at another (Cottrell and Neuberg 2005), and have confirmed that disgust is the emotion most often operative in driving attitudes about the most vilified and dehumanized of out-groups (Harris and Fiske 2006, 2007).

The Co-opt thesis explains these facts by claiming that as human social life became more complex, the disgust response was recruited to play roles in the cognition and motivation associated with social norms and group boundaries. The fusion of the parasite and poison mechanisms created a cognitive system ripe to be co-opted to other purposes: it reliably produced a particular piece of motivation (aversion) and behavior (avoidance), and it was equipped with a flexible acquisition system, primed to be sensitive to a wide range of triggers, including social cues and phenotypic abnormalities in others. Together with the Entanglement thesis that it supplements, the Co-opt thesis also holds that, once recruited, the emotion did not lose the primary functions, features, and sensitivities that allow it to effectively protect against poisons and parasites. Thus when disgust is the emotion recruited to provide motivation and avoidance, be it in conjunction with a certain norm, in response to a particular social practice or to the symbols that mark off an entire group of people, agents not only experience aversion and avoidance motivation but tend to naturally, though often implicitly, think of and treat the elicitor as if it were also tainted, polluted, contaminating, even inhuman.

5.4   New Foundations for Disgust Skepticism

Recall the normative debate over the role that disgust *should* play in morality, broadly construed. Advocates hold that disgust should be accorded a certain moral authority. The argument for this turned on the Deep Wisdom theory of disgust itself, which depicts the emotion as a supra-rational sensitivity and holds that feelings of disgust mark boundaries of naturalness or unnaturalness, even if reason was unable to clearly articulate them or supply clear justification for honoring them. Skeptics, on the other hand, hold that disgust has no moral authority and are deeply suspicious of the influence it can exert on ethical thought and deliberation. The argument for this turned on the Terror Management theory, which depicts disgust as primarily serving to repress thoughts about mortality and death. It sees the emotion as being especially sensitive to anxiety-producing reminders of our fragile animal nature, but holds that this sensitivity paradoxically produces deep discomfort with basic aspects of our own humanity. We resolve this conflict by projecting our own anxiety and discomfort outward onto practices we dislike or even entire groups of people that engage in them.

Against both the Deep Wisdom theory and the Terror Management theory, I have advanced the E&C view, based on the Entanglement thesis and the Co-opt thesis. This view is more evolutionarily grounded, considerably more detailed, and better explains the fine-grained structure revealed by the recent wealth of empirical work on the emotion. In doing so, it also shows how both competing theories are simply wrong about the nature of the emotion itself. At its core, disgust is not repressing reminders of death or projecting uniquely human existential anxiety onto others, nor is it providing any deep wisdom about the putative "unnaturalness" of certain activities or social practices. Rather, it is primarily an element of our defenses against a pair of challenges faced by nearly all creatures in the natural world, namely, toxins and diseases.

In itself, the E&C view undermines one strong type of claim a disgust advocate might make, namely, that eliciting disgust is *sufficient* to show something is immoral, or that feelings of disgust suffice to justify an ethical evaluation. Rather, a large part of what disgust properly responds to has nothing to do with morality but is a reaction to cues likely to mark poisons and parasites. Moreover, this view shows how the primary functions of monitoring food intake and protecting against infection are reflected in the elements and operational features of the response itself. Many of these, I submit, should further undermine our confidence in disgust as a moral authority or source of reliable information about morality. For instance, due to the nature of its proprietary issues, disgust is on a hair trigger, following a "better safe than sorry" rule. Rather than being supra-rational or ungraspable by reason, this simply makes good adaptive sense. It also, however, results in the emotion being extremely susceptible to false positives, and thus in agents easily becoming disgusted by entities that are in fact neither poisonous nor infectious. In this respect, the psychological system is simply a fairly blunt instrument. The mere fact that something is disgusting is a far from fail-safe indicator that something is poisonous or infectious, let alone immoral.

Many disgust advocates appear to be committed to the claim that feelings of disgust are sufficient to justify an ethical evaluation. Some of the things Kass says indicate that he believes that no further justification beyond repugnance is needed, since it is "the emotional expression of deep wisdom," even if that wisdom is "beyond reason's power fully to articulate it." He also implies that repugnance should be allowed to guide ethical thought even if it is "the only voice left that speaks up." Similarly, fellow advocate Robert Streiffer claims that "opponents of the yuck factor must concede that, sometimes, we know that an action is wrong merely on the basis of our reaction to it, even if we cannot satisfactorily justify that reaction" (Streiffer 2003, quoted in Hauskeller 2006, 599).

Needless to say, I find this entire line of thought implausible. Based on what we now know about the emotion, it is unconvincing that feelings of disgust suffice to justify an ethical evaluation. Even less credible would be the claim that they are *necessary* to justify one. So my view is that disgust is neither necessary nor sufficient to justify a moral judgment. But my skepticism runs deeper. It seems clear that the extensions of "disgusting" and "morally wrong" simply crosscut each other.[2] Disgust responds to a wide range of cues that have nothing to do with morality, and actions or practices need not elicit anyone's disgust to be justifiably judged morally wrong. Additional reflection on the empirical work on the emotion and the arguments for the E&C view shows that far from being strictly necessary or sufficient, the fact that something is disgusting is not even remotely a reliable indicator of moral foul play. Disgust is not wise about or acutely attuned to ethical considerations, and "yuck" deserves no special moral credence; rather, repugnance is simply *irrelevant* to moral justification.

Disgust advocates will, of course, disagree. For instance, Hauskeller (2006) argues that feelings of disgust should be taken seriously in moral deliberation until they have been exposed as untrustworthy: "To dismiss as morally irrelevant widespread feelings of disgust . . . is itself in need of justification. In the absence of any good *moral* reasons *not* to trust our intuitions, we should take them seriously and act accordingly" (599–600; italics mine). In case it is not obvious, I should emphasize that the skeptical position I am defending here is exclusively about disgust. I am not making any claims about the trustworthiness of emotions or intuitions in general. Interpreted as also being restricted to feelings of disgust, Hauskeller's claim is less strident than those made by Kass, but it still strikes me as unconvincing. Rather, I think that the *empirical* considerations about the nature of disgust as accounted for by the E&C view, rather than any specifically moral reasons, are more than adequate to show that disgust is not especially sensitive to anything having to do with morality. Therefore the default position toward the use of disgust or repugnance to justify moral condemnation should be one not of trust but of suspicion. Feelings of disgust themselves should be given no weight in deciding whether an issue—be it a norm, an activity, a practice, an outcome, or an ideal—is morally acceptable or morally problematic.

It may help to take a step back and make explicit what I am *not* claiming. I am not claiming that disgust does not, in fact, sometimes influence moral judgments. Nor am I denying that, from a subjective point of view, feelings of disgust can be extremely vivid indeed and so *seem* to be quite authoritative while one is in their grip. Surely no one needs any argumentation or experimental data to be convinced of this.[3] What is at issue between advocates and skeptics, however, is not a straightforward factual matter about whether disgust does or can influence moral judgments—in the heat of the moment, as it were—but a matter of the actual authority or justificatory weight that should be granted those feelings upon reflection, once cooler heads prevail. Consider a scenario in which a particular norm is under consideration, and there are widespread feelings of disgust at violations of that norm. Those widespread feelings of disgust are, I think, simply irrelevant to the question of whether or not the norm itself is morally problematic or acceptable.[4] So I am claiming that, while reflecting on and carefully deliberating about the moral status of a norm, activity, practice, or ideal, the moral significance that should be assigned to the fact that people are disgusted by it is: none.

I have made the preceding argument without even considering the truism that different people, and different groups of people, are often disgusted by different things, including different types of activities, practices, and ideals. Appreciation of the variation in what is considered disgusting only makes the argument for disgust skepticism stronger. Indeed, another advantage that the E&C view has over either of its competitors is that it can shed light on the wide-ranging variation found in what different individuals and cultures consider disgusting, and can furnish an account of the psychological mechanisms that produce that variation. According to the Entanglement thesis, the large proper domain of the parasite mechanism paved the way for the evolution of a highly flexible acquisition system, which now allows environmental variation (physical, social, developmental, etc.) to calibrate individual people's disgust systems in different ways.

This can account for variation in disgust elicitors linked to the emotion's primary functions of protecting against poisons and parasites, but it can account for variation in disgust elicitors linked to its auxiliary functions as well. The Co-opt thesis showed how the disgust system became systematically linked to social norms and sensitivities to group membership and boundaries. The E&C view thus shows that disgust can latch onto locally prevalent norms that delineate certain aspects of a group's way of life and the boundaries it recognizes between itself and other groups. Thus different individuals can come to be disgusted not just by e.g. different foods, but also by different types of groups and social practices, depending on parochial social divisions and on the local norms that prevail in different cultures and shape their different ways of life.

Again, the E&C view begins to explain how feelings of disgust can be directed at different practices and activities, but in doing so, it also shows how, in and of themselves, those feelings are unfit to do any justificatory work. This is an especially important point in cases where there is a disagreement, and members on one side of the dispute claim that their own disgust toward the norm or practice in question shows that their assessment of its moral status is justified, or that their opponent's lack of disgust betrays an impoverished ethical sensibility. Rather, the E&C view shows that in such cases there is not necessarily anything wrong with those who are not disgusted. The failure of any given individual to be disgusted does not reflect some moral superficiality; it reflects nothing more than that she has been socialized differently from those who are disgusted, that a component of her mind designed to be developmentally flexible was calibrated in one way rather than another, and that she has a different set of elicitors in her disgust system's database. This insight into the nature and sources of these types of disagreements undermines some of the strongest and most explicit claims made by the leading disgust advocate Leon Kass. The E&C view provides a principled account of the kind of variation found in what disgusts different people, and thereby discredits any excuse for denigrating large segments of the population as "shallow" because they have "forgotten how to shudder." Who is shallow and who is deep, who is right and who is wrong in such disagreements, needs to be determined on other grounds.[5]

This last point is also worth clarifying. I do not mean to imply that assessing the moral status of the types of practices that have "yuck" potential, such as abortion, stem cell research, cloning, and so on, is easy; these are extremely difficult issues, and I am not here stumping for either a pro or con position with respect to any of them. Mine is a claim about how deliberation over such issues should proceed, and what role a very specific set of considerations should play in debates about them.[6] From the point of view of my disgust skepticism, yuck-inducing activities and practices, and the norms that regulate or prohibit them, and different people's opposing judgments about individuals or groups that engage in them, may or may not be morally justified. My claim is that feelings of disgust are simply irrelevant to this question. Exactly because these issues are so complicated, giving undue credence to the deliverances of a psychological system like disgust can only further muddy already murky waters. I should also stress that I do not have a positive general account of moral justification on offer, either, no list of factors that legitimately *do* provide moral justification. Mine is a skeptical position and so has a negative upshot: feelings of disgust should certainly not be on that list. When the question is one of morality and moral justification, the mere fact that some social practice or the violation of a certain norm induces disgust in some people is neither here nor there, no more to the point than the fact that some people find sushi disgusting, while others relish it.

Finally, the E&C view undercuts another, less common form of disgust advocacy. One might, on the one hand, become convinced that feelings of disgust are not a trustworthy guide to ethical issues, that repugnance is morally irrelevant. At the same time, one could consistently hold that people should be disgusted by certain activities, practices, or groups that *are* genuinely morally problematic. For example, one might hold not just that racists are wrong and immoral but that they should be considered disgusting, that disgust is the justified, morally appropriate response to racism. One might further argue that given its powerful effects on judgment and motivation, mobilizing people's disgust against something like racism, or any other unseemly activity or unethical practice, might be morally appropriate, as well as an effective way to do away with the activity or practice.

Rozin calls this process of bringing disgust to bear on a particular practice "moralization," and he has argued that cigarette smoking, drugs, and even unhealthy eating have been thus moralized recently in the United States (1997, 1999). A disgust advocate might be inspired by this and argue that disgust is the morally appropriate response to racism, and so racism should be moralized in this sense as well. Enthusiastic advocates might be tempted to go one step further, supporting, for instance, a campaign that tried to address the problems of racism by using the latest advertising and marketing techniques to depict racism and racists as not just wrong but disgusting.

Tempting as this may be in some cases, I am dubious of this line of thought, too, and the use of the emotion that it recommends. Even when a disgust- infused moral judgment, social norm, or ideal *is* justified—on other, more defensible grounds—I believe that the E&C view provides reason to be deeply suspicious of the type of influence disgust can have. I do not rest my rejection of moralization or this form of advocacy merely on disgust's record of past offenses, however, or the role the emotion has historically played in many cases of oppression—though that case has powerfully been made elsewhere (Nussbaum 2004a; see also W. Miller 1997). Rather, my suspicions are once again grounded in the E&C view of the nature of the emotion itself: when the features of disgust that are fitting responses to poisons and parasites are brought to bear on whatever else disgust becomes involved with, people will tend to intuitively, if often implicitly, think of any elicitors of disgust as being tainted, polluted, contaminating, or inhuman, as well. I have no doubt that, for example, the judgment that racism is morally wrong is justified. Recommending disgust as the proper, moral response to racism and racists, however, would be to invite the too easy slip into thinking of and treating racists not just as wrong but as dirty, tainted, contaminating, even inhuman. As intuitively correct as disgust could make these further assessments seem, it goes without saying that I do not think they would be appropriate. Neither do I think it acceptable to recommend the deployment of disgust, even in the service of some admirable goal, like moralizing and attempting to do away with racism. My disgust skepticism is, ironically, pure; because of the nature of the emotion itself, the slope

from moralization to demonization and dehumanization is just too slip-
pery to endorse even this form of disgust advocacy.[7]

5.5 Conclusion

Far from disgust being a reliable source of special, supra-rational information about morality, as the disgust advocates would have it, the E&C view
provides a variety of novel reasons to be extremely skeptical of any variation of the idea that disgust deserves some kind of special epistemic credit,
that the emotion is a trustworthy guide to justifiable moral judgments, or
that there is any deep ethical wisdom in repugnance. As vivid and compelling as feelings of disgust can be from the inside, the deliverances of the
emotion in the social domain are explainable in such a way that we can see
they need not be honored as wise. I have also emphasized that while I share
a conclusion with other disgust skeptics, my argument is based on a different, more empirically grounded, and more plausible view of the nature of
disgust and the role it plays in the social and putatively moral domain. The
E&C view also provides grounds for thinking that disgust should not be
regarded as an appropriate response even to ethically questionable activities or practices, and by similar reasoning, that because moralization, in the
technical sense, can easily slide into dehumanization and demonization, it
should be regarded as morally problematic itself.

Finally, it seems to me that the argument presented in this chapter flows
quite naturally from the account of disgust constructed in the first four,
though of course this chapter deals explicitly in normative and prescriptive claims, while the previous chapters dealt in descriptive and explanatory claims. Though somewhere along the way the discussion has made the
reportedly illegitimate leap from "is" to "ought," I remain unable to isolate
the exact step where the reasoning might have gone awry. Indeed, it does
not seem to me to go awry anywhere or that any great conceptual gulf was
leapt over. Moreover, others engaged in the debate at center stage in this
chapter, both advocates and skeptics alike, appear to have done the same
thing in basing their normative conclusions on their accounts of the nature
of disgust itself—I just claim to have a better account of the emotion, and
thus that my normative conclusions are better informed and supported. So
in this case, anyway, I am not terribly troubled by the looming specter of
the naturalistic fallacy (see also Rachels 2000). Quite the contrary, actually;
thinking through these issues has strengthened my admittedly vague suspicion that the relationship between "is" and "ought" is not nearly as simple
as certain familiar timeworn slogans might lead us to believe.

Notes

1   Toward a Functional Theory of Disgust

1. See Keltner and Haidt 1999 for an exploration of some of the intermediate levels, focusing on the various social functions that emotions perform.

2. As has been noted by both Ekman (2003) and Griffiths (1997), affect programs resemble Fodorian modules enough to perhaps constitute being an instance (Fodor 1983). The extent of the overlap is unclear, however, in no small part because the notion of a module has become increasingly vexed in recent years (see Fodor 2000; Carruthers 2006, chap. 1).

3. For a more nuanced discussion of the feeling and first-person aspects of disgust, see W. Miller 1997 and Kolnai 1998. Given my aims and methods, I will not have much more to say about the phenomenology of the emotion (though see hereafter on oral incorporation), as the qualitative aspect of any mental state or process is notoriously difficult to pin down with empirical data or the resources of functionalism (Nagel 1974; Chalmers 2003; but see also Dennett 1991).

4. This appears to be a special case of the more general consistency of the disgust *response* across different domains of disgust *elicitors*. The details of contamination sensitivity, unsurprisingly, get complicated (see Elliott and Radomsky 2009; Radomsky and Elliott 2009). I discuss this issue at greater length in chapter 4.

5. This is not to say that individual elements of the response, or the entire response itself, cannot voluntary be suppressed in certain social contexts, exaggerated in others, or similarly shaped by certain culturally specific norms of expression (though it might be extremely difficult to *completely* block the expression of disgust; see chapter 3).

6. Disgustingness in the first two experiments was measured by self-report of the participants, but in the third, Web-based experiment, disgustingness of urban legends was measured using the Disgust Scale (Haidt et al. 1994).

7. Though the results are not as straightforward or easily interpretable, other studies have indicated how disgust can influence other forms of economic decision making.

For instance, using an fMRI on participants playing the ultimatum game, Sanfey et al. (2003) found heightened activity in the anterior insula (the gustatory cortex associated with disgust) in reaction to unfair offers, and found that increased activity in the same area predicted whether a participant was likely to reject an offer.

8. See also Fessler and Haley 2006 for more on disgust and the bodily perimeter.

9. See also Cottrell and Neuberg 2005 for evidence that different out-groups produce prejudicial attitudes associated with different emotions.

10. In addition to absorbing his or her culture's culinary sensibilities, another way for a food to become disgusting to an individual is for that person to experience intense gastrointestinal sickness after consuming it. I discuss this phenomenon further in chapter 2.

11. Fessler and Navarrete (2003a) document a further wrinkle in the link between disgust and sex. They show that women's sensitivity to sexual elicitors of disgust, but only sexual elicitors, heightens during certain phases of their menstrual cycles, peaking when they are most able to conceive. Rather than indicating a categorically different kind of emotion or capacity, this phenomenon and others like it are best interpreted as revealing unconscious, automatic, but remarkably fine grained and individual specific calibration of the input or detection component of disgust (cf. Carruthers 2006, 200). Fessler and colleagues (2005) also found that pregnant women experience increased disgust sensitivity, especially toward food, in the first trimester of their pregnancies. Another example of this type of domain-specific fine tuning of disgust sensitivity is reported in a study done by Rozin (2008), which found that medical students' sensitivity to a particular set of disgust elicitors— namely, those associated with death and body envelope violations—decreased over the first couple of months they spent dissecting human cadavers. The same participants, however, exhibited no decrease in sensitivity to elicitors from other disgust domains (sexual, moral, social, etc.). In a similar vein, mothers appear to be less disgusted by the smell of their own baby's dirty diapers than by the smell of other babies' (Case et al. 2006).

12. This style of explanation owes much to expositors of homuncular functionalism (Fodor 1968; Dennett 1978; Cummins 1983). There is no easy way to express it pictorially, but I should note here that I intend the model to remain neutral on the issue of whether or not the phenomenological or qualitative aspects of disgust are in fact *caused*, or if they are better explained by one of the other strategies explored in the literature on consciousness and qualia (see Block et al. 1997; Chalmers 2002).

13. There are many ways to flesh out this doctrine, but one of the most influential is via the idea that the program can be expressed in a formal language of mental representations, which are individuated by their syntactic structure (Fodor 1975; Stich 1983). The mental, and thus computational, processes that operate on those representations are sensitive only to that syntactic structure (as opposed to their content,

for instance). In this general picture, mental representations will eventually be paired with neurological states by a function that maps members of one set to members of the other. The discovery and construction of this function can be thought of as one of the general goals of empirical cognitive psychology. The preference for a syntactically structured language as the formalism of choice is based on the hope that the syntactic relations between the mental representations will mimic the causal relations between the neurological states they encode. See also Schiffer 1981 for a much more detailed discussion of the relation between talk about "boxes" and talk about functional roles and mental representations.

2   Poisons and Parasites: The Entanglement Thesis and the Evolution of Disgust

1. Morris et al. (2007) argue that contrary to received wisdom, there is some evidence that several so-called secondary emotions, particularly jealousy, can be found in nonprimate mammals such as dogs and horses. Even with their liberal stance toward the possession of particular emotions in other species, however, Morris et al. find little evidence of any emotion fitting the description of disgust in those same nonprimate mammals. Indeed, it is not clear that other primates possess the emotion of disgust, either; the primatologist Robert Seyfarth reports not having observed anything looking like disgust during his extensive work with baboons (personal communication).

2. Homologies (the term is taken from evolutionary theory) are similar traits or systems found in different species whose similarities can be traced to a shared ancestry. For instance, dolphin fins and human hands are homologies—similarities in the bone structures between the two can be traced to an evolutionarily recent common ancestor, even though fins and hands now serve different functions. Homologies are often contrasted with analogies, similar traits or systems found in different species whose similarities reflect convergent evolution. Similarities in the structure of the eyes of a human and the eyes of a giant squid, or in the structure of the wings of a bat and the wings of a butterfly, are derived not from recent common ancestry but from shared function (for a brief, nontechnical discussion, see Dennett 1995, 136–138).

3. A standard contrast class for parasites is symbionts. In these more reciprocal symbiotic relationships, each organism draws on resources of the other but also contributes in ways that are useful to its counterpart, so that the interaction results in a net overall benefit for each.

4. The example of the lancet fluke also appears in Dennett 2006, 3.

5. There are fascinating literatures on the role of meat consumption in the evolution of human cognition, and the connection between the brain and the gut. The emotion of disgust is rarely discussed, but I take much of this work to be broadly

consistent with the Entanglement thesis. See especially Aiello and Wheeler 1995; Aiello 1997; Sterelny, n.d.; but also see Stanford and Bunn 2001; Stiner 2002.

3   Disgust's Sentimental Signaling System: Expression, Recognition, and the Transmission of Cultural Information

1. A typical gape face involves the following: drawn-down brows; wrinkled nose and forehead; lowered eyes, pushed up and raised (but not tensed); the appearance of deep nasolabial folds with raised cheeks; opened mouth with upper lip raised and lower lip forward and/or out; and, in extreme cases, perhaps an extruded tongue.

2. I should reiterate a point made in chapter 1, note 3. The studies cited in this section and the next key in on the behavior, and in some cases the inferential tendencies and neurological activity, of participants in controlled experimental conditions. They say nothing about whatever qualitative experiences or subjective feelings accompany those behaviors, inferential tendencies, or patterns of neurological activation. I am claiming that the data reported in those studies provide evidence for the claim that expression and recognition of disgust involve the activation of the entire disgust system itself. I am not, however, claiming that from the inside, someone making a microgape (for instance) will be presented with any vivid phenomenology, or even that she would describe herself as "being disgusted" if asked to self-report. That one's disgust system can be activated, and so influence her behavior and thinking in the canonical ways, without that person knowing it, is an implication of this that I do accept. In other words, I am committed to the claim that the disgust system can *sometimes* operate not just automatically but implicitly, or, put slightly differently, that it is possible for a person to "be disgusted" in a very real sense and not even realize it.

3. A couple of studies have also suggested that sufferers of Huntington's disease have a pronounced decrease in their ability to recognize disgust and to produce it (Mitchell et al. 2005; Hayes, Stevenson, and Coltheart 2007), though this result has recently been challenged (Milders et al. 2003; Johnson et al. 2007). The ability to recognize disgust, as opposed to other emotions, appears selectively preserved in Alzheimer's disease (Henry et al. 2008).

4. Defenders (Stevenson 1937, 1944) and critics (Hare 1952) of emotivist theories in metaethics have long noted how expressions of emotions can be remarkably persuasive, in that they tend to tacitly pull others to share the emotions of the expresser. The sorts of mechanisms being described in the main text seem to be the psychological machinery that explains the very phenomenon in which such philosophers have been interested.

5. It is both interesting and unsettling that researchers are already systematically investigating how disgust and its sentimental signaling system can be harnessed in

the service of advertising and marketing (Shimp and Stuart 2004; Morales and Fitzsimons 2007).

6. For an excellent collection of papers on commitment, see Nesse 2001a. In this section, I deliberately describe commitment and commitment devices at an extremely general level, and so the discussion will be rather abstract. I provide examples in the next section to help illustrate and make concrete the ideas and principles described in this one.

7. Not all commitment problems or commitment devices are social in the sense discussed here, and the main difference involves the use and import of signaling. For instance, many discussions of commitment prominently feature the example of Ulysses and the Sirens. Sailing aboard their ship, Ulysses and his crew approach the island of the Sirens and will soon come within hearing range of their famously beautiful but lethally seductive singing. Ulysses wants to hear the song but knows that its beauty will usurp his will, driving him to follow it toward its source and ultimately his own death. To hear the Sirens' song and survive, he needs to commit himself against succumbing to the irresistible call once it is sounded. The commitment device he devises is characteristically shrewd. Ulysses has his crew bind him with ropes to the mast and plug their own ears with wax, rendering them immune to the charms of the song. He orders them to steer the ship close enough to the island that he (and only he) can hear the Sirens, but to continue past it, leaving their ears plugged and ignoring his pleading, thrashing, ordering, and raging until they are far out of hearing range (for more discussion, see Elster 2000).

   Though other people appear in this scenario, it is not social in the way commitment problems typically are. Most noticeable is the lack of any sort of signaling or the need for any signals to be credible to other agents. Ulysses is not binding himself or restricting his range of potential behaviors to strategically influence the expectations, behaviors, or strategic calculations of anyone else (the Sirens or the ship's crew), nor does binding himself to the mast make credible or ensure that he will keep any threats, promises, or pledges he has made to others.

8. Frank's ideas may face insurmountable problems on grounds other than those I consider here, either in their application to particular emotions other than disgust or in general. Since my concern is with disgust, and I will ultimately argue that Frank's Classic Commitment model fails as an account of the expression and recognition facts, I will not go into those types of objections (but see Noel 1990 for early misgivings about Frank 1988).

9. Thus the social emotions, in Frank's account, are paradigmatic examples of mechanisms underlying our capacity for *subjective* commitments (Nesse 2001b).

10. As mentioned earlier, researchers in this tradition have done some work on the cultural variability of emotions and emotional capacities (Matsumoto et al. 2001; Sripada and Stich 2004; Mallon and Stich 2000; cf. Hare 1989). Little of this research

focuses on mechanisms of transmission, acquisition, or the role of emotions in social learning, however.

11. This is not to say that there are *no* routes or mechanisms that facilitate individual learning in the domains associated with disgust and its associated adaptive problems. Indeed, as I discuss later, disgust elicitors can also be individually acquired in a number of different ways. Apparently, humans have evolved multiple ways to be sensitized to the threats of poisons and parasites.

12. They also mention two other domains in which disgust has been shown to operate, namely, social structuring and morality. I take up these issues in chapter 4.

13. What we now recognize as the gape may also include trace elements deriving from disease and parasite avoidance; see Susskind et al. 2008.

14. Another way to put this point is to say that one of the factors leading to the entangling of the poison and parasite mechanisms was a selective pressure generated by what Ryan (1998) calls a receiver-bias process: receivers had a bias toward responding to signals displayed on human faces, and in the absence of a distinctive facial expression associated with disease avoidance, the gape face associated with retching was recruited to perform the relevant signaling function.

15. See chapter 4 for an account of how disgust has become involved in the dynamics of cultural-group selection and may therefore have been co-opted into playing a role in signaling commitment to cultural groups.

16. As far as I know, it remains an open question whether acquired taste aversions produce disgust straightaway or make one more likely to become fully disgusted by the culprit type of food.

17. More speculatively, the phenomenon of genetic sexual attraction provides examples of what can happen when the mechanism is improperly calibrated so as to give false *negatives*. In cases of genetic sexual attraction, opposite-sex siblings who are separated at birth and raised apart but then meet up later in life can find themselves dealing with unwelcome but strong feelings of sexual attraction to each other. A similar phenomenon has also occurred between parents and the children they gave up for adoption at or shortly after birth. Reunions later in life, when the child is fully grown, can be accompanied by uncomfortable sexual feelings in either or both parties. No systematic study has been conducted on these phenomena (though for discussion see Bereczkei et al. 2004; Greenberg and Littlewood 1995), but it is becoming more acknowledged and widely addressed by the institutions that regulate adoption. (For more details, see http://www.reunite.com/adoption-records/genetic-sexual-attraction.html.) The Westermarck view suggests an explanatory hypothesis: what these cases have in common is that kin recognition mechanisms are not activated during the crucial developmental window. As a result, in these anomalous cases, disgust was never recruited to muffle sexual attraction as it usually does, and that attraction is subsequently being allowed to express itself.

4   Disgust and Moral Psychology: Tribal Instincts and the Co-opt Thesis

1. Cultural information can be stored in other mediums, as well, most notably artifacts such as books, computer disks, and so forth.

2. Eventually the repository of cultural information came to contain more than any one person could learn via trial and error and individual problem solving in a single lifetime. The exact conditions under which *cumulative* cultural evolution can be achieved are still not well understood (though for discussion and references, see Sterelny 2006; Caldwell and Millen 2008).

3. As alluded to in the long quotation from Henrich et al. (2005) earlier in the text, many GCC theorists hold a view of the architecture of the human mind that has much in common with classical evolutionary psychology. According to this view, the mind is largely composed of a number of distinct, specialized parts, and those parts individually perform different kinds of functions. Human minds are collections of semiautonomous, domain-specific mental mechanisms, each of which evolved in response to a specific, recurring adaptive problem faced by hominids during their evolutionary past. Each mental mechanism is fairly specialized, both in that it is functionally specialized to solve a specific adaptive problem presented by the physical or social environment, and in that it is activated by a special set of cues relevant to that problem. GCC supplements this picture with the idea that some of the specialized mechanisms found in the human mind have evolved to deal with adaptive problems relating to the use of cultural information, what Henrich and McElreath (2007) call "evolved psychological mechanisms for cultural learning." For classic statements of this type of "Swiss army knife" view of the mind, see Barkow et al. 1992; Pinker 1997; and Tooby and Cosmides 2005. For the most plausible formulation and most sustained defense of the "massively modularity" hypothesis at its core, see Carruthers 2006.

4. See Boehm 1999 for a discussion of the relationship between groups of this size, which he calls "moral communities," intragroup dynamics, and the structuring of social hierarchies.

5. For example, see McElreath et al. 2005 and Henrich et al. 2006 for preliminary attempts to experimentally test empirical predictions specifically derived from the GCC perspective. See also Wilson et al. 2008 for similar suggestions about how theories concerning group structure can inform investigation of psychological architecture at the level of the individual.

6. Another, more controversial part of this story is an appeal to group selection, particularly selection between culturally distinct tribal-sized groups—those tribes whose stock of norms allowed them to better flourish and cooperate usually outcompeted their rivals. For a variety of reasons, group selection fell out of favor among evolutionary theorists for many years. While it is still far from being assimi-

lated to the orthodoxy, it does seem that the community is willing to take (some forms of) group selection seriously again. See Sober and Wilson 1998 and Wilson and Wilson 2007 for well-informed, opinionated canvassing of the history and current state of play. Though the debate over group selection will not be center stage in my discussion in the main text, many of the topics that will be addressed are obviously relevant to it.

7. Other accounts of the psychology of norms and social rules have been offered (Nichols 2004; Prinz 2008; see also Mallon and Nichols, forthcoming). I will focus on Sripada and Stich's theory for expository purposes, but also because it provides a concrete picture of what appear to be the most important elements of the norm system, brings together a wide range of evidence in support of that picture, and was motivated by many of the same types of considerations that drive gene-culture coevolutionary theory.

8. As noted in chapter 3, Fessler and Machery (forthcoming), arguing from evolutionary grounds alone, suggest that human psychology will also include (what they called) domain-specific cultural information acquisition mechanisms dedicated to both social structuring and morality. Norms are crucial to each of these domains.

9. Philosophers debate the significance of the manifest diversity of moral codes and the disagreements that it provokes, but most take as a given that such diversity exists. Doris and Plakias (2007) review the dialectic and philosophical territory and discuss how empirical research can help move the debate forward (see also Machery et al. 2005).

10. See Gil-White 2006 for a discussion of the vexing terminological difficulties that arise for words used to pick out different kinds of in-groups.

11. For a lucid discussion of coordination, see David Lewis's classic *Convention: A Philosophical Study* (1969).

12. This is the case initially, at least. Once ethnic boundary markers have arisen, they are liable to become interwoven with social dynamics involving cooperation and defection. Moreover, certain markers could come to be associated with clusters of prosocial norms that recommend altruistic behavior. This, in turn, would provide an incentive for freeloaders to mimic them. For a brief discussion and further references, see McElreath et al. 2003, 128.

13. For this idea, as well as how it might be applied to issues of racial cognition, see Machery and Faucher 2005a, 2005b.

14. As opposed to the process, the *traits* that have themselves been co-opted are sometimes called preadaptations or exaptations. The term "exaptation" is more often used when the trait in question was not previously adaptive or functional at all (Gould and Vrba 1982), while "preadaptation" is often reserved for traits that performed some other adaptive function before being co-opted to play a new one

(Mayr 1960). Though disgust is clearly an instance of the latter of these, I wish to steer clear of the rhetorical baggage that has been built into these terms, and will avoid using either one.

15. See Sterelny 2003, 192–194, for a clear discussion of a simplified example of how an initially functionally specialized system could become multifunctional in the face of shifting environments and novel selective pressures.

16. For obvious reasons, much work in experimental moral psychology does not involve actual transgressions and punishments but involves asking subjects for their judgments about hypothetical transgressors or moral dilemmas as described in vignettes; see Doris and Nichols (forthcoming) for a discussion of the difficulties these types of laboratory-imposed constraints pose.

17. For elaboration on this line of thought, see Nemeroff and Rozin 2000 for discussion of local variations on the universal themes they identify as the "laws of sympathetic magic," and Mallon and Stich 2000 for discussion of how nativist and social constructivist explanatory resources related to these issues can be integrated. See Goffman 1959 for a locus classicus on the importance and intricacies of such displays in different areas of social life.

18. See Heath et al. 2001 for evidence of a disgust content bias influencing the transmission of cultural items other than norms (namely, urban legends).

19. It is worth pointing out that, according to the Co-opt thesis, expressions of disgust can signal a type of commitment, but it is commitment to a group or tribe, and thus to the norms and moral codes, beliefs, and values that bind the group together. Explanations of the various aspects of human sociality (or ultrasociality) that invoke groups and group membership are importantly distinct from others, enjoying different strengths and suffering from different weaknesses. As a result, the idea that disgust expressions have acquired a role in signaling commitment to groups is distinct from the idea, central to the Classic Commitment model discussed in chapter 3, that the emotion of disgust itself is a classic commitment device of the type suggested by Frank's work. For more discussion of the similarities and differences between these two types of commitment and the different explanations of cooperation they are associated with, see Richerson and Boyd 2001; Boyd and Richerson 2005b, 2006.

20. Indeed, GCC provides the resources to explain related cases of behavior that seem blatantly irrational on their face. For instance, when nutritional resources are scarce, being disgusted by, and thus refusing to eat, an available (non-toxic) type of food is puzzling and plainly maladaptive. Such cases can be made sense of, however: in some of these cases, the refusal to eat an available food source can act as an expression of commitment to the set of food taboos that forbid it. Being disgusted by some food, then, can become a costly signal of one's membership to a particular tribe and its norms. A few striking instances of this have been discussed in more detail (see Henrich 2001 for discussion and references).

21. While I hope this begins to clarify the issue, it certainly does not complete the job. For instance, more needs to be said about the distinction between concrete and abstract, and how each of those two categories is supposed to be related to the category of morality (which, as I argued in the previous section, has its own problems). For instance, I would be skeptical about the claim that only concrete or physical things can trigger genuine disgust; descriptions and figments of the imagination can apparently do the trick, too (Jabbi et al. 2008).

22. See Sockol et al. 2007 for recent discussion and references. Other *psychological* by-product hypotheses have been offered, for instance, to explain features of the character and persistence of religious beliefs (Boyer 2001; Atran 2002; Atran and Henrich 2010), aspects of ethnic and racial cognition (Gil-White 2001), and patterns of homicide involving male sexual jealousy (Daly and Wilson 1988).

5   Disgust and Normative Ethics: The Irrelevance of Repugnance and Dangers of Moralization

1. See also chapter 2 for more discussion of the Terror Management theory.

2. For a somewhat similar line of thought put to different uses, see Nichols's (2004, chap. 1) discussion of the distinction between "bad" and "wrong" and its relevance for understanding other aspects of the cognitive architecture underlying morality.

3. What the E&C view can do, however, is explain how the senses of offensiveness, of contamination sensitivity, of "yuck," however vivid and correct they may seem, are often simply psychological by-products that are projected onto whatever triggers this blunt instrument of an emotion, rather than morally icky features of the triggering entity or practice itself. See chapter 1, section 1.2.1.2.

4. This does not mean that feelings of disgust are irrelevant to *pragmatic* considerations that might arise about what to do about it. For instance, one could easily imagine that in the middle of the last century, feelings of disgust toward something like the racial integration of the school systems were widespread throughout the American South. It is not inconsistent for skeptics like myself to hold, on the one hand, that in situations like this, the presence of such feelings should be taken into account in figuring out the best way to *achieve* integration, but on the other hand, that those feelings were simply irrelevant to the question of whether or not having integrated schools is a morally impermissible, acceptable, or praiseworthy ideal.

5. Many of the things John Kekes (1992) says in his discussion of moral taboos and disgust seem to me to fail to appreciate this type of variability. For instance, he claims that "what elicits them [feelings of disgust] is an act, an event in the world, and if the event has occurred, then it is sufficient to create pollution or to cause deep disgust in people with *appropriate moral commitments*," and cashes this out in terms of "normal standards of decency" (445, 443; italics mine). In cases of disagree-

ment, however, the question of which moral commitments are appropriate or which standards of decency are normal is exactly what is at issue, and appealing to "the bulwark between civilization and barbarism" (445) to decide the matter is unhelpful rhetoric. For all of this, though, it is not clear that Kekes is a straightforward disgust advocate, either, since he also acknowledges that "deep disgust may contribute to the perpetuation of an evil practice or an evil society" (444).

6. In light of this point, perhaps this chapter and the debate on which it focuses are less straightforwardly concerned with standard normative ethical issues than they might first appear. Understood this way, this debate between disgust advocates and skeptics touches on issues that are typically considered the subject matter of metaethics.

7. The legal scholar John Douard (2007), clearly a disgust skeptic, makes a similar argument concerning sex offenders and the way they are treated by the U.S. legal system. He warns that "laws that express disgust are likely to result in the unjust treatment of sex offenders" (36) and goes on to express worries about disgust, demonization, and dehumanization that are similar to my own: "If law functions in part as the expression of disgust or horror, the result may be an unjust exclusion of sex offenders from the human community, or more precisely, the community of citizens who are regarded, by the United States legal system, as capable of acting as free and responsible agents" (37). Douard links the demonization and dehumaniza-tion of this sort to the stirring up of moral panics (Cohen 1972). Another disgust skeptic is Richard Beck (2006), who is concerned with the role of purity and con-tamination in Christian thought and practice, and whose appreciation of the work-ings of disgust leads him to warn that "the deployment of contamination metaphors within Christianity may, unintentionally, undermine the Christian ethic of love" (52). He concludes that "given the ethical implications of sociomoral disgust, purity metaphors should be closely monitored by religious communities," because some-times "the maintenance of sociomoral purity 'justifies' our dark tendencies" (65).

References

Adolphs, R., D. Tranel, and A. Damasio. 2003. Dissociable neural systems for recognizing emotions. *Brain and Cognition* 52: 61–69.

Aiello, L. 1997. Brains and guts in human evolution: The Expensive Tissue Hypothesis. *Brazilian Journal of Genetics* 20 (1): 141–148.

Aiello, L., and P. Wheeler. 1995. The Expensive Tissue Hypothesis: The brain and the digestive system in human and primate evolution. *Current Anthropology* 36: 199–221.

Anderson, M. 2006. Evidence for massive redeployment of brain areas in cognitive function. *Proceedings of the Cognitive Science Society* 28: 24–29.

Anderson, M. 2007a. Evolution of cognitive function via redeployment of brain areas. *Neuroscientist* 13 (1): 13–21.

Anderson, M. 2007b. Massive redeployment, exaptation, and the functional integration of cognitive operations. *Synthese* 159: 329–345.

Anderson, M. 2007c. The massive redeployment hypothesis and the functional topography of the brain. *Philosophical Psychology* 21 (2): 143–174.

Angyal, A. 1941. Disgust and related aversions. *Journal of Abnormal and Social Psychology* 36: 393–412.

Appiah, K. A. 1995. The uncompleted argument: Du Bois and the illusion of race. In *Overcoming Racism and Sexism*, ed. L. A. Bell and D. Blumenfeld, 59–78. Lanham, Md.: Rowman & Littlefield.

Ariew, A. 2003. Ernst Mayr's "ultimate/proximate" distinction reconsidered and restructured. *Biology and Philosophy* 18 (4): 553–565.

Armstrong, D. 1968. *A Materialist Theory of Mind*. London: Routledge & Kegan Paul.

Atran, S. 2002. *In God We Trust: The Evolutionary Landscape of Religion*. New York: Oxford University Press.

Atran, S., and J. Henrich. 2010. The evolution of religion: How cognitive by-products, adaptive learning heuristics, ritual displays, and group competition generate deep commitments to prosocial religions. *Biological Theory* 5 (1): 18–30.

Banaji, M. R. 2001. Implicit attitudes can be measured. In *The Nature of Remembering: Essays in Honor of Robert G. Crowder*, ed. H. L. Roediger III, J. S. Nairne, I. Neath, and A. Surprenant, 117–150. Washington, D.C.: American Psychological Association.

Bandura, A. 1992. Social cognitive theory of social referencing. In *Social Referencing and the Social Construction of Reality in Infancy*, ed. S. Feinman, 175–208. New York: Plenum.

Barkow, J., L. Cosmides, and J. Tooby. 1992. *The Adapted Mind*. New York: Oxford University Press.

Baron-Cohen, S. 1995. *Mindblindness*. Cambridge, Mass.: MIT Press.

Barr, L., J. Kahn, and J. Schneider. 2008. Individual differences in emotion expression: Hierarchical structure and relations with psychological distress. *Journal of Social and Clinical Psychology* 27 (1): 1045–1077.

Barrett, J. 2000. Exploring the natural foundations of religion. *Trends in Cognitive Science* 4 (1): 29–34.

Barth, F., ed. 1969. *Ethnic Groups and Boundaries: The Social Organization of Cultural Differences*. Boston: Little, Brown.

Beck, R. 2006. Spiritual pollution: The dilemma of sociomoral disgust and the ethic of love. *Journal of Psychology and Theology* 34 (1): 53–65.

Becker, E. 1973. *The Denial of Death*. New York: Simon & Schuster.

Bereczkei, T., P. Gyuris, and G. Weisfeld. 2004. Sexual imprinting in human mate choice. *Proceedings: Biological Sciences* 271 (1544): 1129–1134.

Bernstein, I. 1999. Taste aversion learning: A contemporary perspective. *Nutrition* 15 (3): 229–234.

Blackburn, S. 1984. *Spreading the Word*. New York: Oxford University Press.

Blackburn, S. 1993. *Essays in Quasi-Realism*. New York: Oxford University Press.

Blackburn, S. 2000. Critical notice of Frank Jackson, *From Metaphysics to Ethics: A Defense of Conceptual Analysis*. *Australasian Journal of Philosophy* 78 (1): 119–124.

Block, N., O. Flanagan, and G. Güzeldere, eds. 1997. *The Nature of Consciousness: Philosophical Debates*. Cambridge, Mass.: MIT Press.

Bloom, P. 2004. *Descartes' Baby*. New York: Basic Books.

Boehm, C. 1999. *Hierarchy in the Forest*. Cambridge, Mass.: Harvard University Press.

Bowles, S., and H. Gintis. 1998. The moral economy of community: Structured populations and the evolution of prosocial norms. *Evolution and Human Behavior* 19: 3–25.

Bowles, S., and H. Gintis. 2001. Community governance. In *The Evolution of Economic Diversity*, ed. A. Nicita and U. Pagano. London: Routledge.

Boyd, R. 1991. Realism, anti-foundationalism, and the enthusiasm for natural kinds. *Philosophical Studies* 61: 127–148.

Boyd, R., and P. J. Richerson. 1985. *Culture and the Evolutionary Process*. Chicago: University of Chicago Press.

Boyd, R., and P. J. Richerson. 1992. Punishment allows the evolution of cooperation (or anything else) in sizable groups. *Ethology and Sociobiology* 13: 171–195.

Boyd, R., and P. Richerson. 1996. Why culture is common, but cultural evolution is rare. *Proceedings of the British Academy* 88: 77–93.

Boyd, R., and P. Richerson. 2000a. Meme theory oversimplifies cultural change. *Scientific American* (October): 54.

Boyd, R., and P. Richerson. 2000b. Memes: Universal acid or better mousetrap? In *Darwinizing Culture*, ed. R. Aunger. Cambridge: Cambridge University Press.

Boyd, R., and P. Richerson. 2005a. *The Origin and Evolution of Cultures*. New York: Oxford University Press.

Boyd, R., and P. Richerson. 2005b. Solving the puzzle of human cooperation. In *Evolution and Culture*, ed. S. Levinson, 105–132. Cambridge, Mass.: MIT Press.

Boyd, R., and P. Richerson. 2006. Culture and the evolution of the human social instincts. In *Roots of Human Sociality*, ed. N. Enfield and S. Levinson, 453–477. Oxford: Berg.

Boyer, P. 2001. *Religion Explained: The Evolutionary Origins of Religious Thought*. New York: Basic Books.

Brand, R., D. Baldwin, and L. Ashburn. 2002. Evidence for "motionese": Modifications in mothers' infant-directed action. *Developmental Science* 5 (1): 72–83.

Brandt, R. 1946. Moral valuation. *Ethics* 56: 106–121.

Byrne, A., and D. Hilbert. 2003. Color realism and color science. *Behavioral and Brain Sciences* 26 (1): 3–64.

Byrne, R. W., and A. Whiten, eds. 1988. *Machiavellian Intelligence: Social Expertise and the Evolution of Intellect in Monkeys, Apes, and Humans*. Oxford: Oxford University Press.

Calder, A., J. Keane, F. Manes, H. Antoun, and A. Young. 2000. Impaired recognition and experience of disgust following brain injury. *Nature Neuroscience* 3 (11): 1077–1078.

Calder, A., A. Lawrence, and A. Young. 2001. Neuropsychology of fear and loathing. *Neuroscience* 2 (5): 352–363.

Caldwell, C. A., and A. E. Millen. 2008. Studying cumulative cultural evolution in the laboratory. *Philosophical Transactions of the Royal Society B* 363: 3529–3539.

Carpenter, J., P. Matthews, and O. Okomboli. 2004. Why punish? Social reciprocity and the enforcement of prosocial norms. *Journal of Evolutionary Economics* 14 (4): 407–429.

Carruthers, P. 2006. *The Architecture of the Mind.* New York: Oxford University Press.

Case, T., B. Repacholi, and R. Stevenson. 2006. My baby doesn't smell as bad as yours: The plasticity of disgust. *Evolution and Human Behavior* 27 (5): 357–365.

Chalmers, D. 2002. *The Philosophy of Mind.* New York: Oxford University Press.

Chalmers, D. 2003. Consciousness and its place in nature. In *Blackwell Guide to Philosophy of Mind,* ed. S. Stich and F. Warfield. New York: Blackwell.

Chapman, H., D. Kim, J. Susskind, and A. Anderson. 2009. In bad taste: Evidence for the oral origins of moral disgust. *Science* 323: 1222–1226.

Charash, M., and D. McKay. 2002. Attention bias for disgust. *Journal of Anxiety Disorders* 16 (5): 529–541.

Chevalier-Skolnikoff, S. 1973. Facial expression of emotion in nonhuman primates. In *Darwin and Facial Expression,* ed. P. Ekman, 11–89. New York: Academic Press.

Churchland, P. M. 1981. Eliminative materialism and the propositional attitudes. *Journal of Philosophy* 78: 67–69.

Coan, J., and J. Allen. 2003. Varieties of emotional experience during voluntary emotional facial expression. *Annals of the New York Academy of Sciences* 1000: 375–379.

Cohen, S. 1972. *Folk Devils and Moral Panic.* New York: HarperCollins.

Cooper, R. P., and R. N. Aslin. 1990. Preference for infant-directed speech in the first month after birth. *Child Development* 61: 1584–1595.

Cosmides, L., and J. Tooby. 1992. Cognitive adaptations for social exchange. In *The Adapted Mind,* ed. J. Barkow, L. Cosmides, and J. Tooby, 163–228. New York: Oxford University Press.

Cosmides, L., and J. Tooby. 1996. Are humans good intuitive statisticians after all? Rethinking some conclusions from the literature on judgment under uncertainty. *Cognition* 58 (1): 1–73.

Cottrell, C. A., and S. L. Neuberg. 2005. Different emotional reactions to different groups: A sociofunctional threat-based approach to "prejudice." *Journal of Personality and Social Psychology* 88: 770–789.

Csibra, G., and G. Gergely. 2006. Social learning and social cognition: The case for pedagogy. In *Processes of Change in Brain and Cognitive Development: Attention and Performance XXI*, ed. Y. Munakata and M. H. Johnson. Oxford: Oxford University Press, 249–274.

Csibra, G., and G. Gergely. 2009. Natural pedagogy. *Trends in Cognitive Sciences* 13 (4): 148–153.

Cummins, R. 1983. *The Nature of Psychological Explanation*. Cambridge, Mass.: MIT Press.

Cummins, R. 2000. "How does it work?" vs. "What are the laws?": Two conceptions of psychological explanation. In *Explanation and Cognition*, ed. F. Keil and R. Wilson, 117–145. Cambridge, Mass.: MIT Press.

Curtis, V. 2007. Dirt, disgust, and disease: A natural history of hygiene. *Journal of Epidemiology and Community Health* 61 (8): 660–664.

Curtis, V., R. Aunger, and T. Rabie. 2004. Evidence that disgust evolved to protect from risk of disease. *Proceedings of the Royal Society: Biological Science Series B* 271 (4): S131–S133.

Curtis, V., M. DeBarra, and R. Aunger. In press. Disgust as an adaptive system for disease avoidance behaviour. *Philosophical Transactions of the Royal Society B: Biological Sciences*.

Curtis, V., and A. Biran. 2001. Dirt, disgust, and disease: Is hygiene in our genes? *Perspectives in Biology and Medicine* 44 (1): 17–31.

Daly, M., and M. Wilson. 1988. *Homicide*. Hawthorne, N.Y.: Aldine.

Danovitch, J., and P. Bloom. 2009. Children's extension of disgust to physical and moral domains. *Emotion* 9 (1): 107–112.

D'Arms, J., and D. Jacobson. 2000. Sentiment and value. *Ethics* 110: 722–748.

D'Arms, J., and D. Jacobson. 2003. The significance of recalcitrant emotions. In *Philosophy and the Emotions*, ed. A. Hatzimoysis. Cambridge: Cambridge University Press.

D'Arms, J., and D. Jacobson. 2005. Sensibility theory and projectivism. In *The Oxford Handbook of Ethical Theory*, ed. D. Copp. Oxford: Oxford University Press.

Darwall, S., A. Gibbard, and P. Railton. 1993. Toward fin de siecle ethics: Some trends. *Philosophical Review* 101 (1): 115–189.

Darwin, C. 1872. *The Expressions of Emotions in Man and Animals.* 1st ed. New York: Philosophical Library.

Davey, G., L. Forster, and G. Mayhew. 1993. Familial resemblances in disgust sensitivity and animal phobias. *Behaviour Research and Therapy* 31 (1): 41–50.

De Caro, M., and D. Macarthur. 2004. *Naturalism in Question.* Cambridge, Mass.: Harvard University Press.

Dennett, D. 1978. *Brainstorms.* Montgomery, Vt.: Bradford Books.

Dennett, D. 1991. *Consciousness Explained.* Boston: Little, Brown.

Dennett, D. 1995. *Darwin's Dangerous Idea.* New York: Simon & Schuster.

Dennett, D. 2006. *Breaking the Spell: Religion as Natural Phenomenon.* New York: Penguin.

De Sousa, R. 1987. *The Rationality of Emotion.* Cambridge, Mass.: MIT Press.

Doris, J., and S. Nichols. Forthcoming. Broadminded: Sociality and the cognitive science of morality. In *The Oxford Handbook of Philosophy and Cognitive Science,* ed. E. Margolis, R. Samuels, and S. Stich. Oxford: Oxford University Press.

Doris, J., and A. Plakias. 2007. How to argue about disagreement: Evaluative diversity and moral realism. In *Moral Psychology,* vol. 2, *The Biology and Psychology of Morality,* ed. W. Sinnott-Armstrong, 303–332. Oxford: Oxford University Press.

Doris, J., and S. Stich. 2005. As a matter of fact: Empirical perspectives on ethics. In *The Oxford Handbook of Contemporary Philosophy,* ed. F. Jackson and M. Smith. Oxford: Oxford University Press.

Doris, J., and S. Stich. 2006. Moral psychology: Empirical approaches. In *The Stanford Encyclopedia of Philosophy* (summer 2006 edition), ed. Edward N. Zalta, <http://plato.stanford.edu/archives/sum2006/entries/moral-psych-emp>.

Douard, J. 2007. Loathing the sinner, medicalizing the sin: Why sexually violent predator statutes are unjust. *International Journal of Law and Psychiatry* 30: 36–48.

Douglas, M. 1966. *Purity and Danger: An Analysis of Concepts of Pollution and Taboos.* London: Routlegde & Kegan Paul.

Elias, N. [1939] 2000. *The Civilizing Process.* Oxford: Blackwell.

Elliot, C., and A. Radomsky. 2009. Analyses of mental contamination, part I: Experimental manipulation of morality. *Behaviour Research and Therapy* 47 (12): 995–1003.

Elster, J. 2000. *Ulysses Unbound: Studies in Rationality, Precommitment, and Constraints.* Cambridge: Cambridge University Press.

Ekman, P. 1992. An argument for basic emotions. *Cognition and Emotion* 6: 169–200.

Ekman, P. 2003. Darwin, deceit, and facial recognition. *Annals of the New York Academy of Sciences* 1000: 205–221.

Ekman, P., and R. Davidson. 1993. Voluntary smiling changes regional brain activity. *Psychological Science* 4 (5): 342–345.

Fallon, A. E., and P. Rozin. 1983. The psychological bases of food rejections by humans. *Ecology of Food and Nutrition* 13: 15–26.

Fallon, A., R. Rozin, and R. Pliner. 1984. The child's conception of food: The development of food rejections with special reference to disgust and contamination sensitivity. *Child Development* 55: 566–575.

Faulkner, J., M. Schaller, J. Park, and L. Duncan. 2004. Evolved disease-avoidance mechanisms and contemporary xenophobic attitudes. *Group Processes and Intergroup Relations* 7 (4): 333–353.

Fehr, E., and U. Fischbacher. 2004. Third party punishment and social norms. *Evolution and Human Behavior* 25 (2): 63–87.

Fehr, E., and S. Gachter. 2002. Altruistic punishment in humans. *Nature* 415: 137–140.

Fessler, D., A. Arguello, J. Mekdara, and R. Macias. 2003. Disgust sensitivity and meat consumption: A test of an emotivist account of moral vegetarianism. *Appetite* 41: 31–41.

Fessler, D., S. Eng, and C. Navarrete. 2005. Elevated disgust sensitivity in the first trimester of pregnancy: Evidence supporting the compensatory prophylaxis hypothesis. *Evolution and Human Behavior* 26: 344–351.

Fessler, D., and K. Haley. 2006. Guarding the perimeter: The outside-inside dichotomy in disgust and bodily experience. *Cognition and Emotion* 20 (1): 3–19.

Fessler, D., and E. Machery. Forthcoming. Culture and cognition. In *Oxford Handbook of Philosophy and Cognitive Science*, ed. E. Margolis, R. Samuels, and S. Stich. Oxford: Oxford University Press.

Fessler, D., and C. Navarrete. 2003a. Domain specific variation in disgust sensitivity across the menstrual cycle. *Evolution and Human Behavior* 24: 406–417.

Fessler, D., and C. Navarrete. 2003b. Meat is good to taboo: Dietary proscriptions as a product of the interaction of psychological mechanisms and social processes. *Journal of Cognition and Culture* 3 (1): 1–40.

Fessler, D., and C. Navarrete. 2004. Third-party attitudes toward sibling incest: Evidence for Westermarck's hypothesis. *Evolution and Human Behavior* 25: 277–294.

Fessler, D., and C. Navarrete. 2005. The effect of age on death disgust: Challenges to Terror Management perspectives. *Evolutionary Psychology* 3: 279–296.

Fessler, D., E. Pillsworth, and T. Flamson. 2004. Angry men and disgusted women: An evolutionary approach to the influence of emotion on risk taking. *Organizational Behavior and Human Decision Processes* 95: 107–123.

Flanagan, O. 1991. *Varieties of Moral Personality: Ethics and Psychological Realism*. Cambridge, Mass.: Harvard University Press.

Fodor, J. 1968. *Psychological Explanation*. New York: Random House.

Fodor, J. 1975. *The Language of Thought*. Cambridge, Mass.: Harvard University Press.

Fodor, J. 1983. *The Modularity of Mind*. Cambridge, Mass.: MIT Press.

Fodor, J. 2000. *The Mind Doesn't Work That Way: The Scope and Limits of Computational Psychology*. Cambridge, Mass.: MIT Press.

Frank, R. 1988. *Passions within Reason: The Strategic Role of the Emotions*. New York: W. W. Norton.

Fukuyama, F. 1992. *The End of History and the Last Man*. New York: Harper Perennial.

Garcia, J., W. Hankins, and K. Rusiniak. 1974. Behavioral regulation of the milieu interne in man and rat. *Science* 185: 824–831.

Geach, P. 1965. Assertion. *Philosophical Review* 74 (4): 449–465.

Gelman, S. 2003. *The Essential Child: Origins of Essentialism in Everyday Thought*. New York: Oxford University Press.

Gergely, G. 2007. Learning "about" versus learning "from" other minds: Human pedagogy and its implications. In *The Innate Mind*, vol. 3, *Foundations and Future Horizons*, ed. P. Carruthers, S. Laurence, and S. Stich, 170–198. New York: Oxford University Press.

Gergely, G., K. Egyed, and I. Kiraly. 2007. On pedagogy. *Developmental Science* 10: 139–146.

Gert, J. 2005. Neo-sentimentalism and disgust. *Journal of Value Inquiry* 39: 345–352.

Gil-White, F. 2001. Are ethnic groups biological "species" to the human brain? *Current Anthropology* 42 (4): 515–554.

Gil-White, F. 2006. The study of ethnicity and nationalism needs better categories: Clearing up the confusions that result from blurring analytic and lay concepts. *Journal of Bioeconomics* 7: 239–270.

Gil-White, F. n.d. (unpublished manuscript). Is ethnocentrism adaptive? An ethnographic analysis.

Goffman, E. 1959. *The Presentation of the Self in Everyday Life*. New York: Anchor.

Goldman, A. 2006. *Simulating Minds: The Philosophy, Psychology, and Neuroscience of Mindreading*. Oxford: Oxford University Press.

Goldman, A. 2007. A program for "naturalizing" metaphysics, with application to the ontology of events. *Monist* 90: 457–479.

Goldman, A., and C. Sripada. 2005. Simulation models of face-based emotion recognition. *Cognition* 94: 193–213.

Gordon, R. M. 1986. Folk psychology as simulation. *Mind and Language* 1: 158–171.

Gould, S., and R. Lewontin. 1979. The spandrels of San Marco and the Panglossian paradigm: A critique of the adaptationist programme. *Proceedings of the Royal Society of London, Series B: Biological Sciences* 205 (1161): 581–598.

Gould, S., and E. Vrba. 1982. Exaptation: A missing term in the science of form. *Paleobiology* 8: 4–15.

Greenberg, M., and R. Littlewood. 1995. Post-adoption incest and phenotypic matching: Experience, personal meanings, and biosocial implications. *British Journal of Medical Psychology* 68: 29–44.

Greene, J. 2007. The secret joke of Kant's soul. In *Moral Psychology*, vol. 3, *The Neuroscience of Morality: Emotion, Disease, and Development*, ed. W. Sinnott-Armstrong. Cambridge, Mass.: MIT Press.

Greene, J., and J. Haidt. 2002. How (and where) does moral judgment work? *Trends in Cognitive Sciences* 6: 517–523.

Greenwald, A., D. McGhee, and J. Schwartz. 1998. Measuring individual differences in implicit cognition: The implicit association test. *Journal of Personality and Social Psychology* 74 (6): 1464–1480.

Greenwald, A., B. Nosek, and R. Banaji. 2003. Understanding and using the implicit association test: I. An improved scoring algorithm. *Journal of Personality and Social Psychology* 85: 197–216.

Griffiths, P. 1997. *What the Emotions Really Are*. Chicago: University of Chicago Press.

Griffiths, P. 2001. *Emotion and Expression: International Encyclopedia of the Social and Behavioral Sciences*. New York: Pergamon/Elsevier Science.

Griffiths, P. 2003. Basic emotions, complex emotions, Machiavellian emotions. In *Philosophy and the Emotions*, ed. A. Hatzimoysis. New York: Cambridge University Press.

Griffiths, P. E. 2004. Towards a Machiavellian theory of emotional appraisal. In *Emotion, Evolution, and Rationality*, ed. P. Cruse and D. Evans, 89–105. Oxford: Oxford University Press.

Griffiths, P. 2006. "Ask not what your emotions can do for you . . .": Emotions, normativity, and Machiavellian intelligence. Based on a talk given at ISRE Conference, Atlanta, Ga., August 6, 2006.

Guerra, V., and R. Giner-Sorolla. 2010. The Community, Autonomy, and Divinity Scale (CADS): A new tool for the cross-cultural study of morality. *Journal of Cross-Cultural Psychology* 41 (1): 35–50.

Guthrie, S. 1993. *Faces in the Clouds: A New Theory of Religion.* New York: Oxford University Press.

Haidt, J. 2001. The emotional dog and its rational tail: A social intuitionist approach to moral judgment. *Psychological Review* 108: 814–834.

Haidt, J. 2006. *The Happiness Hypothesis: Finding Modern Truth in Ancient Wisdom.* New York: Basic Books.

Haidt, J., and M. Hersh. 2001. Sexual morality: The cultures and emotions of conservatives and liberals. *Journal of Applied Social Psychology* 31: 191–221.

Haidt, J., and C. Joseph. 2007. The moral mind: How 5 sets of innate moral intuitions guide the development of many culture-specific virtues, and perhaps even modules. In *The Innate Mind*, vol. 3, ed. P. Carruthers, S. Laurence, and S. Stich, 367–391. New York: Oxford University Press.

Haidt, J., S. Koller, and M. Dias. 1993. Affect, culture, and morality, or is it wrong to eat your dog? *Journal of Personality and Social Psychology* 65 (4): 613–628.

Haidt, J., C. McCauley, and P. Rozin. 1994. Individual differences in sensitivity to disgust: A scale sampling seven domains of disgust elicitors. *Personality and Individual Differences* 16: 701–713.

Haidt, J., P. Rozin, C. McCauley, and S. Imada. 1997. Body, psyche, and culture: The relationship between disgust and morality. *Psychology and Developing Societies* 9: 107–131.

Hardin, C. 1988. *Color for Philosophers: Unweaving the Rainbow.* Indianapolis: Hackett.

Hare, R. 1952. *The Language of Morals.* Oxford: Clarendon Press.

Hare, R., ed. 1989. *The Social Construction of Emotions.* New York: Blackwell.

Harris, L. T., and S. T. Fiske. 2006. Dehumanizing the lowest of the low: Neuroimaging responses to extreme outgroups. *Psychological Science* 14 (10): 847–853.

Harris, L. T., and S. T. Fiske. 2007. Social groups that elicit disgust are differentially processed in mPFC. *Social Cognitive Affective Neuroscience* 2: 45–51.

Hatfield, E., J. Cacioppo, and R. Rapson. 1994. *Emotional Contagion.* New York: Cambridge University Press.

Hauser, M. 2006. *Moral Minds: How Nature Designed Our Universal Sense of Right and Wrong*. New York: HarperCollins.

Hauskeller, M. 2006. Moral disgust. *Ethical Perspectives: Journal of the European Ethics Network* 13 (4): 571–602.

Hayes, C., R. Stevenson, and M. Coltheart. 2007. Disgust and Huntington's disease. *Neuropsychologia* 45: 1135–1151.

Heath, C., C. Bell, and E. Sternberg. 2001. Emotional selection in memes: The case of urban legends. *Journal of Personality and Social Psychology* 81: 1028–1041.

Hejmadi, A., P. Rozin, and M. Siegal. 2004. Once in contact, always in contact: Contagious essence and conceptions of purification in American and Hindu Indian children. *Developmental Psychology* 40 (4): 467–476.

Henrich, J. 2001. Cultural transmission and the diffusion of innovations: Adoption dynamics indicate that biased cultural transmission is the predominate force in behavioral change. *American Anthropologist* 103 (4): 992–1013.

Henrich, J. 2004. Cultural group selection, coevolutionary processes, and large-scale cooperation. *Journal of Economic Behavior and Organization* 53 (1): 3–35.

Henrich, J., R. Boyd, S. Bowles, C. Camerer, et al. 2005. "Economic man" in cross-cultural perspective: Behavioral experiments in 15 small-scale societies. *Behavioral and Brain Sciences* 28: 795–855.

Henrich, J., and R. Boyd. 1998. The evolution of conformist transmission and the emergence of between group differences. *Evolution and Human Behavior* 19: 215–241.

Henrich, J., and F. Gil-White. 2001. The evolution of prestige: Freely conferred deference as a mechanism for enhancing the benefits of cultural transmission. *Evolution and Human Behavior* 22: 165–196.

Henrich, J., and N. Henrich. 2007. *Why Humans Cooperate: A Cultural and Evolutionary Perspective*. New York: Oxford University Press.

Henrich, J., and R. McElreath. 2003. The evolution of cultural evolution. *Evolutionary Anthropology* 12: 123–135.

Henrich, J., and R. McElreath. 2007. Dual inheritance theory: The evolution of human cultural capacities and cultural evolution. In *Oxford Handbook of Evolutionary Psychology*, ed. R. Dunbar and L. Barrett. New York: Oxford University Press.

Henry, J., T. Ruffman, S. McDonald, M. Peek O'Leary, L. Phillips, H. Brodaty, and P. Rendell. 2008. Recognition of disgust is selectively preserved in Alzheimer's disease. *Neuropsychologia* 46 (5): 1363–1370.

Hess, U., R. B. Adams Jr., and R. E. Kleck. 2004. Facial appearance, gender, and emotion expression. *Emotion* 4: 378–388.

Hess, U., and P. Thibault. 2009. Darwin and emotion expression. *American Psychologist* 64: 120–128.

Heyes, C. M. 1993. Imitation, culture, and cognition. *Animal Behaviour* 46: 999–1010.

Hinde, R. 1985a. Expression and negotiation. In *The Development of Expressive Behavior: Biology-Environmental Interactions*, ed. G. Zivin. New York: Academic.

Hinde, R. 1985b. Was "the expression of the emotions" a misleading phrase? *Animal Behaviour* 33: 985–992.

Hume, D. 1975. *Enquiries Concerning Human Understanding and Concerning the Principles of Morals*. Ed. P. Nidditch. Oxford: Clarendon Press.

Hume, D. 1978. *A Treatise of Human Nature*. Ed. P. Nidditch. Oxford: Clarendon Press.

Humphreys, N. 1976. The social function of the intellect. In *Growing Points in Ethology*, ed. P. P. G. Bateson and R. A. Hinde. Cambridge: Cambridge University Press.

Inbar, Y., D. Pizzaro, J. Knobe, and P. Bloom. 2009. Disgust sensitivity predicts intuitive disapproval of gays. *Emotion* 9 (3): 435–439.

Jabbi, M., J. Bastiaansen, and C. Keysers. 2008. A common anterior insula representation of disgust observation, experience, and imagination shows divergent functional connectivity pathways. *PLoS ONE* 3 (8): e2939.

Johnson, S., J. Stout, S. Solomon, D. Langbehn, E. Aylward, C. Cruce, C. Ross, M. Nance, E. Kayson, E. Julian-Baros, M. Hayden, K. Kieburtz, M. Guttman, D. Oakes, I. Shoulson, L. Beglinger, K. Duff, E. Penziner, J. Paulsen, and the Predict-HD Investigators of the Huntington Study Group. 2007. Beyond disgust: Impaired recognition of negative emotions prior to diagnosis in Huntington's disease. *Brain* 130 (7): 1732–1744.

Jones, A., and J. Fitness. 2008. Moral hypervigilance: The influence of disgust sensitivity in the moral domain. *Emotion* 8 (5): 613–627.

Kass, L. 1997. The wisdom of repugnance. *New Republic* 216 (22). <http://www.catholiceducation.org/articles/medical_ethics/me0006.html>.

Kass, L. 2002. *Life, Liberty, and the Defense of Dignity: The Challenge to Bioethics*. New York: Encounter Books.

Keane, J., A. J. Calder, J. R. Hodges, and A. W. Young. 2002. Emotion recognition in frontal variant fronto-temporal dementia. *Neuropsychologia* 40: 655–665.

Kekes, J. 1992. Disgust and moral taboos. *Philosophy* 67 (262): 431–446.

Kelly, D. In press. Moral disgust and tribal instincts: A by-product hypothesis. In *Signaling, Commitment, and Emotion*, ed. R. Joyce, K. Sterelny, and B. Calcott. Cambridge, Mass.: MIT Press.

Kelly, D. n.d. (unpublished manuscript). Projectivism psychologized.

Kelly, D., E. Machery, and R. Mallon. 2010. Race and racial cognition. In *The Oxford Handbook of Moral Psychology*, ed. J. Doris and the Moral Psychology Research Group. New York: Oxford University Press.

Kelly, D., E. Machery, R. Mallon, K. Mason, and S. Stich. 2006. The role of psychology in the study of culture. *Behavioral and Brain Sciences* 29 (4): 355.

Kelly, D., and S. Stich. 2007. Two theories of the cognitive architecture underlying morality. In *The Innate Mind*, vol. 3, *Foundations and Future Horizons*, ed. P. Carruthers, S. Laurence, and S. Stich, 348–366. New York: Oxford University Press.

Kelly, D., S. Stich, K. Haley, S. Eng, and D. Fessler. 2007. Harm, affect, and the moral/conventional distinction. *Mind and Language* 22 (2): 117–131.

Keltner, D., and J. Haidt. 1999. Social functions of emotions at four levels of analysis. *Cognition and Emotion* 13: 505–521.

Keysers, C., B. Wicker, V. Gazzola, J. Anton, L. Fogassi, and V. Gallese. 2004. A touching sight: SII/PV activation during the observation and experience of touch. *Neuron* 42: 335–346.

Kim, J., and E. Sosa. 1999. *Metaphysics: An Anthology*. New York: Blackwell.

Kinomura, S., R. Kawashima, K. Yamada, S. Ono, M. Itoh, S. Yoshioka, T. Yamaguchi, H. Matsui, H. Miyazawa, H. Itoh, R. Goto, T. Fujiwara, K. Satoh, and H. Fukuda. 1994. Functional anatomy of taste perception in the human brain studied with positron emission tomography. *Brain Research* 659: 263–266.

Kolnai, A. 1998. The standard modes of aversion: Fear, disgust, and hatred. *Mind* 102 (427): 581–596.

Knapp, C. 2003. Demoralizing disgustingness. *Philosophy and Phenomenological Research* 66 (2): 253–276.

Knobe, J. 2007. Experimental philosophy. *Philosophy Compass* 2 (1): 81–92.

Knobe, J., and S. Nichols. 2008. *Experimental Philosophy*. New York: Oxford University Press.

Krolak-Salmon, P., M. A. Henaff, J. Isnard, C. Tallon-Baudry, M. Guenot, A. Vighetto, O. Bertrand, and F. Mauguiere. 2003. An attention modulated response to disgust in human ventral anterior insula. *Annals of Neurology* 53: 446–453.

Kurzban, R., and M. Leary. 2001. Evolutionary origins of stigmatization: The functions of social exclusion. *Psychological Bulletin* 127 (2): 187–208.

Kurzban, R., J. Tooby, and L. Cosmides. 2001. Can race be erased? Coalitional computation and social categorization. *Proceedings of the National Academy of Sciences of the United States of America* 98 (26): 15387–15392.

Laird, J., and C. Bressler. 1992. The process of emotion experience: A self-perception theory. In *Review of Personality and Social Psychology: Emotion and Social Behavior*, vol. 13, ed. M. Clark, 213–234. Newbury Park, Calif.: Sage.

Lane, K. A., M. R. Banaji, B. A. Nosek, and A. G. Greenwald. 2007. Understanding and using the implicit association test: IV. Procedures and validity. In *Implicit Measures of Attitudes: Procedures and Controversies*, ed. B. Wittenbrink and N. Schwarz, 59–102. New York: Guilford Press.

Leakey, R. 1994. *The Origin of Humankind*. New York: Basic Books.

Lerner, J., D. Small, and G. Loewenstein. 2004. Heart strings and purse strings: Carryover effects of emotions on economic decisions. *Psychological Science* 15 (5): 337–341.

Levenson, R. 1992. Autonomic nervous system differences among emotions. *Psychological Science* 3 (1): 23–27.

Leslie, A. 1987. Pretence and representation: The origins of "theory of mind." *Psychological Review* 94: 412–426.

Levenson, R. 1992. Autonomic nervous system differences among emotions. *Psychological Science* 3 (1): 23–27.

Lewis, D. 1969. *Convention: A Philosophical Study*. Cambridge, Mass.: Harvard University Press.

Lieberman, D., J. Tooby, and L. Cosmides. 2003. Does morality have a biological basis? An empirical test of the factors governing moral sentiments relating to incest. *Proceedings of the Royal Society of London, Series B: Biological Sciences* 270: 819–826.

Machery, E., and L. Faucher. 2005a. Why do we think racially? In *Handbook of Categorization in Cognitive Science*, ed. H. Cohen and C. Lefebvre, 1009–1033. Orlando, Fla.: Elsevier.

Machery, E., and L. Faucher. 2005b. Social construction and the concept of race. *Philosophy of Science* 72: 1208–1219.

Machery, E., D. Kelly, and S. Stich. 2005. Moral realism and cross-cultural normative diversity. *Behavioral and Brain Sciences* 28 (6): 830.

Machery, E., and R. Mallon. 2010. Evolution of morality. In *The Oxford Handbook of Moral Psychology*, ed. J. Doris and the Moral Psychology Research Group. New York: Oxford University Press.

Mackie, J. L. 1977. *Ethics: Inventing Right and Wrong*. New York: Penguin.

Mallon, R., and S. Nichols. 2010. Rules. In *The Oxford Handbook of Moral Psychology*, ed. J. Doris and the Moral Psychology Research Group. New York: Oxford University Press.

Mallon, R., and S. Stich. 2000. The odd couple: The compatibility of social construction and evolutionary psychology. *Philosophy of Science* 67: 133–154.

Malson, L. 1972. *Wolf Children*. London: NLB.

Marcus, G. 2007. *Kluge: The Haphazard Construction of the Human Mind*. Boston: Houghton Mifflin.

Mason, W. 1985. Experiential influences on the development of expressive behaviors in rhesus monkeys. In *The Development of Expressive Behavior: Biology-Environmental Interactions*, ed. G. Zivin. New York: Academic Press.

Matsumoto, D., B. Franklin, J.-W. Choi, D. Rogers, and H. Tatani. 2001. Cultural influences on the expression and perception of emotion. In *Handbook of International and Intercultural Communication*, ed. W. Gudykunst and B. Mody, 107–126. Newbury Park, Calif.: Sage.

Mayr, E. 1960. The emergence of evolutionary novelties. In *Evolution after Darwin*, vol. 1, *The Evolution of Life*, ed. S. Tax. Chicago: University of Chicago Press.

Mayr, E. 1961. Cause and effect in biology: Kinds of causes, predictability, and teleology are viewed by a practicing biologist. *Science* 134: 1501–1506.

McDowell, J. 1985. Values and secondary qualities. Reprinted in J. McDowell, *Mind, Value, and Reality*, 131–150. Cambridge, Mass.: Harvard University Press, 1998.

McDowell, J. 1987. Projection and truth in ethics. Reprinted in J. McDowell, *Mind, Value, and Reality*, 151–166. Cambridge, Mass.: Harvard University Press, 1998.

McDowell, J. 1998. *Mind, Value, and Reality*. Cambridge, Mass.: Harvard University Press.

McElreath, R., R. Boyd, and P. Richerson. 2003. Shared norms can lead to the evolution of ethnic markers. *Current Anthropology* 44 (1): 123–129.

McElreath, R., M. Lubell, P. J. Richerson, T. M. Waring, W. Baum, E. Edsten, C. Efferson, and B. Paciotti. 2005. Applying evolutionary models to the laboratory study of social learning. *Evolution and Human Behavior* 26: 483–508.

Medin, D., and S. Atran, eds. 1999. *Folkbiology*. Cambridge, Mass.: MIT Press.

Mesoudi, A., A. Whiten, and K. Laland. 2006. Towards a unified science of culture. *Behavioral and Brain Sciences* 29: 329–383.

Milders, M., J. Crawford, A. Lamb, and S. Simpson. 2003. Differential deficits in expression recognition in gene-carriers and patients with Huntington's disease. *Neuropsychologia* 41: 1484–1492.

Miller, S. 1986. Disgust: Conceptualization, development, and dynamics. *International Review of Psycho-Analysis* 13: 295–307.

Miller, S. 1993. Disgust reactions: Their determinants and manifestations in treatment. *Contemporary Psychoanalysis* 29 (4): 711–735.

Miller, W. 1997. *The Anatomy of Disgust*. Cambridge, Mass.: Harvard University Press.

Mitchell I., H. Heims, E. Neville, and H. Rickards. 2005. Huntington's disease patients show impaired perception of disgust in the gustatory and olfactory modalities. *Journal of Neuropsychiatry Clinical Neurosciences* 17: 119–121.

Moll, J., R. Oliveira-Souza, F. Moll, F. Ignacio, I. Bramati, E. Caparelli-Daquer, and P. Eslinger. 2005. The moral affiliations of disgust: A functional MRI study. *Cognitive and Behavioral Neurology* 18 (1): 68–78.

Morales, A., and G. Fitzsimons. 2007. Product contagion: Changing consumer evaluations through physical contact with "disgusting" products. *JMR: Journal of Marketing Research* 44: 272–283.

Morris, P., C. Doe, and E. Godsell. 2007. Secondary emotions in non-primate species? Behavioural reports and subjective claims by animal owners. *Cognition and Emotion* 22: 3–20.

Murphy, D., and M. Bishop. 2009. *Stich and His Critics*. New York: Oxford University Press.

Murphy, S., J. Haidt, and F. Bjorkland. 2000 (unpublished manuscript). Moral dumbfounding: When intuition finds no reason.

Nabi, R. 2002. The theoretical versus the lay meaning of disgust: Implication for emotion research. *Cognition and Emotion* 16 (5): 695–703.

Nado, J., D. Kelly, and S. Stich. 2009. Moral judgment. In *The Routledge Companion to the Philosophy of Psychology*, ed. John Symons and Paco Calvo, 621–633. New York: Routledge.

Nagel, T. 1974. What is it like to be a bat? *Philosophical Review* 83: 435–450.

Navarrete, C., and D. Fessler. 2006. Disease avoidance and ethnocentrism: The effects of disease vulnerability and disgust sensitivity on intergroup attitudes. *Evolution and Human Behavior* 27 (4): 270–282.

Nemeroff, C., and P. Rozin. 2000. The makings of the magical mind: The nature and function of sympathetic magical thinking. In *Imagining the Impossible*, ed. K. Rosengren, C. Johnson, and P. Harris. New York: Cambridge University Press.

Nesse, R., ed. 2001a. *Evolution and the Capacity for Commitment*. New York: Russell Sage Foundation.

Nesse, R. 2001b. Natural selection and the capacity for subjective commitment. In *Evolution and the Capacity for Commitment*, ed. R. Nesse. New York: Russell Sage Foundation.

Nichols, S. 2001. Innateness and moral psychology. In *The Innate Mind: Structure and Content*, ed. P. Carruthers, S. Laurence, and S. Stich. New York: Oxford University Press.

Nichols, S. 2002a. Norms with feeling: Towards a psychological account of moral judgment. *Cognition* 84: 221–236.

Nichols, S. 2002b. On the genealogy of norms: A case for the role of emotion in cultural evolution. *Philosophy of Science* 69: 234–255.

Nichols, S. 2004. *Sentimental Rules: On the Natural Foundations of Moral Judgment*. New York: Oxford University Press.

Nichols, S., and R. Mallon. 2006. Moral dilemmas and moral rules. *Cognition* 100 (3): 530–542.

Nichols, S., and S. Stich. 2004. *Mindreading: An Integrated Account of Pretence, Self-Awareness, and Understanding Other Minds*. Oxford: Clarendon Press.

Noel, J. 1990. Review of *Passions within Reason*. *Studies in Philosophy and Education* 10 (2): 175–178.

Nosek, B. A., A. G. Greenwald, and M. R. Banaji. 2007. The implicit association test at age seven: A methodological and conceptual review. In *Automatic Processes in Social Thinking and Behavior*, ed. J. A. Bargh, 265–292. Philadelphia: Psychology Press.

Nucci, L. 2001. *Education in the Moral Domain*. Cambridge: Cambridge University Press.

Nussbaum, M. 2004a. *Hiding from Humanity: Disgust, Shame, and the Law*. Princeton, N.J.: Princeton University Press.

Nussbaum, M. 2004b. Danger to human dignity: The revival of disgust and shame in the law. *Chronicle of Higher Education* 50 (48): B6.

Ohman, A. 2002. Automaticity and the amygdala: Nonconscious responses to emotional faces. *Current Directions in Psychological Science* 11 (2): 62–66.

Park, J., J. Faulkner, and M. Schaller. 2003. Evolved disease-avoidance processes and contemporary anti-social behavior: Prejudicial attitudes and avoidance of people with physical disabilities. *Journal of Nonverbal Behavior* 27 (2): 65–87.

Parker, R. 1983. *Miasma: Pollution and Purification in Early Greek Religion*. Oxford: Clarendon Press.

Penfield, W., and M. E. Faulk. 1955. The insula: Further observations on its function. *Brain* 78: 445–470.

Phillips, M. L., A. W. Young, C. Senior, M. Brammer, C. Andrew, A. J. Calder, E. T. Bullmore, et al. 1997. A specific neural substrate for perceiving facial expressions of disgust. *Nature* 389 (6650): 495–498.

Pinker, S. 1997. *How the Mind Works.* New York: W. W. Norton.

Place, U. T. 1956. Is consciousness a brain process? *British Journal of Psychology* 47: 44–50.

Prinz, J. 2004. *Gut Reactions: A Perceptual Theory of Emotion.* New York: Oxford University Press.

Prinz, J. 2008. *The Emotional Construction of Morals.* Oxford: Oxford University Press.

Radomsky, A., and C. Elliot. 2009. Analyses of mental contamination, part II: Individual differences. *Behaviour Research and Therapy* 47 (12): 1004–1011.

Raafat, R., N. Chater, and C. Frith. 2009. Herding in humans. *Trends in Cognitive Sciences* 13 (10): 420–428.

Rachels, J. 2000. Naturalism. In *The Blackwell Guide to Ethical Theory*, ed. Hugh LaFollette, 74–91. Oxford: Blackwell.

Richerson, P., and R. Boyd. 1998. The evolution of human ultra-sociality. In *Ideology, Warfare, and Indoctrinability*, ed. I. Eibl-Eibisfeldt and F. Salter. Oxford: Oxford University Press.

Richerson, P., and R. Boyd. 1999. Complex societies: The evolutionary origins of a crude superorganism. *Human Nature* 10: 253–289.

Richerson, P., and R. Boyd. 2000. Climate, culture, and the evolution of cognition. In *The Evolution of Cognition*, ed. C. M. Heyes. Cambridge, Mass.: MIT Press.

Richerson, P., and R. Boyd. 2001. The evolution of subjective commitment to groups: A tribal instincts hypothesis. In *Evolution and the Capacity for Commitment*, ed. R. Nesse. New York: Russell Sage Foundation.

Richerson, P., and R. Boyd. 2005. *Not by Genes Alone.* Chicago: University of Chicago Press.

Richerson, P., R. Boyd, and J. Henrich. 2003. Cultural evolution and human cooperation. In *Genetic and Cultural Evolution of Cooperation*, ed. P. Hammerstein. Cambridge, Mass.: MIT Press.

Rozin, P. 1997. Moralization. In *Morality and Health*, ed. A. Brandt and P. Rozin. New York: Routledge.

Rozin, P. 1999. The process of moralization. *Psychological Science* 10 (3): 218–221.

Rozin, P. 2008. Hedonic "adaptation": Specific habituation to disgust/death elicitors as a result of dissecting a cadaver. *Judgment and Decision Making* 3 (2): 191–194.

Rozin, P., and A. Fallon. 1987. A perspective on disgust. *Psychological Review* 94: 23–41.

Rozin, P., A. Fallon, and M. Augustoni-Ziskind. 1985. The child's conception of food: The development of contamination sensitivity to "disgusting" substances. *Developmental Psychology* 21: 1075–1079.

Rozin, P., J. Haidt, and K. Fincher. 2009. From moral to oral. *Science* 323: 1179–1180.

Rozin, P., J. Haidt, and C. McCauley. 2008. Disgust. In *Handbook of Emotions*, 3rd ed., ed. M. Lewis, J. M. Haviland-Jones, and L. F. Barrett. New York: Guilford Press.

Rozin, P., J. Haidt, C. McCauley, and S. Imada. 1997. Disgust: Preadaptation and the cultural evolution of a food-based emotion. In *Food Preferences and Taste: Continuity and Change*, ed. H. M. Macbeth. Oxford: Berghahn.

Rozin, P., L. Hammer, H. Oster, T. Horowitz, and V. Marmora. 1986. The child's conception of food: Differentiation of categories of rejected substances in the 16 months to 5 year age range. *Appetite* 7: 141–151.

Rozin, P., L. Lowery, and R. Ebert. 1994. Varieties of disgust faces and the structure of disgust. *Journal of Personality and Social Psychology* 66 (5): 870–881.

Rozin, P., L. Lowery, S. Imada, and J. Haidt. 1999. The CAD triad hypothesis: A mapping between three moral emotions (contempt, anger, disgust) and three moral codes (community, autonomy, divinity). *Journal of Personality and Social Psychology* 76 (4): 574–586.

Rozin, P., M. Markwith, and C. Nemeroff. 1992. Magical contagion beliefs and fear of AIDS. *Journal of Applied Social Psychology* 22 (14): 1081–1092.

Rozin, P., L. Millman, and C. Nemeroff. 1986. Operation of the laws of sympathetic magic in disgust and other domains. *Journal of Personality and Social Psychology* 50: 703–712.

Rozin, P., and C. Nemeroff. 1990. The laws of sympathetic magic: A psychological analysis of similarity and contagion. In *Cultural Psychology: Essays in Comparative Human Development*, ed. J. Stigler, R. Schweder, and G. Herdt. Cambridge: Cambridge University Press.

Rozin, P., C. Nemeroff, M. Wane, and A. Sherrod. 1989. Operation of the sympathetic magical law of contagion in interpersonal attitudes among Americans. *Bulletin of the Psychonomic Society* 27: 367–370.

Rozin, P., C. Nemeroff, M. Horowitz, B. Gordon, and W. Voet. 1995. The borders of the self: Contamination sensitivity and potency of the body apertures and other body parts. *Journal of Research in Personality* 29: 318–340.

Rozin, P., and M. Siegal. 2003. Vegemite as a marker of national identity. *Gastronomica: The Journal of Food and Culture* 3 (4): 63–67.

Ruiz-Belda, M.-A., J.-M. Fernandez-Dols, and P. Carrera. 2003. Spontaneous facial expressions of happy bowlers and soccer fans. *Cognition and Emotion* 17 (2): 315–326.

Ryan, M. 1998. Sexual selection, receiver biases, and the evolution of sex differences. *Science* 281: 1999–2003.

Ryle, G. 1949. *The Concept of Mind*. London: Hutchinson.

Sanfey, A., J. Rilling, J. Aronson, L. Nystrom, and J. Cohen. 2003. The neural basis of economic decision-making in the ultimatum game. *Science* 300: 1755–1758.

Schaich Borg, J., D. Lieberman, and K. A. Kiehl. 2008. Infection, incest, and iniquity: Investigating the neural correlates of disgust and morality. *Journal of Cognitive Neuroscience* 20: 1529–1546.

Schnall, S., J. Haidt, and G. Clore. 2008. Disgust as embodied moral judgment. *Personality and Social Psychology Bulletin* 34 (8): 1096–1109.

Schiffer, S. 1981. Truth and the theory of content. In *Meaning and Understanding*, ed. H. Parret and J. Bouvaresse. Berlin: Walter de Gruyter.

Shennan, S. 2002. *Genes, Memes, and Human History: Darwinian Archaeology and Cultural Evolution*. London: Thames & Hudson.

Shepher, J. 1983. *Incest: A Biosocial View*. New York: Academic Press.

Shimp, T., and E. Stuart. 2004. The role of disgust as an emotional mediator of advertising effects. *Journal of Advertising* 33 (1): 43–53.

Shweder, R., N. Much, M. Mahapatra, and L. Park. 1997. The "big three" of morality (autonomy, community, and divinity), and the "big three" explanations of suffering. In *Morality and Health*, ed. A. Brandt and P. Rozin. New York: Routledge.

Siegal, M. 1988. Children's knowledge of contagion and contamination as causes of illness. *Child Development* 59: 1353–1359.

Siegal, M., and D. Share. 1990. Contamination sensitivity in young children. *Developmental Psychology* 26 (3): 455–458.

Simpson, J., S. Carter, S. Anthony, and P. Overton. 2006. Is disgust a homogenous emotion? *Motivation and Emotion* 30 (1): 31–41.

Singer, P. 1981. *The Expanding Circle: Ethics and Sociobiology*. New York: Farrar, Straus & Giroux.

Singer, P. 2005. Ethics and intuitions. *Journal of Ethics* 9: 331–352.

Small, D., D. Zald, M. Jones-Gotman, R. Zatorre, J. Pardo, S. Frey, and M. Petrides. 1999. Brain imaging: Human cortical gustatory areas; A review of functional neuroimaging data. *Neuroreport* 10: 7–14.

Smith, R. 2007. Language of the lost: An explication of stigma communication. *Communication Theory* 17: 462–485.

Sober, E., and D. S. Wilson. 1998. *Unto Others: The Evolution and Psychology of Unselfish Behavior.* Cambridge, Mass.: Harvard University Press.

Sockol, M. D., D. A. Raichlen, and H. Pontzer. 2007. Chimpanzee locomotor energetics and the origin of human bipedalism. *Proceedings of the National Academy of Sciences of the United States of America* 30: 12265–12269.

Sperber, D. 1996. *Explaining Culture: A Naturalistic Approach.* New York: Blackwell.

Sprengelmeyer, R., A. Young, A. Calder, A. Karnat, H. Lange, V. Homberg, D. Perrett, and D. Rowland. 1996. Loss of disgust: Perception of faces and emotions in Huntington's disease. *Brain* 119 (5): 1647–1665.

Sprengelmeyer, R., A. Young, I. Pundt, A. Sprengelmeyer, A. Calder, G. Berrios, R. Winkel, et al. 1997. Disgust implicated in obsessive-compulsive disorder. *Proceedings of the Royal Society of London* 264: 1767–1773.

Sripada, C. 2005. Punishment and the strategic structure of moral systems. *Biology and Philosophy* 20: 767–789.

Sripada, C. 2007. Adaptationist and culturist explanations of human behavior. In *Innateness and the Structure of the Mind: Foundations and the Future,* ed. P. Carruthers, S. Laurence, and S. Stich, 311–329. New York: Oxford University Press.

Sripada, C., and S. Stich. 2004. Evolution, culture and the irrationality of the emotions. In *Emotion, Evolution, and Rationality,* ed. D. Evans and Cruse, 133–158. Oxford: Oxford University Press.

Sripada, C., and S. Stich. 2007. A framework for the psychology of norms. In *The Innate Mind: Culture and Cognition,* ed. P. Carruthers, S. Laurence, and S. Stich, 280–301. New York: Oxford University Press.

Stanford, C., and H. Bunn, eds. 2001. *Meat Eating and Human Evolution.* New York: Oxford University Press.

Sterelny, K. 2003. *Thought in a Hostile World.* New York: Blackwell.

Sterelny, K. 2006. The evolution and evolvability of culture. *Mind and Language* 21 (2): 137–165.

Sterelny, K. n.d. (unpublished manuscript). The fate of the third chimpanzee. Nicod lectures, <http://www.institutnicod.org/lectures2008_outline.htm>.

Stevenson, C. 1937. The emotive meaning of ethical terms. In *Facts and Values*, ed. C. Stevenson. New Haven: Yale University Press.

Stevenson, C. 1944. *Ethics and Language*. New Haven: Yale University Press.

Stich, S. 1983. *From Folk Psychology to Cognitive Science: The Case against Belief.* Cambridge, Mass.: MIT Press.

Stich, S. 1996. Naturalism, positivism, and Puritanism. In *Deconstructing the Mind*. New York: Oxford University Press.

Stich, S. 2006. Is morality an elegant machine or a kludge? *Journal of Cognition and Culture* 6 (1): 181–189.

Stich, S. 2007. Nicod lectures on morality. Videos available at <http://www.institutnicod.org/lectures2007_outline.htm#1>.

Stich, S., D. Fessler, and D. Kelly. 2009. On the morality of harm: A response to Sousa, Holbrook, and Piazza. *Cognition* 113 (1): 93–97.

Stich, S., J. Henrich, and T. David. In preparation. Survey on norms.

Stich, S., and S. Laurence. 1994. Intentionality and naturalism. In *Midwest Studies in Philosophy*, vol. 19, *Philosophical Naturalism*, ed. P. A. French and T. E. Uehling Jr. Notre Dame: University of Notre Dame Press.

Stich, S., and S. Nichols. 1993. Folk psychology: Simulation or tacit theory? *Mind and Language* 7 (1–2): 35–71.

Stiner, M. 2002. Carnivory, coevolution, and the geographic spread of the genus *Homo*. *Journal of Anthropological Research* 10 (1): 1–63.

Streiffer, R. 2003. In defense of the moral relevance of species boundaries. *American Journal of Bioethics* 3 (3): 37–38.

Susskind, J., D. Lee, A. Cusi, R. Feiman, W. Grabski, and A. Anderson. 2008. Expressing fear enhances sensory experience. *Nature Neuroscience* 11 (7): 843–849.

Tajfel, H., C. Flament, M. G. Billig, and R. P. Bundy. 1971. Social categorization and intergroup behaviour. *European Journal of Social Psychology* 1: 149–175.

Taylor, K. 2007. Disgust is a factor in extreme prejudice. *British Journal of Social Psychology* 46: 597–617.

Tetlock, P. E., O. Kristel, B. Elson, M. Green, and J. Lerner. 2000. The psychology of the unthinkable: Taboo trade-offs, forbidden base rates, and heretical counterfactuals. *Journal of Personality and Social Psychology* 78: 853–870.

Tomasello, M. 1999. *The Cultural Origins of Human Cognition*. Cambridge, Mass.: Harvard University Press.

Tomasello, M., A. C. Kruger, and H. H. Ratner. 1993. Cultural learning. *Behavioral and Brain Sciences* 16: 495–552.

Tooby, J., and L. Cosmides. 2005. Evolutionary psychology: Conceptual foundations. In *The Handbook of Evolutionary Psychology*, ed. D. Buss. New York: Wiley.

Trivers, R. 1971. The evolution of reciprocal altruism. *Quarterly Journal of Biology* 46: 35–57.

Trivers, R. 2002. *Natural Selection and Social Theory*. Oxford: Oxford University Press.

Turiel, E. 1983. *The Development of Social Knowledge*. Cambridge: Cambridge University Press.

Turner, J. C. 1984. Social identification and psychological group formation. In *The Social Dimension: European Developments in Social Psychology*, vol. 2, ed. H. Tajfel. Cambridge: Cambridge University Press.

Vasquez, K., D. Keltner, D. Ebenbach, and T. Banaszynski. 2001. Cultural variation and similarity in moral rhetorics: Voices from the Philippines and the United States. *Journal of Cross-Cultural Psychology* 32: 93–120.

Wallbott, H. 1991. Recognition of emotion from facial expression via imitation? Some indirect evidence for an old theory. *British Journal of Social Psychology* 30: 207–219.

Wang, K., R. Hoosain, R. Yang, Y. Meng, and C. Wang. 2003. Impairment of recognition of disgust in Chinese with Huntington's or Wilson's disease. *Neuropsychologia* 41: 527–537.

Ware, J., K. Jain, I. Burgess, and G. Davey. 1994. Disease-avoidance model: Factor analysis of common animal fears. *Behaviour Research and Therapy* 32 (1): 57–63.

Webb, K., and G. Davey. 1993. Disgust sensitivity and fear of animals: Effect of exposure to violent and revulsive material. *Anxiety, Coping, and Stress* 5: 329–335.

Westermarck, E. A. 1891/1921. *The History of Human Marriage*. London: Macmillan.

Wheatley, T., and J. Haidt. 2005. Hypnotic disgust makes moral judgments more severe. *Psychological Science* 16 (10): 780–784.

Whiten, A., N. McGuigan, S. Marshall-Pescini, and L. Hopper. 2009. Emulation, imitation, overimitation, and the scope of culture for child and chimpanzee. *Philosophical Transactions of the Royal Society B* 364: 2417–2428.

Wicker, B., C. Keysers, J. Plailly, J. Royet, V. Gallese, and G. Rizzolatti. 2003. Both of us disgusted in *my* insula: The common neural basis of seeing and feeling disgust. *Neuron* 40: 655–664.

Wilson, D., M. Van Vugt, and R. O'Gorman. 2008. Multilevel selection theory and major evolutionary transitions: Implications for psychological science. *Current Directions in Psychological Science* 17 (1): 6–9.

Wilson, D. S., and E. O. Wilson. 2007. Rethinking the theoretical foundation of sociobiology. *Quarterly Review of Biology* 82 (4): 327–348.

Wolf, A. P. 1995. *Sexual Attraction and Childhood Association: A Chinese Brief for Edward Westermarck*. Stanford, Calif.: Stanford University Press.

Zhong, C., and K. Liljenquist. 2006. Washing away your sins: Threatened morality and physical cleansing. *Science* 313 (5792): 1451–1452.

Index

Note: Figures and tables are indicated by "f" or "t," respectively, following page numbers.

Acquisition subsystem, 4, 6, 36–38
Adaptation. *See* Evolution
Advertising, 151, 156n5
Advocates. *See* Disgust advocacy
Affect programs, 15–17, 18, 39, 46–48, 153n2
Anderson, Michael, 132
Anger, 73–74
Animals. *See also* Primates
  disgust not found in, 43–45, 55–56, 155n1
  as elicitors, 31
  taste aversion in, 44
Anterior insula, 17, 18
Applied ethics. *See* Normative and applied ethics
Attention, 23

Beck, Richard, 163n7
Becker, Ernest, 43
Behavioral profile of disgust, 3, 13–34
"Better safe than sorry" logic, 50, 90, 147
Bloom, Paul, 129–130
Body
  as elicitor of disgust, 28, 51–52
  Terror Management theory and, 139
Boxologies, 36
Boyd, Robert, 79, 107, 124

Brain
  and moral disgust, 131
  part of, associated with disgust, 17, 67
  and prejudice, 30, 125
By-product hypotheses, 133–135

Capacities
  for cultural transmission, 80–85
  defining and distinguishing, 21–22
  for disgust, 22, 35–36, 66–68
CCM. *See* Classic Commitment model
Chapman, H., 130
Christianity, 163n7
Classic Commitment model (CCM), 5, 62, 63, 69–78
  application of, 75–78
  commitment problems and devices, 70–73
  CTM compared to, 87–88, 94, 95t
  social emotions, 73–75
Cognitive architecture
  defined, 36
  disgust-related, 36–39, 37f, 67
  evolutionary psychology's conception of, 159n3
  gene-culture coevolution and, 105, 106f
  tribal instincts and, 106–116

Cognitive sciences, 3, 12
Commitment, 62. *See also* Classic Commitment model
   co-opt thesis and, 161n19
   defined, 70
   nonsocial, 157n7
   problems and devices concerning, 70–73
   social emotions and, 73–75
Communication. *See* Cultural transmission; Information sharing
Computational theory of mind, 36, 154n13
Conformity biases, 85
Conspecifics, 4, 49–50, 55, 116, 118
Contamination, inappropriate imputation of, 134–135, 151–152, 163n7. *See also* Purity norms
Contamination sensitivity, 19–21
Content biases, 86, 122
Context biases, 85–86
Conventional norms, 126–127
Cooperation, 75–77, 87, 92, 107, 113
Co-opt thesis, 6–7, 116–125. *See also* E&C view
   by-product hypotheses and, 134
   ethnic boundaries and, 123–125
   and moral disgust, 131–133
   new problems and functions and, 116–119
   overview of, 143–146
   social norms and, 119–122
   underlying principle of, 117
Coordination, social, 111–113
Core coevolutionary feedback loop, 105, 107, 110, 113, 118–119
Core disgust, 17–21, 39, 48–52
Cottrell, C. A., 115
CTM. *See* Cultural Transmission model
Cultural transmission, 78–86. *See also* Cultural Transmission model; Information sharing
   biases in, 85–86

   cognitive architecture required for, 105, 106f
   gene-culture coevolution and, 103–106
   psychology of, 80–86
   receptive capacities for, 82–85, 90
   sending capacities for, 81–82
Cultural Transmission model (CTM), 5–6, 62–63, 78–98
   application of, 87–98
   CCM compared to, 87–88, 94, 95t
   Entanglement thesis and, 88–92
   evidence for, 92–94
   evolutionary advantages of, 90–92
   gene-culture coevolution and, 103
   psychology of, 80–86
   underlying principles of, 78–80
Culture. *See* Social norms

Darwin, Charles, 15, 64
Death, 43–44, 139
Deception, 75, 77, 87, 92
Deep Wisdom theory, 138–139, 140, 146
Defection, 112–113
Dehumanization, 30, 125, 152, 163n7
Descent with modification, 53
Diet, 54, 56, 89, 120. *See also* Eating; Food
Digestion. *See* Food
Disease, 29, 48–52
Disgust, human vs. animal experience of, 43–45, 55–57, 155n1
Disgust advocacy, 8, 138–139, 146–152, 162n5
Disgustingness. *See also* Elicitors
   asymmetry in, 20
   metaethics and, 9, 101
   as property, 8–9
Disgust response, 15–26. *See also* Elicitors
   affect program of, 15–17, 46–48
   by-products of, 133–135
   characteristics of, 1, 63

core disgust, 17–21, 39, 48–52
  diversity/variability of, 40–41, 58
  downstream effects of, 21–26, 39–40
  hair trigger of, 51, 90, 132, 147
  nature vs. nurture concerning, 11, 122
  phenomenology of, 153n3
  physiological aspects of, 16–17
  projective character of, 9, 21, 27
  recognition of, 66–68
  as uniquely human, 4, 43–44, 55–57
  unity of, 33–34, 40, 58
  universality of, 15
Disgust skepticism, 8, 139–140, 146–
  152, 163n7
Disgust system, 36–40, 37f, 59f, 99f, 136f
Domain-specific cultural information
  acquisition mechanisms, 83–85,
  89–90
Douard, John, 163n7
Downstream effects of disgust response,
  21–26, 39–40
Dual inheritance theory, 103

E&C view, 140–152
Eating, 51–52. See also Diet; Food
Ekman, Paul, 15
Elicitor neutrality, 19–20
Elicitors, 27–33. See also Disgustingness;
  Disgust response
  common themes involving, 29–33
  database of, 38–39
  diversity/variability of, 2, 27, 29, 32,
    34, 94, 96–98, 135–136, 149–150
  experience-derived, 39
  innate, 39
  nature vs. nurture concerning, 11
  neutrality of, 19–20
  physical, 1, 28–29
  social, 1–2, 31–33
  universal, 28–29, 39, 96–97
  variability of (see diversity/variabil-
    ity of)
Emotion. See also Disgust response

  communication of, 61–64, 69
  evolutionary account of, 76–77
  social, 73–76
Empathy, 5, 27, 66–68, 90
Endowment effect, 26
Entanglement thesis. See also E&C view
  disease/parasite avoidance and, 48–52
  evidence for, 52–53, 56–59
  evolution and, 45–59
  factors leading to, 53–55
  overview of, 4, 52, 141–143
  sentimental signaling system and,
    88–92
  taste aversion and, 46–48
Essentialization, of ethnic properties,
  114
Ethics. See Metaethics; Moral disgust;
  Morality; Normative and applied
  ethics
Ethnic boundaries, 7, 111–115, 123–
  125, 134–135
Ethnic psychology, 113–115
Ethnocentrism, 124
Etiquette, 23, 93
Evaluative judgment, 23–26
Evolution
  and cognitive architecture, 159n3
  co-opt thesis and, 116–125
  CTM and, 90–92
  and descent with modification, 53
  disease/parasite avoidance and, 48–52
  emotion and, 76–77
  Entanglement thesis and, 4–5, 45–59
  gene-culture coevolution, 103–116
  taste aversion and, 46–48
  tribal instincts hypothesis and,
    103–116
Exaptations, 160n14
Execution subsystem, 4, 37–39
Explanations, proximate vs. ultimate, 35

Facial expressions, communicative function of, 55, 61–66. See also Gape face

Facial feedback, 66
Facial leakage, 65
False negatives, 158n17
False positives, 4, 47, 50, 51, 147
Fessler, D., 83–84, 89–90, 97, 154n11
Fiske, S. T., 30
Food. *See also* Diet; Eating
  central role of, in disgust, 17–18,
    30–31
  Entanglement thesis and, 46–48, 54–55
  and ethnic boundaries, 123
  irrational taboos concerning, 161n20
Frank, Robert, 5, 62, 69–70, 73, 75–77
Functionalism, 36

Gape face
  automatic nature of, 65, 92, 156n2
  as characteristic feature, 5, 47, 64
  communication of disgust via, 5, 55,
    64–66, 93
  components of, 93, 156n1
  derivation of, 16, 47, 64
  description of, 16
  and disease/parasite avoidance, 91,
    158n14
  as elicitor, 27, 65–66
  and empathy, 5, 27, 66–68, 90
  in primates, 44
Garcia aversions, 47
Garcia effect, 47
Gene-culture coevolution (GCC), 6
  and cognitive architecture, 106f,
    159n3
  and ethnic boundaries, 111–115
  overview of, 103–106
  and social norms, 108–111
Gil-White, F., 113–114, 124
Greece, 32–33
Group membership, 6, 7, 32, 93,
    161n19. *See also* Ethnic boundaries;
    Tribal instincts hypothesis
Group selection, 159n6
Gustatory cortex, 17

Haidt, Jonathan, 24, 54
Harris, L. T., 30
Hauskeller, M., 148
Heath, C., 93
Henrich, J., 113
Hitler, Adolf, 20
Homologies, 44–45, 56, 155n2
Hopi, 32–33
Human disgust system, 4
Hume, David, 9

Imitation, 82–83
Impetus to act, 70–71
Incest, 98, 158n17
Individual learning, 38
Infection, 29, 48–52
Inferential signature, 21
Information sharing. *See also* Cultural
    transmission
  disgust as promoting, 23, 93
  emotion and, 61–64, 69
  evolutionary advantages of, 55
  expression and, 64–66
  gape face as means of, 5, 55, 64–66
  recognition and, 66–68
  sentimental signaling system, 68–69
Inheritance systems, 103–104
Insular cortex, 67

Japan, 32–33
Judgment, 23–26

Kass, Leon, 138, 147, 148, 150
Kekes, John, 162n5
Kin recognition, 98, 158n17
Kurzban, R., 49

Language
  acquisition and comprehension of, 82
  disgust-related, 23
  production capacities for, 81
Learning. *See also* Cultural transmission
  individual and social, 38

mechanisms contributing to, 97–98
natural pedagogy, 81–82
one-shot, 46–47
of taste aversion, 46–47
variation in elicitors attributed to, 96
Leary, M., 49
Lorenz, Konrad, 15
Love, 73

Machery, E., 83–84, 89–90
Marketing, 151, 156n5
Marriage, 98
McElreath, R., 113
Meat, 31, 54, 56
Medial prefrontal cortex, 30
Memory, 23
Metaethics, 8–9, 101, 156n4, 163n6
Metaphysics, 8–9
Microexpressions, 65
Mill, John Stuart, 128
Moll, J., 131
Mood congruency, 23
Moral disgust, 6–7, 125–135. *See also*
    Morality, judgments associated with
    disgust pertaining to; Normative and
    applied ethics
    as actual or metaphorical disgust,
        128–132
    co-opt thesis and, 131–133
    moral domain and, 126–128
    value of studying, 9
Moral dumbfounding, 24
Moral hypervigilance, 24
Morality. *See also* Metaethics; Moral dis-
    gust; Normative and applied ethics
    contamination sensitivity and, 20
    demarcating domain of, 126–128
    judgments associated with disgust per-
        taining to, 24–26, 137–140, 147–151,
        162n4, 162n5
    and tribal instincts hypothesis,
        103–116
Moralization, 151–152

Morris, P., 155n1
Mouth, 17–18. *See also* Food

Natural pedagogy, 81
Nature–nurture controversy, 11
Nausea, 16–17, 47–48
Navarrete, C., 154n11
Neuberg, S. L., 115
Nichols, S., 93
Normative and applied ethics, 7–8, 101–
    102, 137–152
    E&C view and, 140–146
    role of disgust in, 146–152, 162n4
    role of disgust in morality, 137–140
Norm psychology, 108–110
Nussbaum, Martha, 139–140

Offensiveness, 18
Omnivore's dilemma, 46–48
One-shot learning, 46–47
Oral incorporation, 17–18
Organic materials, 28
Orwell, George, 1

Parasite mechanism, 52
Parasites, 29, 48–52
Phenotypic abnormality, 29–30, 49–50,
    118
Pinker, Stephen, 61–63
Pinker's Puzzle, 62, 69, 76, 92
Poison mechanism, 48, 52
Preadaptations, 160n14
Prestige biases, 85
Primates
    disgust in, 44
    evolution of, 55–56
Proximate explanations, 35
Psychological model of disgust, 35–40,
    45
Purity norms, 121. *See also* Contamina-
    tion, inappropriate imputation of
Putamen, 67
Pygmalion (play), 1

Reciprocity, 76–77, 87, 92, 94, 107
Religion, 86, 121, 163n7
Repugnance, 138
Response. *See* Disgust response
Richerson, Peter, 79, 107, 124
Risk aversion, 26
Rozin, Paul, 12, 17, 19–20, 30, 44, 46, 51, 93, 97, 140, 151

Schaich Borg, J., 131
Scholarship on disgust, 2–3, 8–9, 11–14
Sentimentalist tradition, 9
Sentimental signaling system, 5–6, 68–69, 88–92
Sex, 31, 51–52, 154n11, 163n7
Shepher, J., 98
Shweder, R., 121
Simple Continuity view, 5, 44, 56–57
Skeptics. *See* Disgust skepticism
Social emotions, 73–76
Social learning, 38, 104. *See also* Cultural transmission; Cultural Transmission model
Social norms, 6
  co-opt thesis and, 119–122
  disgust and, 31–33
  tribal instincts hypothesis and, 108–111
Sripada, C., 108–110, 119
Stich, S., 108–110, 119
Streiffer, Robert, 147
Symbolic markings, 111–115

Taste aversion, 46–47. *See also* Food
Terror Management theory, 5, 44, 56–57, 139–140, 146
Theory of disgust. *See also* Entanglement thesis
  constraints on, 33–34, 40–41, 58
  psychological model for, 35–40
Tinbergen, Nikolaas, 15
Transmission biases, 85–86
Tribal instincts hypothesis, 6, 103–116. *See also* Group membership

  cognitive architecture pertinent to, 106–116
  and ethnic boundaries, 111–115
  gene-culture coevolution and, 103–106
  and social norms, 108–111

Ultimate explanations, 35
Ultrasociality, 107
United States, 32–33
Urban legends, 23, 93

Vocabulary, 23

Westermarck, E. A., 98, 158n17
Withdrawal, from disgusting stimuli, 16, 39, 47–48
Wolf, A. P., 98

Xenophobia, 30, 124

Yuck factor, 7, 137

DATE DUE

MAY 0 8 2012	

DEMCO, INC. 38-2931